CHARLES VAN DER LEEUW

Cold War II: Cries in the Desert

- or how to counterbalance NATO's propaganda from Ukraine to Central Asia

abcgallery.com - Internet's biggest art collection

Hieronymus Bosch: Hell

Published in United Kindom
Hertfordshire Press Ltd © 2015

9 Cherry Bank, Chapel Street
Hemel Hempstead, Herts.
HP2 5DE, UK

e-mail: publisher@hertfordshirepress.com
www.hertfordshirepress.com

COLD WAR II: CRIES IN THE DESERT
or how to counterbalance NATO's propaganda
from Ukraine to Central Asia

Text copyright to Charles Van Der Leeuw © 2015

Typeset by Allwell Solutions
Cover design by Aleksandra Vlasova
Printed & bound in Great Britain

British Library Catalogue in Publication Data
A catalogue record for this book is available from the British Library
Library of Congress in Publication Data
A catalogue record for this book has been requested

ISBN 978-1-910886-07-6

*A todos, a vosotros, los silenciosos seres de la noche que tomaron mi mano en las
tinieblas, a vosotros, lámparas de la luz inmortal, líneas de estrella, pan de las
vidas, hermanos secretos, a todos, a vosotros, digo: no hay gracias, nada podrá
llenar las copas de la pureza, nada puede contener todo el sol en las banderas de
la primavera invencible, como vuestras calladas dignidades.*

*To all, to you, silent creatures of the night holding my hand amidst the
darkness, to you, lamps shining immortal light, lines of stars, bread of the lives,
secret brothers, to all, to you I say: there is no gratitude, nothing shall be able to
fill the cups of purity, nothing can contain the entire sun on the banners of the
invincible spring, like your quiet dignity.*

Pablo Neruda: Canto General

US-steered NATO plots to spread the havoc it caused in Ukraine further east
across the southern Caucasus into Central Asia by trying to provoke more
"coloured revolutions" with the aim to install US puppet regimes. Sinister
fifth-columnists penetrating into the region on behalf of the so-called
Islamic State in the Near-East. Attempts on the "Eurasian" subcontinent
by existing, legitimate states to consolidate and stay aloof from economic
degradation under US hegemony. All that and a bit more is at stake for
Central Asia in what is often dubbed Cold War II – a continuous around-
the-clock propaganda battle in which calls for reason and realism have only
recently become stronger. Written in the peaceful and pleasant centre of
Bishkek, this modest monograph is a journey through the whirlwind of
false arguments and attempts to expose them, using a number of examples,
countered by increasing attempt to tear off the veils and reveal America's war
mongers' true faces and intentions.

ABOUT THE AUTHOR

Charles van der Leeuw was born in The Hague, The Netherlands, in 1952. He started working as an independent reporter on cultural issues in a wide variety of publications back in 1977. Ten years later, he settled down in war-torn Beirut as an international war correspondent, following a first experience in Iraq in 1985 which resulted in his first book on the Iraq-Iran war. After his kidnapping and release in 1989, his second book «Lebanon - the injured innocence» came out, followed, in early 1992, by «Kuwait burns». Later in the year, he settled down in Baku, Azerbaijan, as a war correspondent. «Storm over the Caucasus» on the southern Caucasus geopolitical conflicts, came out in 1997 in the Dutch language and two years later in the first English edition. It was followed by «Azerbaijan - a quest for identity» and «Oil and gas in the Caucasus and Caspian - a history», both published in 2000, and "Black&Blue" published in Almaty in summer 2003 about the stormy rise of Russia's present-day oil and gas companies. His latest publication before this work was a bipartite book about the histories of Kazakhstan and Kyrgyzstan.

1986-1991:
De Golfoorlog/Iraq-Iran (Het Spectrum, Netherlands)
Libanon/De vermoordeonschuld (Jan Mets, Netherlands, Kritak, Belgium)
Koeweitbrandt (EPO, Belgium)

1996-2008:
Storm over the Caucasus (Babylon De Geus, Netherlands, Curzon Press, UK, St. Martin's Press, USA)
Azerbaijan/a quest for identity (Curzon Press, UK, St. Martin's Press, USA)
Caspian and Caucasian oil and gas: a history (Curzon Press, UK, St. Martin's Press, USA)
Kazakhstan/a quest for statehood (Caspian Publishing House, Kazakhstan)
Black & Blue: The turbulent formation of new giants: the Russian oil and gas industry
    (Caspian Publishing House, Kazakhstan)

2012-2014:
Fugitive long-fingered gentry from the plains: Banking fraud's impact on economics and financials
    in Kazakhstan and beyond – the affair of BTA's former management and affiliated cases (Caspian
    Library, Almaty)
A tale of two lands, two nations: Histories of Kazakhstan and the Kazakhs, Kyrgyzstan and the Kyrgyz

CONTENTS

INTRODUCTION

El Greco. The Dream of Philip II. 1579. Oil on canvas.
Real Monasterio, Escorial, Spain

Watch out: there is gunfire in the air here, and heavy it is indeed. Any doubt? Is Russia under Vladimir Putin's government keen on conquering the world? Hardly so. Is China keen on doing so? Hardly so. Is America's ruling elite keen on disintegrating Russia and the rest of the Eurasian mega-continent and divide it into dictatorial banana republics which it can rape and reap at its whim? Quite so. Is Washington's end goal to subdue the European Union to America's supremacy on world markets and economies in order to make America richer and richer and the rest of the world poorer and poorer? Quite so. Is there a pending danger that Central Asia will be hit by massive "Islamic" terror possibly going to control entire territories undermining national states? Quite so. Is America's ruling elite playing out the "Islamic" card as one of its tools to destroy supranational economic and political blocks consisting of legitimate governments of UN member states and prevent emerging blocks from consolidating? Quite so. Are, therefore, Kyrgyzstan and other Central-Asian former Soviet republics under threat from either Russia or China? Hardly so. Are they under threat from the USA? Quite so. What about the European Union? The answer is blowing in the wind…. So, in the end, who is telling lies here from beginning to end? The American regime – both to its own people and the world. This is not a problem in itself. The core problem is the absence of disbelief among its audiences…

The timeline at the bottom of it all is longer than what mass media want people to believe. That started with the last-minute refusal of President Viktor Yanukovich to sign the so-called association treaty with the European Union in November 2013 followed by the first mass demonstrations, soon deteriorating to violent riots and clashes and ending, towards the end of February, by crowds toppling the government. Loyalist forces, however, persisted on the Crimea and in the eastern provinces of Donbas and Lugansk, which ended with the three of them declaring "provisional independence". While the latter two have maintained that position ever since, the Crimea went one step further and claimed adherence to the Russian Federation, which was granted on condition that it would be confirmed through a referendum – which took place soon afterwards with more than the expected result: not only the roughly 70 per cent ethnic Russians populating the peninsula but also a majority of ethnic Ukrainians living on it voted in favour.

It was this "Russian invasion" in the words of US-led propagandists that brought Cold War II into the open. Loyalists in the other two breakaway areas were dubbed "pro-Russian rebels" and suggestions that Russian troops were pouring into Ukraine were poured into the minds of western audiences on an hour-to-hour basis around the clock, accompanied by "economic sanctions" meant to undermine Russia's economic development. In the process, no lies were blunt enough, no fake information was shunned, not even the most shameful demagogy was left unused to create the image of the Bear stretching out its claws, including the demonisation of the alleged man behind the alleged scheme – Russia's President Vladimir Putin. One could expect that he would have to take the blame in case Peru would be hit by a tsunami at any time. Over the winter of 2014/'15, with the worst fighting in Ukraine drawing to a close and a stalemate on the ground more and more seen as inevitable, criticism in Europe but also inside the USA was growing and more and more openly expressed. This prompted US warmongers to extend attention from the northern coast of the Black Sea to beyond the Caspian, where the overthrow of Washington's puppet Kurmanbek Bakiyev in Kyrgyzstan back in 2010, followed by the closure of the US military base in the country had caused a setback for Washington's longstanding plan to encircle the Russian Federation and make it disintegrate from within. The argument: the US would "help" Central Asia's former Soviet republics against the Russian "threat" – in the same way it has "helped" Ukraine into a civil war and economic bankruptcy…

In the Oxford Concise Dictionary, brainwashing is defined as "systematic replacement of established ideas in a person's mind by new ones". In the Encyclopedia of psychology, Vol. 1 (pp. 463-464) of the American Psychological Association, the phenomenon is described as "an impairment of autonomy, an inability to think independently, and a disruption of beliefs and affiliations. In this context, brainwashing refers to the involuntary reeducation of basic beliefs and values." In practice, one could thereby describe brainwashing as it exists today as spreading fantasy so extensively and intensively that in the end it has a chance to become reality. The way in which this is practiced by western parties in Cold War II means, above all, that people are coming to put notions before facts and select the facts and their interpretations in a manner subordinate to what they are wanted to believe. The process appears to be so massive that even normally independent mass media have fallen victim to it and become instrumental in it – reducing critics to the level of lonely individuals.

In the process, the role of western diplomats in general and American ones in particular has become pivotal. Traditionally, a diplomat's role is to defend the interests of the country he or she has been sent by, and perceive the interests of his host country to explain them objectively and realistically to his masters in his home country. Meanings of the word diplomatic, according to the Oxford dictionary, thereby also include "tactful", "uncandid", "subtle" and "exactly reproducing the original". A superficial read through Wikileaks, just to mention one source, has revealed quite different characteristics where it comes to today's US diplomacy. Digging deeper, information often overlooked by popular mass media reveals even worse. Today, diplomats are supposed to be doing what up till about a hundred years ago used to be done by gunboats: pushing sovereign states into turmoil, overthrow governments and states, and brainwashing people to believe somebody else is doing it.

To all who have even briefly visited Central-Asian cities such as Almaty, Bishkek, Shymkent or Tashkent (let alone Moscow or St.-Petersburg in neighbouring Russia) it must have become clear that few things remind one of the stereotypes western propaganda machineries depicted the average Soviet citizen throughout the Cold War and beyond. These days, people are dressed in modern fashion, go shopping in modern, well-equipped supermarkets and malls, wine and dine in a wide variety of restaurants and take their exercises in modern-day fitness centres. The homo sovieticus, as the stereotype was often dubbed, has ceased to exist. Surprise: it never really existed to begin with.

The fabricated image featured a stereotype representing a plump, dull, sad-looking person wearing a shapeless, tasteless and colourless standard suit, while standing motionlessly staring into the void, under the watchful eyes of grim-looking faces topping out of uniforms or plain clothes, representing a sterile state apparatus constantly reading citizens' minds in search for "deviations" from an iron doctrine imposed on the entire society. Obedience was strictly required an disobedience cruelly punished.

Western propagandists, however, made one formidable mistake by ignoring a hardly less formidable weapon in the hands of the Soviet government. This was not the often exaggerated but still immense arsenal of military equipment including multi-range missiles with nuclear ammunition the Red Army had at its disposition. This was the huge and well-organised state corporation called Intourist, which throughout the Soviet period organised all-in holidays for tourists from all over the world to virtually all parts of the USSR. Tours included museums, theatres, nature resorts and other attractions. But during free time, tourists were allowed to walk around in city centres on their own, only to discover swiftly that people on the spot were as diverse in character, features and attitude as they tend to be in any country wherever in the world. The only type of citizen they found hard to find was the one corresponding to the stereotype they had been brainwashed wigh back home.

Some if not many social scientists in Central Asia and elsewhere in the former USSR fully recognise the misleading image western propaganda tried to impose. "In the West, a negative stereotype of the Soviet past lingers: Its totalitarian political system, the KGB, the Lada automobile, homo sovieticus people standing in long lines to buy bread, etc.," a recently published dissertation by **Ulugbek Badalov, an Uzbek scholar who** received his PhD in political anthropology from the School for Advanced Studies in Social Sciences (EHESS) in Paris in 2011 reads. "But in the collective memory of former Soviet citizens, the past is essentially associated with a time when people lived in similar conditions with little social differentiation. Common values, like friendship, solidarity and neighborhood were important. For many people, the era embodies nostalgia for their own youth, with its train of dreams and illusions, gone now forever. [...] Almost all the population in Central Asia, as in other parts of the ex-USSR, who knew communism would prefer a return of the 'protector' regime in all areas rather, than perpetuate the current system. For many, this is a generator of disappointment for reasons readily perceptible. Older people who lived in the previous period often speak with pride and even with tears in their eyes. It was a pride of belonging to a powerful country whose authority was recognized worldwide in military and scientific fields. But today, their countries are in distress." 1)

This distress, however, is quite different from the imaginary distress on western minds during Soviet rule. Widespread social and other abuses are a result of "imported values" from the west imposed on Central Asia's and other former Soviet republics, which for many are not valuable at all but have allowed the entry of wild capitalism, in the absence of a solid ideology that could have replaced the one cherished under Soviet rule. The quest for renewed common ideological thinking has brought Central Asia closer, once more, to Russia which is widely seen as the new cradle of a reconciliation between state rule and private entrepreneurship, accessible to all but protected under the law at the same time.

Not everybody, though, seems to share that view and try to depict Vladimir Putin's Russia and its allies as a source of evil similar to that cultivated by the west in Soviet times. "Putin's kleptocratic system [...] has redistributed hydrocarbon profits in exchange to both the so-called core elites (people from the closest pro-Putin circles) and mass constituencies through pay increases for public sector employees who constitute about 70% of Russia's middle class in exchange for unquestioned loyalty," one article in an American magazine called New Republic written by a certain Maria Snegovaya, "a Ph.D. student at Columbia University" and published recently read. "Putin's main problem is that the system he built up is almost entirely based on material reimbursement. Personalistic regimes like the one he has built sustain the loyalty of their supporters almost entirely through access to material rewards, and they are extremely vulnerable to economic catastrophe."2)

Ironically, the student-columnist hits the bull's eye where the importance of "material reimbursement" is concerned. Only this is not the problem in Russia and its partners in the nascent Eurasian Economic Union (Kazakhstan, Kyrgyzstan, Belarus and Armenia). It is the solution. If 70 per cent of the population has "access to material rewards" a nation is not "extremely vulnerable to economic catastrophe" but rather protected against it, as "middle class" people will observe that economic setbacks are shared by most if not all, without certain parties taking advantage of them. For Central Asia's homo postsovieticus, this is the only realistic response in a world were crises have become camouflage for political subversion – something nobody in the region wants to see again.

It is just one striking example of not just US war-driven propaganda, but most of all how easily pundits (often presenting themselves as "experts" or "analysts" waving some academic certificate) put themselves under the instruction of US intelligence (how intelligent remains subject to dispute) services. They include not only mavericks popping up out of nowhere but also longstanding critical, independent and democratic-minded mass media. The brutality with which this process has taken place, often leaving "Russian-minded" counterparts dumbfounded, is the main topic of this modest work. At the time of writing, more and more counter-voices are being heard denouncing the impudent US-led propaganda campaign making the latter look as hilarious as it is if the consequences would not be so tragic. It is likely to take a long haul, but only in this way the American and European nations' respectability can be regained in the eyes of the world at large.

Many people may have wondered what ever happened to pacifism in Europe and the Americas. The middle- and elder generations may well remember the likes of Bob Dylan and John Lennon and a small army of artists, writers, journalists and intellectuals staging profound and high-profile action, first against America's war against Vietnam, later against its treacherous acts of aggression against several democratic Latin American states while maintaining oppressive dictators in power in others, and ending in campaigns against America's nuclear umbrella aimed against the USSR and the People's Republic of China, thereby representing a threat of global destruction. With the break-up of the Soviet Union, the voices of protest died down – wrongly so since the event was abused by NATO and its political backers to seek hegemony in what was now considered a fractured part of the world taking after Africa and Latin America. This goal was stopped by Russia, which maintained its position as a political, economic and military super power, flanked by China and India – the latter being a superpower in the making rather than a postcolonial satellite. This and little else made western cold war mongers realise that the "end" of "Sovietism" had in fact been a Pyrrhus victory upon which old methods of undermining states were revived. Code-name: "Colour Revolution".

But what started, and still continues, as an aggressive campaign through western media with little discord on the campaigning side with the aim to vilify everything Russian and put pro-western rebels in Ukraine seizing power and toppling a legitimate elected regime using mobs and mobsters, has now been joined by a growing chorus of American and European protests against NATO's aggression – by proxy for now but moving eerily towards all-out confrontation. Warnings are increasingly profiled that not Russia, but NATO represents the present-day danger to peace in the world.

This strange-looking book is an attempt to guide sideliners and outsiders through a labyrinth of polemics – in the hope that at the end of the search some light will shine into their eyes. It is not for nothing in this context that the illustrations chosen for this edition include Hiëronimus Bosch together with El Greco and mostly Pavl Filonov. All three of them tried to look through the trends of their times trying to identify the timeless truth, horrible and at the same time fascinating as it might seem. Contemplating on their speechless but at the same time revealing visions might give readers extra inspiration to give shape to each individual's own reflections – hopefully leading to a world where real people in mutual understanding put current trends of self-interest and hysteria to a definite end.

CHAPTER I

THE US/NATO PROPAGANDA MACHINERY AND COUNTER-VOICES

Pavel Filonov. October. Landscape. Formula. 1921. Oil on plywood. 47 x 40.5 cm. The Russian Museum, St. Petersburg, Russia

One would be inclined to think that state propaganda, meaning making things look different from what they are in the eyes of the general public in the interest of state executive powers, has been an invention made by councils to authoritarian monarchs who have ruled the world and its nations for thousands of years. This is not true, for the simple reason that image-forging was not needed since the monarch's word was the only reality, the only incentive for action in society. It was only when that incentive shifted, stage-wise and with significant limits, towards other layers of society than just the very top, that the need to steer those limits by executive powers arose, from which the notion of propaganda was born – unsurprisingly, in the USA. So-called leaders can no longer dictate people's actions with no reasons needed to be given, they have to "sell" those reasons to the public in order for the latter to let them go ahead. The system was first explained between the two World Wars by an American public relations entrepreneur named Edward Bernays, for all it mattered a nephew of Siegmund Freud, who wrote a classic on his ideas simply titled Propaganda.

"The conscious and intelligent manipulation of the organised habits and opinions of the masses is an important element in democratic society," the book reads in its opening chapter. "Those who manipulate this unseen mechanism of society constitute an invisible government which is the true ruling power of our country. We are governed, our minds are molded, our tastes formed, our ideas suggested, largely by men we have never heard of. This is a logical result of the way in which our democratic society is organized. Vast numbers of human beings must cooperate in this manner if they are to live together as a smoothly functioning society. Our invisible governors are, in many cases, unaware of the identity of their fellow members in the inner cabinet. They govern us by their qualities of natural leadership, their ability to supply needed ideas and by their key position in the social structure. Whatever attitude one chooses to take toward this condition, it remains a fact that in almost every act of our daily lives, whether in the sphere of politics or business, in our social conduct or our ethical thinking, we are dominated by the relatively small number of persons—a trifling fraction of our hundred and twenty million—who understand the mental processes and social patterns of the masses. It is they who pull the wires which control the public mind, who harness old social forces and contrive new ways to bind and guide the world."

Not that this is something new. The world's history is full of shady figures behind the throne trying to steer almighty monarchs in the direction they desired. The difference is that these days each and every citizen needs to be steered in such a manner. "It is not usually realised how necessary these invisible governors are to the orderly functioning of our group life," the text reads further down. "In theory, every citizen may vote for whom he pleases. Our Constitution does not envisage political parties as part of the mechanism of government, and its framers seem not to have pictured to themselves the existence in our national politics of anything like the modern political machine. But the American voters soon found that without organization and direction their individual votes, cast, perhaps, for dozens or hundreds of candidates, would produce nothing but confusion. Invisible government, in the shape of rudimentary political parties, arose almost overnight. Ever since then we have agreed, for the sake of simplicity and practicality, that party machines should narrow down the field of choice to two candidates, or at most three or four. In theory, every citizen makes up his mind on public questions and matters of private conduct. In practice, if all men had to study for themselves the abstruse economic, political, and ethical data involved in every question, they would find it impossible to come to a conclusion about anything. We have voluntarily agreed to let an invisible government sift the data and high-spot the outstanding issues so that our field of choice shall be narrowed to practical proportions. From our leaders and the media they use to reach the public, we accept the evidence and the demarcation of issues bearing upon public questions; from some ethical teacher, be it a minister, a favorite essayist, or merely prevailing opinion, we accept a standardized code of social conduct to which we conform most of the time."

So far, so good. But further down, the author switches from technical issues to ideological ones, displaying sheer disdain for the public's ability to think independently. "No serious sociologist any longer believes that the voice of the people expresses any divine or specially wise and lofty idea," the book's chapter on political propaganda reads. "The voice of the people expresses the mind of the people, and that mind is made up for it by the group leaders in whom it believes and by those persons who understand the manipulation of public opinion. It is composed of inherited prejudices and symbols and clichés and verbal formulas supplied to them by the leaders. [...] The political apathy of the average voter, of which we hear so much, is undoubtedly due to the fact that the politician does not know how to meet the conditions of the public mind. He cannot dramatise himself and his platform in terms which have real meaning to the public. Acting on the fallacy that the leader must slavishly follow, he deprives his campaign of all dramatic interest. An automaton cannot arouse the public interest. A leader, a fighter, a dictator, can. But, given our present political conditions under which every office seeker must cater to the vote of the masses, the only means by which the born leader can lead is the expert use of propaganda. Whether in the problem of getting elected to office or in the problem of interpreting and popularising new issues, or in the problem of making the day-to-day administration of public affairs a vital part of the community life, the use of propaganda, carefully adjusted to the mentality of the masses, is an essential adjunct of political life."

On March 11 2015, the US monthly periodical The Diplomat, known for its long list of ferocious attacks and false insinuations against Kyrgyzstan and other former Soviet republics, assailed one of its peers, this time over Kazakhstan, in a report against a news outlet known as Silk Road Reporters which it accused of being on the payroll of Astana to report "selectively" on Kazakh affairs. "While no paperwork linking Silk Road Reporters to Astana has emerged, numerous signs surrounding the publication point to the outlet as yet another effort at Astana's image-burnishing efforts in the United States – an effort that has not only roped in Tony Blair, but has already extended to assorted American media outlets," the article read. "Silk Road Reporters, which first began publishing stories on the region last January, says it offers 'compelling original reporting, analysis, interviews, and investigations from Central Asia'. The publication is run by James Kimer, the site's self-described 'owner and editor'. In an interview, Kimer said that he had visited Central Asia multiple times over the past decade, and wanted to give a voice to those in the region 'who had almost no coverage in English-language media'. With his own money and an 'inheritance' from his grandmother, Kimer began Silk Road Reporters in early 2014, and has been publishing regularly ever since." 3)

14

It is sufficient just to take a glance at the time table of the first Cold War. NATO emerged first, and the Warsaw Pact only years later in response to it – meaning that the "threat" against the west only took shape years after warnings against it had been spread all over the world. The aim of NATO was to destroy the USSR's image of an ally against nazi-Germany and to make the world forget the crucial role it had played in the final victory over it. To reach that goal, no means were spared – including engaging a large number of surviving Nazis in propaganda and terror campaigns first against communist parties in Western Europe and later against Warsaw Pact member states directly. Initially, the reaction consisted of indifference, accompanied by the traditional personality cults surrounding Lenin and Stalin. This changed under Nikita Khrushchev, who changed the overall attitude into a more activist one: we do not have to say that we are better – we shall simply prove it. Stalin's paranoid security policy was softened, and construction and industry were booming, boosting the former Russian Empire's economy to unprecendented levels, the remains of which can still be seen throughout the former Soviet Union including Central Asia. This was the very opposite of what Washington and its allies wanted to happen, and the pseudo-ideological campaign that followed, today known as Cold War, was the result, while its true intention was little else than for America to lay its hands on its former ally's immense natural and industrial resources in the name of economic "freedom" – read: usurpation.

Today, like it or not: with Cold War II in full swing, economics and business have become more political than ever, and attempts by corporate enterprises to stay out of the Dirty Information War accompanying it have remained by and large futile. It all began on the very first day of the so-called Maidan Revolution which was to result in the violent overthrow of the government of Ukraine. Ever since, the western Brotherhood of Hatred has subsequently bombarded audiences around the globe with propaganda under the guise of so-called information, full-heartedly aided by both traditional news media and new, mainly cybernetic outlets.

Throughout the process, reactions from Russia and other former Soviet republics remained by and large cool and even today the ferocious attacks preaching hell and damnation over the former USSR are merely shrugged off by politicians and commentators in the region alike. As a result of this, as well as the rise of critical movements versus the US/EU war trumpeting machinery in Europe and the Americas, a propaganda war between media outlets themselves seems to have broken out, with some of them accusing others of spreading biased information under the guise of news and analyses on the payroll of various parties in the "New Great Game". Most of the fighting takes place in the cyberspace, as its flexible time schedules allow swift tit-for-tat attacks between newsmongers. And the name Kyrgyzstan almost never fails to pop up in the continuing campaigns of mutual mud-throwing.

1. Media Relations Counsels

Pavel Filonov. Countenances (Faces on an Icon). 1940.
Oil on paper. 64 x 56 cm. The Russian Museum, St. Petersburg, Russia

From there on, a quest starts to find "links" and "interests" of people connected with SRR which should result in nailing them – for what remains unclear since there is no law in the world that prohibits media and PR firms to serve governments of UN member states as clients. "Silk Road Reporters is not Kimer's main focus," the article continues. "He also runs K Social Media Consulting, a Washington-based PR firm that claims to stand as a 'new breed of public relations' agency. Kimer's work in communications and spin has previously extended to Central Asia – including work with the law firm that represented Mina Corp., the fuel company accused of providing kickbacks to the autocratic Bakiyev family that was toppled in Kyrgyzstan's 2010 revolution. But Kimer's links to Central Asia don't exist solely within this specific consulting firm. He is also listed as one of two Media Relations Counsels with the Amsterdam Group, a separate PR firm run by Sam Amsterdam. Amsterdam, as it is, maintains his own intimate contacts with

Central Asia – with Kazakhstan, in particular. Amsterdam works for BGR Gabara, one of two firms that, until 2014, represented Kazakhstani interests in Washington. In his position as the head of digital communications with BGR Gabara, Amsterdam led 'traditional and social media campaigns' for Kazakhstan. (BGR President Ivo Ilic Gabara told this reporter via email that the company did not work with Kazakhstan in 2014, and denied any involvement with Silk Road Reporters.) That is to say, the head of a putatively 'independent news' outlet – with no obvious means of external funding, as neither subscriptions nor advertisements are available on the site – has worked directly for the man charged with leading Kazakhstan's media outreach in the United States. When asked about his links to Amsterdam, Kimer repeatedly denied any connection between his work with Silk Road Reporters and his work with Amsterdam, or any of Amsterdam's clients. He also denied any slant to material published with Silk Road Reporters."

In mainly stranding attempts to identify contributors to SRR as "collaborators" of the Kazakh government which The Diplomat vilifies as though it were evil itself, the article finds only one "suspect" named under vague and inconsistent arguments. "To be fair, after the interview with Kimer, certain stories moved beyond brushing Kazakhstan's image, including one focusing on Kazakhstan's human rights issues," the article's conclusion reads. "Unfortunately, the author of the story, Kseniya Bondal, is best-known for her work with a propaganda site run by U.S. Central Command. No direct link has appeared between Silk Road Reporters and Astana. All that exists is an 'independent' publication with a distinct string of pro-Kazakhstani articles, run by a professional consultant who is listed as one of two media relations counsels for the man charged with leading Kazakhstan's media engagement in the U.S. – and stocked with 'contributors' who have been scrubbed from the site, whose contact information has been repeatedly withheld, and whose prior publications seem nonexistent. Kazakhstan already has a notable history of media manipulation in the West, and considering the product and slant of Silk

Road Reporters, Kimer's consultancy firm may well not be his only project focusing on a new breed of public relations."

Smearing campaigns between media outlets are not that new, though. A similar attack on Central Asia Online by The Diplomat's US rival Foreign Policy took place back in late 2011, well before the outbreak of the Ukrainian conflict even though trouble was already in the air. Interesting enough, the author of the article, this time targeting the government of Uzbekistan, was David Trilling, editor of another trouble-making publication known as EurasiaNet, George Soros' propaganda machine which can hardly be considered impartial in the cyberspace battle marking Cold War II. EurasiaNet maintains close cooperation with CIA mouthpiece "Radio Free Europe/Radio Liberty", a relic from Cold War I but still a core vehicle to spread Washington's campaigns against Russia and other FSU states. Ironically, it is the US Defence Department which is attacked here for allegedly "polishing" the image of Central Asia's former USSR member states through, among others, Central Asia Online. 4)

"Over the past three years, a subdivision of Virginia-based General Dynamics has set up and run a network of eight 'influence websites' funded by the Defense Department with more than $120 million in taxpayer money,," the article reads. "The sites, collectively known as the Trans Regional Web Initiative (TRWI) and operated by General Dynamics Information Technology, focus on geographic areas under the purview of various U.S. combatant commands, including U.S. Central Command. In its coverage of Uzbekistan, a repressive dictatorship increasingly important to U.S. military goals in Afghanistan, a TRWI website called Central Asia Online has shown a disturbing tendency to downplay the autocracy's rights abuses and uncritically promote its claims of terrorist threats. Central Asia Online was created in 2008, a time when Washington's ability to rely on Pakistan as a partner in the U.S.-led operation in Afghanistan was steadily waning. In the search for alternative land routes to supply U.S. troops, Uzbekistan seemed the best option. Nearby Iran was a non-starter, and Uzbekistan's infrastructure — used by the Soviets to get in and out of Afghanistan during their ill-fated war there — was far superior to that of neighbouring Tajikistan."

"In the past, Karimov has responded to U.S. criticism by threatening to shut down the supply route to Afghanistan. In 2005, after Washington demanded an investigation into the massacre of hundreds of civilians in the eastern city of Andijan, he closed the American airbase at Karshi-Khanabad. So Washington's expressions of disapproval have given way to praise. In September, Secretary of State Hillary Clinton cautiously commended Tashkent for its 'progress' on political freedoms, and, more significantly, President Barack Obama moved to end restrictions on military aid, in place since 2004. Then, during an Oct. 22 visit to Tashkent, Clinton thanked the Uzbek leader in person for his cooperation. A State Department official traveling with her said he believed Karimov wants to leave a democratic legacy for 'his kids and his grandchildren'. Theoretically, with the restrictions lifted, General Dynamics stands to profit. The company has already shown interest in finding clients in Central Asia, hawking its wares at a defense exposition in Kazakhstan last year. This potential self-interest casts an unflattering light on Central Asia Online's flattering coverage of the region's calcified dictatorships, especially Uzbekistan." "Over the past two years, the budget for the TRWI websites has increased from $10.1 million to $121 million, according to DOD records. But the parties involved in the project have been reluctant to discuss details. Central Asia Online did not respond to repeated requests for comment, sent via the website, over the course of six months. General Dynamics Information Technology referred questions to U.S. Special Operations Command (SOCOM). A spokesman for SOCOM in Tampa would not provide details on why the budget grew so quickly. He said the websites' content is coordinated with regional embassies, but 'developed in support of a set of combatant command-assigned objectives'. Representatives of all five U.S. embassies in Central Asia, however, told me they have nothing to do with Central Asia Online. In Tajikistan, where the U.S. embassy has a commendable record of defending media freedoms, a press attaché volunteered that Central Asia Online does not even receive the embassy's press releases. A spokesman for another embassy in the region said he had never heard of the site. All this raises the question: Is U.S. taxpayer money being given to a for-profit military contractor to shill for a Central Asian dictator, just because he's a useful ally in the war on terror?"

The question remains who is accusing whom of what in the ongoing cyber space wars, now that the initially unison anti-Russian wolf-crying chorus' harmony appears to have made place for dissonance. Those Kyrgyz, Kazakh and other former Soviet citizens who bother to follow the endless avalanches of fairy tales – about new "revolutions" in Kyrgyzstan and other FSU states that never took place, about looming wars between Central Asia solely existing in the imagination of the spreaders of such "information", about the Russian Federation falling apart because Vladimir Putin takes a holiday and last but not least about the Caucasus and Central Asia falling into the claws of Middle East "Islamic" radicals who are only developing because the USA is condoning and according to some discretely supporting them. In the midst of such a whirlwind of contradicting lies and half-truths, it can hardly come as a surprise that the protagonists responsible for passing them on now seem to be at each other's throats...

2. Historic roots and neo-imperialism

Pavel Filonov. Colonial Policy. 1926. The Russian Museum,
St. Petersburg, Russia

The hero-versus-villain rhetoric made in USA and copied in Brussels has come back to the surface in full flood after everybody was made to believe that it had been buried following the break-up of the USSR back in 1991. Buried alive, that is: it is simply impossible to make nearly half a billion people in the world change their minds overnight and throw a deep conviction which may have its faults but was and still is profoundly based on human solidarity and prosperity sharing through communal harmony rather than internal struggle falsely dubbed competition down the drain without much further thinking. Now, the vampires have crawled out of their coffins once more. Championed by the United States of America, or rather its ruling elites since within America's society there are plenty who still rightly refuse to believe Washington's propaganda machinery, the much-trumpeted "western victory" sealing the end of the Cold War did not end in a lasting peace. And as it used to be, vilifying the adversary can only be done if there is an adversary. And where it is not in place, it will be invented which it has been. A glance at pre-modern, modern and post-modern history clarifies it all. During the so-called Great Game which dominated the second half of the XIX Century, Britain, which was then the main player in global geopolitics, tried to maintain its south-Asian colonial empire supporting medieval-style local tyrants in exchange for the latter's support to Whitehall and its policies. On the empire's outskirts, a number of khanates were given similar support, though not included in Britain's colonial domain. These khans used to maintain a regime marked by cruel oppression, usurpation, slavery, torture and public murders inherited from their Mongol ancestors, the breed of Dzhengiz Khan.

Among the subdued communities fighting for their freedom were the Kyrgyz, but no western politician even remotely thought of coming to their aid. The only half-western government to do so turned out to be Russia's czarist regime, which, once its mission was completed, imposed (though far from perfectly) laws applicable to all inhabitants, no more slavery and other forms of civil abuse, education for all, and freedom to produce and trade for all – something the Kyrgyz nation under dominion of the Kokand khanate in which it used to be included could previously hardly dream of.

After the czars had come to an end, the new Soviet regime consolidated "Russian" control over Kyrgyzstan – even though workers' rights were enforced and social welfare, health care, education and employment were open to all. Until the end of the Second World War, the USSR remained by and large left in peace by Western power blocks. This changed shortly after the war, when the west, and in particular the USA, enhanced a more aggressive stand in attempts to push the Soviet Union and its allies against the wall.

What caused the end of the USSR remains subject to dispute but one thing can be safely assumed: it was not the way in which Washington and its allies endeavoured to promote their self-proclaimed values in the form of provocations inside the Soviet block. Instead, the break-up came from within. But though the system in which ideas dating from the XIX Century socialist movement in Europe had materialised fell through, the ideas themselves had lost none of their virtue. This must have led to a sense of frustration especially in the United States, where leading political and business elites, by tradition narrowly intertwined, had hoped for a new round of neocolonial plunder of a prostrated former world power.

Combined with a desperate need for a new enemy powerful enough to justify America's costly role as a world bully, this has led straight to the situation as it is right now and of which Kyrgyzstan finds itself caught right in the middle. One can believe it or not – but this long history has everything to do with the diplomatic warfare waged on Kyrgyzstan and its government by all kinds of western-powered red carpet machinery deployed behind the walls of official premises downtown Bishkek. While pretending to be glorifying Kyrgyzstan's longstanding tradition of communal rule which, as many westerns remain unaware of, goes centuries back in time and distinguished the nation from most others in the region ever since the middle ages.

3. "The spread of democracy"

Pavel Filonov. Head. 1924. Watercolor, Indian ink, feather on paper.
The Russian Museum, St. Petersburg, Russia

A perfect example of the ammunition used by US propaganda gun batteries is an open letter published on a US government website and written by departing American ambassador to Kyrgyzstan Pamela Spratlen (her new post was to be just around the corner in Tashkent) and widely posted by local news media. The article pretends (quite rightly so) that Kyrgyzstan has come a long way in determining its own future but raises the suggestion that this was by and large thanks to the generous support by the USA and that this generosity is now under threat by the Russian bear stretching its claws and baring its teeth to the poor Kyrgyz. For all it matters, the very word China appears nowhere in the lengthy article – but that is an issue deserving a separate close look. 5)

The article makes a start that on the surface looks friendly enough. "Surrounded by autocratic dictatorships and heavily dependent on Russian political and economic support, Kyrgyzstan appears to some pundits to be no more than a pawn in Russia's 'Great Game' ambitions in the region, leading many to conclude that democracy in Central Asia is not sustainable," the text begins. "But Kyrgyzstan has so far proved resistant to one-man rule, and few people in Kyrgyzstan see autocracy as inevitable. Since one of the highest priorities for US foreign policy is supporting the growth of accountable government and democracy in the world, it is worth reflecting on Kyrgyzstan's experience and its future prospects as a lesson in what is possible for the spread of democracy in the most difficult regions of the world."

So far, so good. But it is further down that the article seems to take a nasty turn. "The 2011 presidential elections solidified the democratic transition to a new regime under President Almazbek Atambayev," the article reads further down. "The success of these three largely free and fair early elections was an early win for democracy, but the new government faced enormous challenges in low governance capacity, absence of rule of law, rampant corruption, human rights challenges, and external pressures. [...] While we see signs of hope in the younger generation, change is incremental. And so while Kyrgyzstan's people largely supported the 2010 revolution, they remain disappointed with the lack of improvement in their daily lives. Nostalgia for the Soviet Union remains high in the older generation, while many in the younger generation gravitate to cynicism or, in a small minority of cases, religious extremism."

From there on, the article not only gets blurrier, but also betrays the author's and her supreme commanders' true intentions. "Another challenge to our efforts to support Kyrgyzstan's democracy is its growing partnership with Russia," the text continues bluntly. "Confronted with a sea of internal and external challenges, President Atambayev has forged a strong partnership with Russian President Putin, seeing Russia as one of his few options for much needed assistance. This partnership has had its impact on our efforts, leading to the closure of the United States military presence at the Transit

Center at Manas International Airport, while Russia retains its Kant Air Base outside of Bishkek."

But that is not the end of it. Teeth-grinding follows: "Kyrgyzstan's new leadership would welcome a partnership with the United States, but places a priority on its relationship with Russia, which often comes at our expense. It remains an unanswered question how Kyrgyzstan can maintain its democratic trajectory while pursuing this partnership. President Atambayev's decision to enter the protectionist Customs Union by the beginning of 2015 exemplifies this challenge. Both officials and business leaders appear unenthused, but resigned to this choice, seeing a lack of better options. Strong US and European support for democratic transitions in Georgia and Ukraine fuels the impression locally that Kyrgyzstan must "go it alone" in Central Asia, even though our assistance levels for Kyrgyzstan are the highest in Central Asia."

So what does this "assistance" consist of? While Russian and Chinese enterprises, both public and private, are building power generating installations, power lines, oil and gas infrastructure, textile and chemical factories, gold and other metal mining combines, roads and other facilities throughout the country, investing billions in greenbacks, creating tens of thousands of jobs, American companies are absent in Kyrgyzstan. And the US government's "assistance" appears to consist of a lot of noise but hardly anything tangible. Yet, according to Her Excellency, Russia's assistance is the very evil threatening Kyrgyzstan – and all that through messengers of good news the diplomat would like to see beheaded since for America they are supposed to bring bad news.

"Along with political influence, Russia enjoys heavy cultural influence in Kyrgyzstan, both through legacy Soviet institutions and through Russian media. Most of Kyrgyzstan's people get their news from Russian-language sources. In particular, following the crisis in Ukraine, the strident anti-American tone taken by Russian propaganda has crystallised local public opinion around Moscow's narrative of events there. Although the domestic media remain free and diverse, they are far from professional and can be easily influenced by powerful political leaders. Kyrgyzstan's open society remains one of its great achievements, but its media need to make significant strides to make to become a true pillar of its democracy." In other words: journalists, take heed, listen to Uncle Sam and ignore the rest – and all that under the misleading banner of freedom…

4. "A fragile success facing serious risks"

Pavel Filonov. Untitled (Heads, a Boot, a Fish). 1920s. Watercolor, Indian ink, feather on paper. 22 x 23 cm. The Russian Museum, St. Petersburg, Russia

Further down, the article sums up the "achievements" America's "assistance" is supposed to have blessed poor Kyrgyzstan with. "Our core investment in civil society over the past 20 years successfully 'seeded' civil society organisations (CSOs) that not only survived the lean years of the late Akayev and Bakiyev presidencies, but unified the sector's voice," the text reads. "They now act as a key government partner, when given the space. Consistent, multi-year engagement with these organisations—including the Coalition for Democracy and Civil Society, Interbilim, Foundation for Tolerance International, and Association of Civil Society Support Centers—also helped ensure that key pro-civil society voices ascended to influential positions in Parliament, the President's Office, and relevant ministries. Civil society is also widely represented in Public Advisory Boards, a type of oversight and advisory committee attached to over 40 government ministries and agencies. In recent years, home-grown CSOs have made significant contributions on supporting democracy and human rights, de-escalating interethnic conflict, fighting corruption, eliminating torture and supporting a free media. In short, Kyrgyzstan's civil society has deep roots and is well organised to protect democratic gains."

Now if that is enough to fill millions of empty stomachs, it is hard to imagine what is, is it not? According to the lady diplomat, the blessings Kyrgyzstan receives from benevolent America include "the ability to think critically along Western-oriented lines" and "the capacity of Kyrgyzstani citizens to compete in the global economy, as well as to address drivers of instability in the country". There is definitely some need for that, but pretending that the USA is all Kyrgyz people need to realise that is simply preposterous. "Central Asia's only democracy remains a fragile success facing serious risks of economic under-development, low governance capacity, absence of rule of law, rampant corruption, human rights challenges, and external pressures," the article concludes. "But since gaining independence Kyrgyzstan has charted a course different from that of its Central Asian neighbors, one that the United States should continue to support as a beacon of hope in the region."

A beacon of hope for whom? Putting US "national interests" on one and the same level with "democratic values" is not something history over the last seven decades justifies. Nations' "right of self-determination" goes as far as any nation's willingness to dance to Washington's tune. Should it wish to take a different direction, that tune becomes less sweet than it sounds today, as the cases of Vietnam, Chili, Nicaragua, Panama, Grenada and Iraq (just to name a few) amply demonstrate – not to speak of the cruel oppression and near-annihilation of the Palestinian nation carried out with full support of Washington. There is little reason for Kyrgyzstan to expect anything better. One hopeful thought, however: as history shows, it could turn out for US propaganda soldiers and their commanders to twist the mind of a European than that of a Kyrgyz...

CHAPTER II

MAIDAN AND THE REBIRTH OF GLADIO

Pavel Filonov. Victory over Eternity. 1920-21. Oil on plywood.
41 x 37.5 cm. The Russian Museum, St. Petersburg, Russia

Who would have thought, or even dreamt, that after the end of the Cold War the two former opposite sides would turn to business (in fact, neither of them had ever left it and throughout Soviet times trade between "east" and "west" ever flourished) and politics would be out of the game, has had a cruel wakeup call. Mechanisms in place in the west, conducted by Washington through NATO, throughout the Soviet period seem to be reactivated, and Kyrgyzstan is among the nations placed in the hot seat in a "New Great Game" which is a lot less great than its nickname suggests. The overall aim, according to many observers, is to maintain the US dollar's dominance in the world economy. To this purpose, Washington deems it necessary to lay its hands on Russia's and other former Soviet republics' resources and China's cash… On the surface, it does not look related but that is exactly what it is. In last fall 2014, Kyrgyzstan was among the majority of United Nations member states which voted in favour of a resolution that called for rejection of and vigilance against neofascist movements popping up time and again around the world. Pro-neonazi voters were the USA, Canada and – less surprisingly – Ukraine.

"Russia's Foreign Ministry regrets the U.S., Canada and Ukraine have voted against the UN resolution on fighting glorification of Nazism, and the EU countries' delegations have abstained from voting," Russia's former state (now privately run) news agency Itar Tass reported on November 22 2014. "Ukraine's position is especially regretful. It is tough to realise how a country, in which people had experienced the horrors of Nazism and had made a major input in the common Victory over it, could be voting against a document, which condemns is glorification," the agency quoted a statement from the Russian foreign ministry published little earlier as reading. "We hope adoption of this resolution will send a clear signal to the countries, which have been facing the necessity of most decisive measures to fight the growing attempts to glorify Nazism," the statement was quoted as noting. "The third committee of the UN General Assembly on Friday adopted a resolution urging countries to undertake more efficient measures to struggle against glorification of Nazism and other forms of racial discrimination, xenophobia and intolerance," the news report read further down. "A total of 115 out of 193 UN member-states voted in favour of the document, initiated by Russia. Three countries opposed the document - Canada, the United States and Ukraine. Another 55 delegations, including those from the European Union countries, abstained. The resolution expresses concerns over spread across the world of various extremist political parties, movements and groups, including neo-Nazis as well as racist extremist movements and ideologies. The text also warns against glorification of the Nazi movement and former members of the Waffen-SS organisation and against erecting monuments and memorials to them. Therefore the document calls on states to take more efficient measures in line with international standards in the human rights sphere to fight these developments and extremist movements posing a real threat to democratic values. The resolution unequivocally condemns any denial of the Holocaust and calls for ensuring ratification and implementation of the International Convention on the Elimination of All Forms of Racial Discrimination (ICERD)." 6)

The fact that Ukraine voted against the resolution can hardly come as a surprise. "The acting president of the coup regime in Kiev announces that he is ordering an 'anti-terrorist' operation against pro-Russian protesters in eastern Ukraine, while his national security chief says he has dispatched right-wing ultranationalist fighters who spearheaded the Feb. 22 coup that ousted elected President Viktor Yanukovych," an article by the renowned American investigative journalist Robert Parry who broke many of the Iran-Contra stories in the 1980s for the Associated Press and Newsweek, posted in the winter of 2014/'15 reads. The article focuses on Andriy Parubiy, the recently appointed head of the Ukrainian National Security Council. "Parubiy himself is a well-known neo-Nazi, who founded the Social-National Party of Ukraine in 1991. The party blended radical Ukrainian nationalism with neo-Nazi symbols. Parubiy also formed a paramilitary spinoff, the Patriots of Ukraine, and defended the awarding of the title, 'Hero of Ukraine,' to World War II Nazi collaborator Stepan Bandera, whose own paramilitary forces exterminated thousands of Jews and Poles in pursuit of a racially pure Ukraine. During the months of protests aimed at overthrowing Yanukovych, Parubiy became the commandant of 'Euromaidan,' the name for the Kiev uprising, and – after the Feb. 22 coup – Parubiy was one of four far-right Ukrainian nationalists given control of a ministry, i.e. national security." 7)

"Everyone should understand by now that 'anti-terror' suggests extrajudicial killings, torture and 'counter-terror'," the article continues. "Yet, with much of the Ukrainian military of dubious loyalty to the coup regime, the dispatch of the neo-Nazi militias from western Ukraine's Right Sektor and Svoboda parties represents a significant development. Not only do the Ukrainian neo-Nazis consider the ethnic Russians an alien presence, but these right-wing militias are organized to wage street fighting as they did in the February uprising. Historically, right-wing paramilitaries have played crucial roles in "counter-terror" campaigns around the world. In Central America in the 1980s, for instance, right-wing 'death squads' did much of the dirty work for U.S.-backed military regimes as they crushed social protests and guerrilla movements."

1. America's warfare laboratory

Pavel Filonov. Man and Woman. 1912-13. Watercolor, brown ink, Indian ink, feather, brush on paper. 31 x 23.3 cm. The Russian Museum, St. Petersburg, Russia

Commentators tend to focus on a most remarkable couple at the bottom of of the wave of trouble haunting the former USSR today. "Neoconservative pundit Robert Kagan and his wife, Assistant Secretary of State Victoria Nuland, run a remarkable family business: she has sparked a hot war in Ukraine and helped launch Cold War II with Russia -- and he steps in to demand that Congress jack up military spending so America can meet these new security threats," another article by Parry posted in March 2015 was to read. This extraordinary husband-and-wife duo makes quite a one-two punch for the Military-Industrial Complex, an inside-outside team that creates the need for more military spending, applies political pressure to ensure higher appropriations, and watches as thankful weapons manufacturers lavish grants on like-minded hawkish Washington think tanks. Not only does the broader community of neoconservatives stand to benefit but so do other members of the Kagan clan, including Robert's brother Frederick at the American Enterprise Institute and his wife Kimberly, who runs her own shop called the Institute for the Study of War. Robert Kagan, a senior fellow at the Brookings Institution (which doesn't disclose details on its funders), used his prized perch on the Washington Post's op-ed page on Friday to bait Republicans into abandoning the sequester caps limiting the Pentagon's budget, which he calculated at about $523 billion (apparently not counting extra war spending). Kagan called on the GOP legislators to add at least $38 billion and preferably more like $54 billion to $117 billion: 'The fact that [advocates for more spending] face a steep uphill battle to get even that lower number passed by a Republican-controlled Congress says a lot -- about Republican hypocrisy. Republicans may be full-throated in denouncing [President Barack] Obama for weakening the nation's security, yet when it comes to paying for the foreign policy that all their tough rhetoric implies, too many of them are nowhere to be found'...' If it weren't for Nuland's efforts as Assistant Secretary of State for European Affairs, the Ukraine crisis might not exist. A neocon holdover who advised Vice President Dick Cheney, Nuland gained promotions under former Secretary of State Hillary Clinton and received backing, too, from current Secretary of State John Kerry." 8)

The combination of names should strike a sensitive chord for those keen on unraveling the structure of reactionary and pro-violence forces within the upper echelons of American society. It should come as no surprise that the names of the entire Bush clan, from grandfather who also happened to be Adolf Hitler's financial genius through a bank based in Rotterdam, The Netherlands, which he controlled, to grandson George Jr. who waged America's robber war against Iraq while having over 50 billion greenbacks in oil stolen in the process, appear on the list of members of an occult and subversive organisation known as Skull and Bones – the age-old emblem of pirates.

Skull and Bones goes back to late the XIX Century and was founded in the wake of the American Civil War at the University of Yale. Its main example is said to have been a German university. Blood rituals, secret oaths and other occult practices were its main features from the very beginning, but it was only after the First World War that the movement developed into an underground power house where secret deals were clinched between corporate tycoons, politicians and military. The arrival of fascist regimes in Italy and Germany was widely seen within Skull and Bones as a beacon for the future, and striving for an alliance between the USA and nazi Germany became its most prominent activity. 9)

As related by Denis Wheatly in his series of profound studies on Skull and Bones and its colourful past and present, the movement had more than skin-deep similarities with the cults maintained by Europe's fascists. "Adolf Hitler was obsessed with the occult, in his case the Thule Society, closely inter-connected with German Theosophists," in the author's words. "The jolly roger, skull and cross bones, 'der Totenkopf' was an emblem worn by Hitler's SS soldiers and was emblazoned on SS armoured cars and tanks. The SS was a religious cult of sworn Hitler/German ancestor worship. If the Nazis' occult lodges had been exposed then shut down, not treated as a taboo, millions of lives could have been saved. A small price to pay for insane racism and the blood of millions of people. The second world war need never have happened. Unless you want the occult fuelling a totalitarian West's Third World War 'on terror' and their 'New World Order' - please - do your bit to expose George W. Bush, the bonesmen and other interconnected lodges round the world.'

The first Cold War represented a chance of revival for Skull and Bones – which it took with unprecedented endeavour (using nazi contacts of old to put them forward on the chessboard against the Warsaw Pact through an organisation known as Gladio – see below) which far from ended with the break-up of the USSR in 1991. A shortlist of prominent names illustrates how dangerous the movement has always been and remains up to this very day – turning it into an almost natural cradle for new threats to the world including provocations against the Russian Federation and other former Soviet republics. "Among prominent alumni are former President and Supreme Court Justice William Howard Taft (a founder's son); former Presidents George H. W. Bush and his son, George W. Bush; Supreme Court Justices Morrison R. Waite and Potter Stewart; James Jesus Angleton, 'mother of the Central Intelligence Agency'; Henry Stimson, U.S. Secretary of War (1940-1945); U.S. Secretary of Defense Robert A. Lovett, who directed the Korean War; and Henry Luce, founder and publisher of Time, Life, Fortune, and Sports Illustrated magazines," information posted on Wikipedia concerning the organisation reads. "John Kerry, U.S. Secretary of State and former U.S. Senator; Stephen A. Schwarzman, founder of Blackstone Group; Austan Goolsbee, Chairman of Barack Obama's Council of Economic Advisers; Harold Stanley, co-founder of Morgan Stanley; and Frederick W. Smith, founder of FedEx, are all reported to be members. [...] The group Skull and Bones is featured in conspiracy theories, which claim that the society plays a role in a globalist/corporatist conspiracy for world control. Theorists such as Alexandra Robbins suggest that Skull and Bones is a branch of the Illuminati, or that Skull and Bones itself controls the Central Intelligence Agency." 10)

What has happened on the ground and behind the screen can only affirm such suggestions and brings us back to the likes of Victoria Nuland. "Confirmed to her present job in September 2013, Nuland soon undertook an extraordinary effort to promote "regime change" in Ukraine," Robert Parry relates further down in his paper quoted earlier. "She personally urged on business leaders and political activists to challenge elected President Viktor Yanukovych. She reminded corporate executives that the United States had invested $5 billion in their 'European aspirations', and she literally passed out cookies to anti-government protesters in Kiev's Maidan square. Working with other key neocons, including National Endowment for Democracy President Carl Gershman and Sen. John McCain, Nuland made clear that the United States would back a 'regime change' against Yanukovych, which grew more likely as neo-Nazi and other right-wing militias poured into Kiev from western Ukraine. In early February 2014, Nuland discussed U.S.-desired changes with U.S. Ambassador to Ukraine Geoffrey Pyatt (himself a veteran of a "regime change" operation at the International Atomic Energy Agency, helping to install U.S. yes man Yukiya Amano as the director-general in 2009). Nuland treated her proposed new line-up of Ukrainian officials as if she were trading baseball cards, casting aside some while valuing others. 'Yats is the guy', she said of her favourite Arseniy Yatsenyuk. [...] The coup against Yanukovych played out on Feb. 22, 2014, as the neo-Nazi militias and other violent extremists overran government buildings forcing the president and other officials to flee for their lives. Nuland's State Department quickly declared the new regime 'legitimate' and Yatsenyuk took over as prime minister."

But as it would soon appear, that was never the end purpose. "Russian President Vladimir Putin, who had been presiding over the Winter Olympics at Sochi, was caught off-guard by the coup next door and held a crisis session to determine how to protect ethnic Russians and a Russian naval base in Crimea, leading to Crimea's secession from Ukraine and annexation by Russia a year ago," the article continues. "Though there was no evidence that Putin had instigated the Ukraine crisis -- and indeed all the evidence indicated the opposite -- the State Department peddled a propaganda theme to the credulous mainstream U.S. news media about Putin having somehow orchestrated the situation in Ukraine so he could begin invading Europe. Former Secretary of State Clinton compared Putin to Adolf Hitler. As the new Kiev government launched a brutal "anti-terrorism operation' to subdue an uprising among the large ethnic Russian populations of eastern and southern Ukraine, Nuland and other American neocons pushed for economic sanctions against Russia and demanded arms for the coup regime. Amid the barrage of "information warfare" aimed at both the U.S. and world publics, a new Cold War took shape. Prominent neocons, including Nuland's husband Robert Kagan, a co-founder of the Project for the New American Century which masterminded the Iraq War, hammered home the domestic theme that Obama had shown himself to be 'weak', thus inviting Putin's 'aggression'."

So where is the line between strategy and ideology? Very simple: there is no such thing since "strategic" aims set by America's war schemers are not based on any ideology, but rather dressed up with pseudo-ideologies to fool the general public. "Whenever peace threatens to break out in Ukraine, Nuland jumps in to make sure that the interests of war are protected. Last month, German Chancellor Angela Merkel and French President François Hollande hammered out a plan for a cease-fire and a political settlement, known as Minsk-2, prompting Nuland to engage in more behind-the-scenes manoeuvering to sabotage the deal. [...] Nuland sounded determined to sink the Merkel-Hollande peace initiative even though it was arranged by two major U.S. allies and was blessed by President Obama. And, this week, the deal seems indeed to have been blown apart by Nuland's hand-picked Prime Minister Yatsenyuk, who inserted a poison pill into the legislation to implement the Minsk-2 political settlement. The Ukrainian parliament in Kiev added a clause that, in effect, requires the rebels to first surrender and let the Ukrainian government organize elections before a federalized structure is determined. Minsk-2 had called for dialogue with the representatives of these rebellious eastern territories en route to elections and establishment of broad autonomy for the region. Instead, reflecting Nuland's hard-line position, Kiev refused talks with rebel leaders and insisted on establishing control over these territories before the process can move forward. If the legislation stands, the result will almost surely be a resumption of war between military forces backed by nuclear-armed Russia and the United States, a very dangerous development for the world. Not only will the Ukrainian civil war resume but so will the Cold War between Washington and Moscow with lots of money to be made by the Military-Industrial Complex."

But Nuland is just a face with behind her an impressively sophisticated and extensive network of schemers and imposters. "Do not think that this unlocking of the U.S. taxpayers' wallets is just about this one couple," in Parry's words. "There will be plenty of money to be made by other neocon think-tankers all around Washington, including Frederick Kagan, who works for the right-wing American Enterprise Institute, and his wife, Kimberly, who runs her own think tank, the Institute for the Study of War [ISW]. According to ISW's annual reports, its original supporters were mostly right-wing foundations, such as the Smith-Richardson Foundation and the Lynde and Harry Bradley Foundation, but it was later backed by a host of national security contractors, including major ones like General Dynamics, Northrop Grumman and CACI, as well as lesser-known firms such as DynCorp International, which provided training for Afghan police, and Palantir, a technology company founded with the backing of the CIA's venture-capital arm, In-Q-Tel. Palantir supplied software to U.S. military intelligence in Afghanistan. Since its founding in 2007, ISW has focused mostly on wars in the Middle East, especially Iraq and Afghanistan, including closely cooperating with Gen. David Petraeus when he commanded U.S. forces in those countries. However, more recently, ISW has begun reporting extensively on the civil war in Ukraine."

Reporting or inventing? Looking a bit more closely at the forces, and in particular some individuals behind those forces, behind Ukraine's latest so-called revolution sheds a lot of awesome light upon the future of the former Soviet republics should America's war gang get its way. It looks indeed like a spitting image of Operation Gladio, the process put in place by NATO in the wake of World War II – or rather during the war only to be activated after its end. No deceit, forgery, selective fact finding and fact twisting, corruption and blackmail, extending to terrorism in the end, has been shunned in the American propaganda factory – not then and not now.

2. Some "revolutionaries" revisited

Pavel Filonov. The Dray-Men. 1915. Watercolor, brown ink,
Indian ink, feather, brush, graphite pencil on paper. 45 x 58 cm.
The Russian Museum, St. Petersburg

The Ukrainian extremist conglomerate features, among others, Yuri Marchuk, an open neo-nazi from Lvov, his peer Oleksandr Muzychko who in late March died in a shoot-out, according to some with police forces while others suggest neofascist groups' infighting, and Right Sektor leader Roman Koval. As already noted, on the outside, support has been mostly provided in the public domain by Assistant Secretary of State for European Affairs Victoria Nuland. "Nuland is married to neoconservative superstar Robert Kagan, a founder of the Project for the New American Century," Parry notes. "During the protests, neocon Sen. John McCain, R-Arizona, took the stage with leaders of Svoboda – surrounded by banners honoring Stepan Bandera – and urged on the protesters. Even before the demonstrations began, prominent neocon Carl Gershman, president of the U.S.-funded National Endowment for Democracy, had dubbed Ukraine 'the biggest prize'."

In a separate report, another author by the name of Walter Uhler focuses on a certain Oleh Tiahnybok, dubbed "…the leader of Svoboda, a right-wing party that captured 38 seats and 10 percent of the vote in the last parliamentary elections and played a significant role in the violent overthrow of President Yanukovych," the report reads. Nevertheless, the New York Times on May 6 this year generously offered its columns to the inheritor of Hitler's fifth-columnists in Ukraine and an open admirer of them.

Outstanding, though, remains the name of Igor Kolomoisky, Ukraine's second-richest tycoon and hawkish anti-federalist campaigner, recently appointed governor of the Dnepropetrovsk province. Kolomoisky has his own "private army" consisting of mercenaries, originating, among other sources, of soldiers of Fortune sent by America's Blackwater corporation. His militiamen have been responsible for the mass murder in Odessa in the winter of 2013/'14. But Kolomoisky also happened to own the country's largest bank, Privat Bank, which in the winter of 2014/'15 was in the process of being bailed out for the equivalent of roughly a billion US dollar, following fund diversion schemes during the previous decade. It was not so much the government bailing out the faltering bank, but the International Monetary Fund. According to available information, part of the money "lost" on non-repaid loans at the time include part of those funneled away through Privat Bank by Mukhtar Ablyazov, Kazakhstan's banker/swindler who robbed the bank he used to control, BTA, of billions in dollars using the same method. 11)

Mukhtar Ablyazov was a banker from Kazakhstan who embezzled worth between 10 and 12 billion US dollar in lent cash and submitted collateral from the local Bank TuranAlem (BTA), as the bank's president, CEO and major shareholder. In early spring 2009, a $10 billion hole in the balance sheet was disclosed, leading to the bank's bail-out by the Kazakh state and the latter becoming a 78 per cent majority shareholder in it. Ablyazov fled to Britain, where the bank pursued numerous court cases against him with the aim to recover part of the stolen money and assets, about 3.5 million

Sterling of which was stashed through circuits of offshore mailbox firms registered on British territory. In early 2012, faced with a 22-months prison term for perjury, Ablyazov fled the UK in turn. He was to be arrested in France in summer 2014, and due to be extradited either to Russia or to Ukraine, both of which were the jurisdictions where the fund-diversion and conversion into illegaly bought assets have taken place, since extradition to Kazakhstan was not possible. At the time of writing, proceedings regarding his extradition have not finished, but it is clear that Ukraine, where his former accomplices are now in power, is where the culprit's hopes lie.

In the case of Privat Bank, there appears to be blood on the trail. "Russian investigators have launched a criminal case against Ukraine's Interior Minister and the Dnepropetrovsk region's governor on suspicion of the "organised murder" of civilians in eastern Ukraine," The Moscow Times wrote in a recent news report published on June 18. "Investigators plan to explore further charges against Interior Minister Arsen Avakov and billionaire governor Igor Kolomoisky, including the use of prohibited means and methods of warfare, as well as the abduction of journalists and obstruction of their lawful activities, the statement added. The two will soon be placed on an international wanted list. Since early April, the two have "knowingly and with the intention of killing civilians" orchestrated a series of criminal activities committed by Ukrainian troops, the National Guard and the ultranationalist group Right Sector, as well as members of the special Dnyepr" battalion, which was created and financed by Kolomoisky, Investigative Committee spokesman Vladimir Markin said. Investigators further allege that the pair ordered the abductions of Russian journalists reporting on events in eastern Ukraine." 12)

As for Kolomoisky's financial dealings, the western backers of the "revolution" apparently prefer to look the other way – and the IMF appears to be no exception to that. "The Ukrainian revolution has been very bad for business in the country. But for Igor Kolomoisky's Privatbank there has been compensation of almost a billion dollars in state funds: publicly, rival Ukrainian commercial banks call that favouritism; privately, Ukrainian business as usual, one report on the development reads. "Privatbank is Ukraine's largest commercial bank. Since the replacement of the Ukrainian Government in February, and the start of the International Monetary Fund's (IMF) financial aid programme in April, Privatbank has been the largest beneficiary of what the IMF and the Ukrainian Ministry of Finance are calling Emergency Liquidity Assistance (ELA) to the country's banks. Published measurements of Privatbank's share of ELA range from 36% to more than 40% of the additional financing which has flowed out of Ukrainian state funds into the commercial banks. Just how much Kolomoisky benefits, along with related companies to which Privatbank lends much of its loan book, is one of the control operations being performed this week, as the IMF's Ukraine mission starts its first inspection since the IMF transferred $3.2 billion to the National Bank of Ukraine on May 7. This is the first tranche of the $17.1 billion committed to Kiev by the IMF. The next tranche of $1.4 billion, according to the IMF's published schedule, is due to be paid on July 25." 13)

There have been dozens of cases pointing at "revolutionary" Ukraine's current state of affairs similar to those concerning the Ablyazov/Kolomoisky files. The irony is that the thievery has paid well, the thieves got away with it and there was, as things looked into 2015, little hope for their victims to recover their money but to tap it from international loans – which in the end would have to be paid back, and guess by whom. **The Deposit Insurance Fund of Ukraine will not be able to repay people their losses and will have to rely on the external funding from the EU and, in particular, European taxpayers," a report by Sputnik posted in April 2015 was to read.** "Forty-six banks went bankrupt in Ukraine over the course of one year, Managing Director of the Ukrainian Deposit Insurance Fund Konstantin Woruschilin told the Ukrainian news agency UNIAN. He explained that there are several reasons for the mass bankruptcy of Ukrainian finance institutions. First of all, it is "the immoral behavior of bank managers".

According to Woruschilin, bank employees had been stealing the money and used it for their own purposes. The second reason is the drop in exports, the consumption decline as well as high production costs, Woruschilin said. The Deposit Insurance Fund makes every effort to repay Ukrainians their losses. However, the financial resources of the fund are insufficient, reaching a total of 16.1 billion dollars as of April 1. In order to meet its obligations to the banks' customers, the fund will have to rely on external funding. According to the German magazine Deutsche Wirtschafts Nachrichten, the main burden will ultimately fall on the EU taxpayers who will have to pay for the mismanagement in the Ukrainian banking sector." 14)

It all meant that America's "revolution" in Ukraine left the country bankrupt and the people with it. "With each passing day the Ukrainian debt bomb ticks closer to a sovereign default, which can now only be defused by Western creditors. With the economy expected to contract by 8% this year, and Western bailouts becoming its only salvation, the country is going through a difficult phase. Standard & Poor's cut Ukraine's long term foreign debt rating to CC from CCC-. The rating C, is used when a debtor is in the process of filing for bankruptcy protection," a separate Sputnik report posted on April 11 2015 read. "The foreign investors holding $10 billion of Ukrainian bonds "joined forces to develop a restructuring plan" for the country's debt. The plan does not include a decrease in debt, but interest payments on the other hand are impossible to manage at such rates. Ukraine's immediate future is now firmly in the hands of Western bond funds and the IMF, Forbes reports. Nobody knows what is happening in Ukraine, says Ukrainian lawyer Marlen Kurzkhov, a partner with Gusrae Kaplan in New York. Kurzkhov has been working with high net worth Ukrainians trying to get their money out of the country. All I know for sure is that whatever money the IMF gives to them, the government will steal some of it, at least that's the word on the street. A lot of Ukrainian businessmen are hoping things will blow over, or are dealing with authorities on the ground, says Kurzkhov. The IMF approved the provision of $17.5 billion to Ukraine in February as part of a four-year extension that replaced the original deal made in 2014. The IMF program targets a total of $40 billion in loans, nearly seven times what the Central Bank of Ukraine has in reserves. It is planned that this year Ukraine will be granted $10 billion, but this may not happen if Kiev does not pay the debt of $3 billion to Moscow, the due date of which is set for December." In all: a terrible mess and all thanks to the likes of McCain and Barroso... 15)

3. A plane crash and juggling with facts

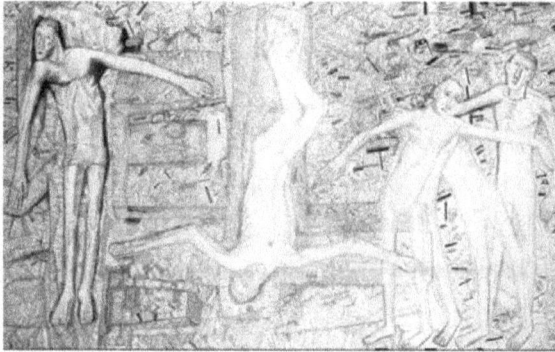

Pavel Filonov. Execution. 1912. The Russian Museum, St. Petersburg, Russia

Then came that fateful day of July 14 2014, when a Malaysia Air Boeing 777-200ER on flight MH17 from Amsterdam to Kuala Lumpur was travelling over the conflict-hit region till it disappeared from radar. All of the 283 passengers, including 80 children, and the 15 crew members on board perished as the plane exploded in the air and crashed on territory controlled by the self-declared Donetsk People's Republic loyal to the previous Ukrainian regime. Almost a year later, the results of the forensic expertise carried out on the spot by Dutch, Malaysian and other experts had still not been publicised and a full report could only be expected to bring things to light over summer 2015. This, however, did not prevent the US-led propaganda machinery to seize the opportunity to accuse the "pro-Russian rebels" and Russia itself to have shot the plane down from the very beginning. News media of name and fame once more fell into the trap with open eyes – resulting in a stream of dubious reporting.

"Western nations said there was growing evidence that the plane was hit by a Russian-supplied missile fired by rebels. Russia blamed Ukrainian government forces," the BBC wrote in an aftermath article posted on September 9 the same year. "US officials from the Office of the Director of National Intelligence said there was a 'solid case' that a SA-11 missile - also known as Buk - was fired from eastern Ukraine under 'conditions the Russians helped create'. They said the 'most plausible explanation' for the shooting down of the plane was that rebels mistook it for another aircraft. Evidence included images purportedly showing a surface-to-air missile launcher in the area, analysis of voice recordings of pro-Russian rebels apparently admitting bringing the airliner down and social-media activity pointing to rebel involvement." 16)

But worse was to follow when experts of various nationalities not only found out that the plane had been hit by a missile shot from behind apparently from a war jet on its tail – where its fuel tank is, a plane's most vulnerable spot – but identified the plane's pilot as well. Rather than taking it as a wake-up call, western media only scowled more brutally for it. "A shadowy Russian organisation claiming to be investigating the MH17 crash has claimed that a Ukrainian pilot fired a missile on the day the Malaysia Airlines plane went down, killing 298 people," a report by The Guardian posted by the end of the year was to read. "The group said a witness, who was not named, worked at an airfield in the Ukrainian city of Dnipropetrovsk where he claimed to have seen a warplane take off on 17 July with air-to-air missiles and return without them, a Russian report said. The group describing itself as a Russian investigative committee said the testimony of the man 'is important proof that Ukrainian military was implicated in the crash of the Boeing 777'. However, previous claims of Ukrainian involvement in shooting down the civilian passenger jet have been roundly dismissed. Efforts to shift the blame from the Kremlin have extended to supposed satellite photos that were said to implicate the Ukrainians but were quickly identified as crude fakes and dismissed." 17)

"Crude fakes"? Hardly so, as it would appear pretty soon. "Malaysia Airlines' flight MH17 that crashed in southeastern Ukraine in July 2014 was shot down by a Buk surface-to-air missile from a location where Kiev's Buk systems were stationed," Sputnik News reported on May 6 2015 referring to a report by Russian military engineers that had been grabbed by one of Russia's main opposition newspapers Novaya Gazeta. The most likely reason for the destruction of Malaysia Airlines' Boeing-777 (MH17) in the air was the impact of a 9M38M1 antiaircraft guided missile from a Buk-M1 missile system," the document was quoted as reading – adding that "…the area over which the plane was shot down was the spot where Ukraine's Buk missile systems were stationed". The document had been sent to the Dutch expertise team for its information, but no comment from its side was ever published. 18)

A month earlier, the Dutch authorities had published over 500 documents related to the crash, Sputnik News reported on April 10. "However, some 150 of the requested documents remain classified, triggering discussions in the media about the controversial progress of the investigation," the agency noted - quoting Jean Fransman, deputy head of press briefings and policy presentations at the Ministry of Security and Justice as commenting: "Under the Dutch law it is possible to make exemption on these document of the government. Those exemptions are for example national security or private opinions of civil servants. On every document is stated why (parts of) information is not made public." 19)

Since the information is kept classified, the last observation is of course hard to check. Has any information be held back because it did indicate that the Ukrainian armed forces were indeed the perpetrators? The suggestion itself was already far from secret. Thus, Sputnik News reported on the previous 20 March: "Captain Voloshin, the Ukrainian pilot implicated in bringing down flight MH17, may have gone missing. An unnamed source earlier identified him as the perpetrator behind the plane's tragic crash last July, and according to Russia's Investigative Committee, the individual even passed a polygraph. The still unnamed source visited the editorial office of Russia's Komsomolskaya Pravda newspaper earlier this week and provided his eye-witness account of what happened on July 17th. He claims that a Su-25 fighter jet flown by Cpt. Voloshin departed from Aviatorskoye air base carrying two air-to-air missiles but returned without them, and that the pilot frighteningly muttered such statements as 'wrong plane' and that 'the plane happened to be in the wrong place at the wrong time'. Such a version of events could have been easily been taken for a lie had the witness not passed a polygraph administered by Russia's Investigative Committee. Deepening the intrigue, Voloshin, the prime suspect, seems to have disappeared. Provided that the account is true (which has thus far not been disproven, even by polygraph), then an absolutely different picture begins to emerge about the devastating events of July 17th that completely contrasts with Kiev's official narrative." 20)

4. "The structure of the threat"

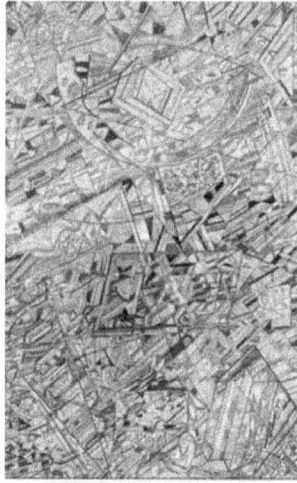

*Pavel Filonov. Formula of the Universe. 1920-22. Watercolor on paper.
35.6 x 22.2 cm. The Russian Museum, St. Petersburg, Russia*

To get back to the financial dimensions of the story, the banking and finance scandal is more than incidental. For also prominent in the (yet incomplete) file of Ablyazov's connections with the powers-that-be in present-day Ukraine (or most of it) is that of the Finance Minister, Alexander Shlapak. "Shlapak acknowledges that between 1994 and at least 1998 he was an executive at Privatbank's Lviv branch, and then vice-chairman of Privatbank in charge of its western Ukraine operations, an investigative report published recently by long-experienced news analyst in the former USSR John Helmer, reads. "Since then Shlapak has been in and out of Ukrainian government. From 2010 until his February appointment to be finance minister, he was a senior executive at IMG International Holding Company. In the Ukrainian records, this is a 6-year old insurance brokerage and fund manager, with a conglomerate of insurance companies in Ukraine, Russia and Kazakhstan. The records also reveal that while Shlapak was in charge at IMG, an investment in Oranta Insurance Company, a related party, disappeared when the latter lost its operating licence and was ordered into bankruptcy administration. Oranta has been part-owned by the controversial Kazakh business figure, Mukhtar Ablyazov, and by a Cyprus front company controlled by Victor Pinchuk. At the time Pinchuk was also operating Rossiya Insurance in Russia, but it has subsequently collapsed into bankruptcy amid allegations of cash stripping through fraudulent reinsurance schemes. Who controls IMG is not known. Shlapak was asked if he continued to have a business association with Privatbank after he left its employ. His spokesman refused to say. Asked the same question Privatbank spokesman in Dniepropetrovsk, Oleg Serga, also declined to answer. A well-known financial reporter in Kiev comments: "[Shlapak] cannot be called an agent of Kolomoisky." Asked to confirm how much Privatbank has received to date from NBU in ELA payments, Serga will not disclose how much ELA Privatbank has been receiving, but he disputes the timing that has been reported."

All this demonstrates that American flirtations with far-right extremists are a lot more than just coincidence or even mere opportunism. They fit into a pattern the dimensions of which are hair-raising. In late 2014, Kyrgyz security agencies announced a court case under preparation against a US NGO called Advocacy Center, suspected as preparing provocations among Kyrgyz and Uzbek communities in the west of the country, which has been the scene of bloody confrontations in 1990 and once more in 2010. The NGO is funded by Freedom House, which receives some of its funding from the US Agency for International Development (USAID). US representatives balked and barked at the allegation – without, however, going into detail. After President Atambayev announced that the case had been "dropped" the affair fell swiftly into oblivion. But all the same, it seems that there is more to this than some overzealous civil servants' curiosity. The main element is that economic and monetary interests at stake here are astronomic. "As more and more of the world moves against the US dollar, at some point in the near future the US economy will plunge into a free-fall nosedive of a severe depression. But then this also has been the oligarchs' eventual plan in the making for some time," a paper by Global Research posted on June 9 2014 reads. "In fact the biggest East vs. West geographical bone of contention covers the elongated stretch of land 10,000 miles long spanning every country bordering Russia and China, all those onetime outer Soviet state nations that end in 'stan' that Americans can neither pronounce nor remember. From Europe through the trans-Caucasus of Central Asia to Tibet all the way to East Asia, the big East vs. the big West face-off in recent months has been heating up with noticeable mounting tensions throughout. [...] All along the Russia-China bloc's own backyard, the West is fomenting and creating dirty secret wars spilling death squad bloodshed in any number of these highly unstable, corrupt, resource-rich borderlands. The strategy is to head Russia off at the pass from forming its own Eurasian Union [EAU – meant here is the EEU] by next year with Kazakhstan and Belarus. A number of other nations in the region like Armenia, Kyrgyzstan and Tajikistan that may even include prior Western leaning nations like Georgia have all expressed an interest in also joining this EAU as well. If Putin succeeds in acquiring these pivotal nations on its side, the EAU would rival the EU and NATO in economic and military power. This development would weaken and potentially threaten the oligarchs' central banking cabal."

The structure of the threat as propagated by Washington is a combination of military and industrial clout and increasing monetary tools to impose on the world by the Sino-Russian tandem. "Russia, China and Iran are the only major nations outside Latin America that serve as serious barriers to American worldwide military expansion and dominance. By driving into former Soviet territory in the Caspian Sea basin and Central Asia, the Pentagon and NATO are completing their military advance on all three nations. Azerbaijan, Kazakhstan, Kyrgyzstan, Tajikistan, Turkmenistan and Uzbekistan are situated in a compact zone between China, Iran and Russia, and all but Uzbekistan border one or more of the three nations,"

an earlier report by Global Research dated August 12 2010 was to read.
"Notwithstanding the deadly upheavals in Kyrgyzstan this April and June,
the U.S. and NATO have substantially increased the deployment of troops –
at least 50,000 a month – and equipment through the nation for the West's
150,000-troop, nine-year war in Afghanistan. Washington and Brussels
have activated the Northern Distribution Network to transport supplies to
the Afghan war front from ports on the Baltic, Black and Caspian Seas
through the Caucasus and Central Asia, pulling Azerbaijan and the five
Central Asian states deeper into the Western military phalanx. This year
leading Pentagon, State Department and NATO officials have paid visits to
Azerbaijan, Kazakhstan, Kyrgyzstan, Tajikistan and Uzbekistan, including
the first trip by a U.S. secretary of defense in five years and a secretary of
state in eighteen years to the first-named state. In April President Obama
secured military overflight and transit rights from his Kazakh opposite
number, President Nursultan Nazarbayev, in a nation adjoining China and
Russia." 21)

Meanwhile, on the ground in Bishkek, the alarm was sounded as early
as shortly after the restoration of legitimate government authority in
spring 2010. Already then, it became clear that the USA had been a lot
happier with the crooked Bakiyev regime than with the newly established
parliamentary democracy. "The August 7 (2010) edition of the Washington
Post substantiated earlier reports that the U.S. plans to establish a comparable
base in Kyrgyzstan, which like Tajikistan borders China," the paper relates.
"The article revealed that 'The United States is planning to move ahead with
construction of a $10 million military training base in Osh, Kyrgyzstan,
the site of a bloody uprising in June....Called the Osh Polygon, the base
was first proposed under former Kyrgyz president Kurmanbek Bakiyev as
a facility to train Kyrgyz troops for counterterrorism operations. After the
ouster of Bakiyev...discussions continued under the new Kyrgyz president,
Roza Otunbayeva, with whose government Washington is trying to broaden
relationships...Osh Polygon will consist of a secure garrison compound with

officers' quarters and barracks for enlisted personnel, plus range facilities, firing pistols, rifles, crew-served weapons and explosive ordnance'." 22)

The overall ideal behind the scheme look all too clear. America's, or rather America's warfare conspiracy clique has set as its goal to grab all the territories surrounding the Russian Federation it possibly can under the pretext of "liberation" and "democratisation" but in reality with no other aim than to usurp and exploit them (especially those with rich natural resources which most of them have) in the process, and with the final purpose to fragmentise the Russian Federation and destroy it from within, since in terms of natural resources Russia outmatches all others by far. Using those resources for the nation's own development is not something America wants to see happen. Anything to prevent that has been used elsewhere in the past: military coups followed by jungle dictatorships, mobsters and terrorists – in the case of Russia and other former Soviet republics, even an "alliance of convenience" with the likes of the so-called Islamic State that terrorises the Near East cannot be overlooked. Located at the gates of China and at the crossroads of smuggling routes, Kyrgyzstan looks like the ideal playground to carry out such schemes.

5. Provocations and intrigues

Pavel Filonov. Untitled (The Riders). 1913. Watercolor, Indian ink,
feather, brush, graphite pencil on paper. 28.8 x 28.8 cm.
The Russian Museum, St. Petersburg, Russia

But at least so far, fortunately, the plans have failed. "Much to the dismay of the United States, Russia has been steadily strengthening its foothold in Kyrgyzstan in recent years," a fresh article on the issue posted by the e-periodical The New Great Game Round-Up in its edition of October 21 2014 was to read. "This became apparent in June of this year, when American troops vacated the important U.S. air base at Manas International Airport after the Kyrgyz government had yielded to Russian pressure and agreed to kick the Americans out. Since 2001, the U.S. had used Manas not only to support U.S. military operations in Afghanistan, but also to engage in all kinds of nefarious activities. After years of unsuccessful attempts to convince Bishkek of closing the base, the Russians finally got their way a few months ago, marking 'Kyrgyzstan's new era as a Russian client state' according to Alexander Cooley, Deputy Director for Social Sciences Programming at Columbia University's Harriman Institute, which is famous for its anti-Russian bias. Cooley's statement shows that the closure of Manas was a heavy blow for the United States. Moscow lost no time in capitalising on the departure of U.S. forces and is now apparently planning to expand Kant Air Base in Kyrgyzstan." 23)

In summer 2015, not a single thread of evidence for ll this was to be found on the ground. What did appear, by contrast, was the presence of one of America's most notorious trouble-spreading agencies known as TechCamp, which had already played a key role in fuelling the Ukrainian civil war. Now, it appeared to be working on a scheme that looked like Ukraine's spitting image using similar methods in the run-up to parliamentary elections due for early October. "Lately, the Kyrgyz authorities have been increasingly suspicious of the activities of American NGOs in the country," the document reads further down. One Kyrgyz MP was particularly concerned about the recent TechCamp event in Bishkek: Kyrgyz MP concerned about meetings held with youth by NGO holding similar meetings in Ukraine prior to unrest MP Irina Karamushkina said at today's plenary session of the Parliament of Kyrgyzstan the NGO TechCamp is holding meetings with youth in Bishkek, which held similar meetings prior to the Maidan events in Ukraine. 'This NGO has been holding meetings with our youth for 2 weeks already. Do our special services have information about what kind of meetings this NGO is holding? This NGO held similar meetings with youth prior to the events on Maidan in Ukraine. Aren't we wasting time, while someone is shaping views of your youth?' the lawmaker interrogated. ... Karamushkina's concerns with regard to the TechCamps initiative, which is led by the U.S. State Department's Office of Diplomacy, might seem absurd at first glance but given that former Ukrainian MP Oleg Tsarov demanded on 20 November 2013 a criminal investigation into the activities of TechCamp in Ukraine because he believed it was part of 'preparations for inciting a civil war', it is probably a good idea to keep a close eye on the TechCamp events."

So what is the overall pattern – at least according to the theories reflected here? Washington seems to be driven by fears that it will lose its monetary grip on the world economy – and determined to stick to that grip and thwart all attempts to circumvent the US dollar as a global clearing tool at all costs – in pretty much the same way it remained determined to maintain its position in the global market place in the wake of the Second World War, after Stalin had refused to cooperate within the Marshall Plan and denominated everything within the USSR's domestic economy in roubles with a fixed exchange rate to western currencies. Fears that the European Union, though then still at a rudimentary stage, might opt for a "third way" made the Americans initiate what has become known as Operation Gladio, using former nazi chiefs and collaborators to spread anti-communist fears in Europe through destabilisation threats in the form of terrorist attacks, the most notorious one was the bomb at the railway station of Bologna, Italy, in 1980, killing close to a hundred, which later appeared to be the work of Gladio-linked neofascist cells. In the course of 2014, fears were raised that Gladio, which in fact never ceased to exist, has come straight home to Kyrgyzstan…

Some people will always be looking for trouble – and if they fail to find it at home, they will simply start looking for it elsewhere. If this is the price one pays for liberty, let it be. But trouble it is. And in a world where macro-political provocations and intrigues are once more in vogue, it will never be too hard to find to begin with. Over the summer of 2014, opposition MP Omurbek Abdyrakhmanov and an "extraparliamentary opposition leader" as he labels himself Ravshan Zheenbekov asked the Ambassador of Kyrgyzstan to arrange a meeting with the United States Senator John McCain, the local independent news agency 24.kg reported on September 19, referring to unnamed "sources in the Parliament" in the agency's words. 24)

"Letter № 6-4610 N/14 to the Ambassador Extraordinary and Plenipotentiary of the Kyrgyz Republic to the United States and Canada Muktar Dzhumaliyev was signed by Omurbek Abdyrakhmanov and Ravshan Zheenbekov," the news report read further down. "The latter is the leader of the national opposition movement, his colleague Abdyrakhmanov also reckons himself to be opposition. Any reason for the meeting has not been specified. 'The date and time can be oriented sooner, convenient for Mr. McCain,' the letter read." It seems that the controversial US ultra-rightist politician has met before – in Kiev at the barricades to be precise. "In December 2013 the domestic media wrote that Ravshan Zheenbekov performed in Kiev on Euromaidan and secretly met with John McCain in that trip," in the news agency's words. "He supports anti-Russian regimes in Ukraine and Georgia."

6. Connections leading to John McCain and cronies

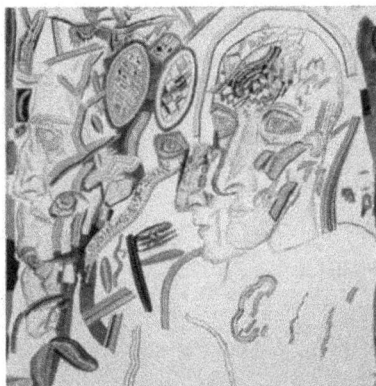

Pavel Filonov. Heads. 1924. Watercolor, Indian ink, feather on paper.
44.3 x 42.5 cm. The Russian Museum, St. Petersburg, Russia

In a follow-up report published in September 22, the agency quoted Zheenbekov as confirming the affair, commenting that ..."our meeting with John McCain is motivated by the desire of opposition to build relations with the democratically-minded politicians and countries. [...] This letter was registered in the General Department of the Parliament. Everything is open and transparent. We have not yet received the answer, and it is far from certain that this meeting will take place at all, but we want to deal with democratically-minded politicians and states, focused on democracy. But our authorities prefer to be friends with authoritarian regimes. We have prepared a strategy for development of Kyrgyzstan and intend to present it in all democratic institutions. In 2009, by the way, there was already a similar meeting with American senators, where we presented the draft constitution. Omurbek Tekebayev, Alibek Dzhekshenkulov, Bolot Sher, Kubatbek Baybolov Omurbek Abdyrakhmanov and me took part there from Kyrgyzstan. If we receive the answer, we will depart for the United States, most likely at our own expense," 25)

61

Democratic-minded? Having begun as an airborne baby killer in the American war against Vietnam, during which his plane crashed upon which he was taken prisoner of war and according to his own account "tortured" leaving him "physically disturbed", he went into politics on his return, ever heftily supporting anti-Soviet feelings and witch hunting parties against alleged "communists" instigated by such sinister characters as Wallace and McCarthy. Once elected senator of his home state Arizona, he got involved in illegal election fund raising, but was put off the hook by the Senate's supervising committee. He tried to run against Obama in the latest presidential election, but lost rather dramatically. Still, the fact that tens of millions of American citizens voted for such a character looks more than a little disturbing.

Through the year 2014, McCain's own disturbance tended to look less and less physical and more and more mental. In Kiev, his role seems to have been a bit more than just sympathetic. He could be suspected to have links with an obscure American organisation known as Blackwater (also as Xe or Academi), operating under the cover of a private security firm but in fact the operator (though possibly not the only one) of a long list of murders, massacres and other terror campaigns staged by US intelligence agencies and the Pentagon. Among the locations of Blackwater's handiwork are Vietnam during the war, and later Iraq. But the misdeeds committed recently in Ukraine, culminating in the massacre of loyalist demonstrators in Odessa who were burnt alive in a building where they had taken refuge with those who escaped being strangled and stabbed to death, have also been put on Blackwater's record. Here as well the name of McCain was bound to pop up which it did.

"Breaking during the weekend was a story by Der Spiegel and Bild that American mercenaries were on the ground in Kiev. According to the report 400 mercenaries from Academi (formerly Blackwater) were on the ground "involved in a punitive operation mounted by Ukraine's new government," a report posted on May 18 2014 by WashingtonsBlog was to read. "Indeed, the German newspaper apparently claims that the American mercenaries are *directing* and *coordinating* the attacks by the fascist Right Sector militia. Blackwater is more or less an extension of the CIA. There are also dozens of CIA and FBI 'advisors' in Ukraine, and the CIA director visited Kiev before the massacres started. [...] While the 'Orange Revolution' was carried out more covertly, the 'Euromaidan' was openly backed by both the US and the European Union. At the height of the protests, US Senator John McCain would literally take the stage with the ultra-right, Neo-Nazi Svoboda Party leaders as well as meet with 'Fatherland Party' member and future 'prime minister', Arseniy Yatsenyuk." 26)

There could even be a reason to track the organisation back to Kyrgyzstan. In the uprising against the Bakiyev regime in April 2010, snipers under the latter's command posted on rooftops surrounding the Ala Too Square in Bishkek have been held responsible for most of the killings on the ground – until autopsies confirmed that a number had been killed not bu bullets coming from upper levels but from the ground, thereby suggesting infiltrators drawing guns at critical moments: a method that bears Blackwater's trade mark. McCain's link with Blackwater was already clearly exposed in an article published back in June 2009 under the header Blackwater Still Working in Iraq for John McCain-linked 'Non-Profit' organisations. "Loosely affiliated with the Republican Party, the International Republican Institute (IRI) works closely with the the National Endowment for Democracy and United States foreign policy instruments, including the U.S. Department of State and the U.S. Agency for International Development, to support economic and political development programs around the world. The organisation is almost exclusively funded by the U.S. government and related agencies. IRI is also closely linked to Sen. John McCain," the report read. 27)

But the story far from ends even there. An even more disturbing connection leading to McCain touches upon a phenomenon which worries authorities in Kyrgyzstan to extremes these days – being the terror-driven self-styled Islamic State of Iraq and Syria (ISIS) stretching over the former's northern and the latter's eastern provinces. The ISIS has been virtually created by American state and state-related institutions, in an attempt to topple the government in Damascus. Starting as of 2014, the ISIS, by then better known as ISIL (Islamic State of Iraq and the Levant) was to be under American bombs with the silent consent of the Syrian and Iraqi governments. At the same time, hundreds if not thousands of "volunteers" (read: desperados) from Central Asia including Kyrgyzstan would appear to be in the service of ISIS and trained in such charming arts as sabotage and massacre.

"Kentucky Republican Senator Rand Paul was walloped on Thursday by a series of media reports that concluded he was wrong to claim fellow GOP Sen. John McCain of Arizona unwittingly met with ISIS terrorists when he held a secret 2013 meeting with rebel leaders in Syria," the Daily Mail in one of its bright-eyed moments reported on September 19 2014, showing photographs of McCain in sinister company. "Paul contends that the Obama administration's effort to 'train and equip' moderate Syrian rebels against ISIS, the self-proclaimed Islamic State of Iraq and al-Sham, is foolhardy because the U.S. could wind up arming radical jihadis if alliances shift in the future. The McCain photos, he said, show 'the quandary of determining who are the moderates and who aren't. ... The objective evidence is that the ones doing most of the fighting and most of the battles among the rebels in Syria are the radical Islamists.' On the Senate floor Wednesday, Paul doubled down. 'We don't even know who is in charge of the Free Syrian Army,' he said 'They voted out one guy, and in another, and he didn't even know they were voting. There are estimates that half of the Free Syrian Army has defected to al Qaeda and ISIS.' McCain has long been an advocate of arming rebel groups, arguing even before ISIS became a regional menace that they should have U.S. support to fight dictator Bashar al-Assad." 28) INTERSPACE Considering it all, it cannot possibly be considered a crime to meet such a man. But whether it is a good idea remains subject to doubt. Almost certain is that far from everybody would think this would be a good idea indeed. Also on September 19 2014, Kyrgyzstan's acting Interior Minister Melis Turganbayev was quoted as declaring that "those persons attempting to destabilise the situation in the country will be toughly punished" in the words of the Bishkek-based news agency AkiPress. "Fight against official crimes, prevention and solution of corruption related crimes are among priority areas in work of the Interior Ministry," the official was quoted as saying. "We should ensure public safety in the country through coordination of actions between involved agencies. Of course, every person in a democratic society has right to freedom of speech, but tough and lawful measures will be applied towards those who try to destabilise the situation in the country, to disturb public order and to involve young people into protest actions," the Acting Interior Minister warned. "We will conduct a merciless fight against crime. Carrying out reforms, the Ministry is open for cooperation. We will take into account the opinion of general public, recommendations of parliamentarians," Therefore, in the unlikely case that the honourable Kyrgyz MP and his associate should bring John McCain to Kyrgyzstan, police could well think of a few good reasons to ask him a few questions at the station...

CHAPTER III

A TALE OF OIL, GAS AND CASH

*Pavel Filonov. Raider (Mugger). 1926-28. The Russian Museum,
St. Petersburg, Russia*

Energy resources have been the cause of armed political confrontations between states and multi-state alliances for a very long time. It started with coal which led to all-out war between France and Prussia on several occasions, and ended with the First World War in which, for all it mattered, oil was playing a key role as well. Baku with its immensely rich oil fields was among the main prizes for Hitler's Germany to invade the USSR. America's two acts of aggression against Iraq were about oil and little else where it comes to reality – as was its and France's support for the so-called Arab spring, especially the one that took place in Libya. In all cases, the aim was to prevent major shifts in the trade flows of energy commodities around the world, which could lead to changes in the so-called world energy map. Ever since the beginning of America's interventions in European affairs which started with World War I, Washington has used all of its military and political clout to keep America in a favourable position to as a major consumer to the detriment of producers.

Today, in the ongoing "Second Cold War" under the pretext of Ukraine's unruly behaviour (the adherence of the Crimea to Russia has all but be forgotten and so will the regions of Donetsk and Lugansk once they consolidate themselves as "unofficially independent" states after the example of Northern Cyprus, Nagorno Karabakh in Azerbaijan, Abkhazia and South-Ossetia in Georgia and the "Trans-Dnyestr Republic" in Moldova), it looks like it is the turn of natural gas which is the main stake in the game. Despite the fact that neither oil nor gas from the former USSR has ever arrived, or will ever arrive, in the USA, Washington's power-wielders "behind the throne" keep trying to dictate the energy balance – or rather the lack of it – between the former Soviet Union and a rather reluctant European Union. It is this pattern, and in particular the FSU's reaction by removing western Europe from the top of its agenda to replace it by China which virtually overnight draws Kyrgyzstan out of its traditional splendid isolation which has given it a chance to develop itself into the region's sole parliamentary republic but also kept it cash-strapped ever since the break-up of the USSR which delivered the country its unsolicited independence. Today, Kyrgyzstan is becoming the very knot that binds cooperation between the Russian Federation and the People's Republic of China to the benefit of both – and as it is hoped for, to the benefit of Kyrgyzstan and its Central Asian neighbours as well.

Even though it has kept the back door open for gas supplies to Europe replacing Ukraine with Turkey, the Kremlin, with overwhelming support of the Russian Parliament and the overall population, has now made it clear that it does not entirely depend on the European Union as a customer for natural gas. Instead, Gazprom which is majority-owned by the state and thereby under the Kremlin's orders is stepping up its supplies to China with incredible speed, leaving Europe with leftovers. By controlling the track from Turkmenistan and Uzbekistan into China, Gazprom is also controlling increasing supplies from western Central Asia to the People's Republic, thereby practically blocking their eventual supplies in the direction of Europe.

1. A China-Russia rapprochement

Pavel Filonov. Composition. 1928-29. Oil on canvas.
The Russian Museum, St. Petersburg, Russia

America's "men behind the throne" are understandably (from Washington's point of view at least) worried about this on one hand while on the other hand trying to make the world believe that the current trend should be considered doomed to fail. In pretty much the same manner, for all it matters, Washington's conflict mongers have tried to thwart the formation of the Eurasian Economic Union – so far in vain. In order not to confuse readers with selected quotes which could blur the overall picture, here follows the integral text of an example of such verbal warfare.

"Some analysts believe that 2014 ushered in a new era of Cold War-style geopolitics. Russian President Vladimir Putin's invasion of Ukraine and annexation of Crimea was met with heavy economic sanctions from Europe and the United States, weakening Russia's ties with the West and leaving the Kremlin eager to strengthen ties with China," an article posted on January 12 written by one of the most prominent men-behind-the-throne named Joseph S. Nye, a former US assistant secretary of defense and chairman of the US National Intelligence Council, nowadays professor at the Harvard

University and a member of the World Economic Forum Global Agenda Council on the Future of Government, was to read. "At first glance, it seems plausible. Indeed, traditional balance-of-power theory suggests that US primacy in power resources should be offset by a Sino-Russian partnership. INTERSPACE Perhaps more convincing, there seems to be historical precedent for such a partnership. In the 1950s, China and the Soviet Union were allied against the US," the article related further down. "After US President Richard Nixon's opening to China in 1972, the balance shifted, with the US and China cooperating to limit what they viewed as a dangerous rise in the Soviet Union's power. With the collapse of the Soviet Union, that *de facto* US-China alliance ended, and a China-Russia rapprochement began. In 1992, the two countries declared that they were pursuing a 'constructive partnership'; in 1996, they progressed toward a 'strategic partnership'; and in 2001, they signed a treaty of 'friendship and cooperation Organisation'." 29)

"In recent years, China and Russia have cooperated closely in the UN Security Council and taken similar positions on Internet regulation," the text reads further down. "They have used diplomatic frameworks – such as the BRICS group of major emerging countries (along with Brazil, India, and South Africa) and the Shanghai Cooperation Organization (along with Kazakhstan, Kyrgyzstan, Tajikistan, and Uzbekistan) – to coordinate positions. And Putin has struck up a good working relationship with Chinese President Xi Jinping, based on their shared domestic illiberalism and desire to counter American ideology and influence. Their economic relationship, too, seems to be progressing. Last May, shortly after the annexation of Crimea, Russia announced a $400 billion deal to supply 38 billion cubic metre (bcm) of gas to China annually for 30 years, beginning in 2019."

"The contract, between Russia's state-owned energy giant Gazprom and the China National Petroleum Corporation, entails the construction of a 2,500-mile gas pipeline to China's Heilongjiang province (where, incidentally, the two countries nearly went to war a few decades ago). Though the exact price remains secret, it appears that Russia offered major concessions, after nearly a decade of negotiations, to ensure the deal's success. Moreover, in November, Gazprom announced a framework agreement to deliver an additional 30 bcm of gas to China's Xingjiang Province from western Siberia for 30 years via another new pipeline. If the "eastern" and "western" pipelines are completed as planned, the 68 bcm they deliver to China annually would dwarf the 40 bcm that Russia exports to its current largest customer, Germany. This may seem to portend an ever-deepening bilateral relationship. But there is a hitch: the gas deals amplify a significant bilateral trade imbalance, with Russia supplying raw materials to China and importing Chinese manufactures. And the gas deals do not make up for Russia's lost access to the Western technology that it needs to develop frontier Arctic fields and become an energy superpower, not just China's gas station."

Just erroneous or deliberately misleading? A bit of both, as it appears. "In fact, the problems with a Sino-Russian alliance run even deeper. With its economic, military, and demographic heft – China generates considerable unease in Russia," the article continues. "Consider the demographic situation in eastern Siberia, where six million Russians live across the border from up to 120 million Chinese. Furthermore, Russia's economic and military power has been in decline, whereas China's has exploded. Anxiety over China's conventional military superiority probably motivated, at least partly, Russia's 2009 announcement of a new military doctrine explicitly reserving the right to first use of nuclear weapons – a stance that resembles America's Cold War force posture, aimed at deterring superior conventional Soviet forces in Europe. These imbalances suggest that Russia would resist a tight military alliance with China, even as the two countries pursue mutually beneficial tactical diplomatic coordination. China's willingness to cooperate with Russia also has its limits. After all, China's development strategy depends on its continued integration into the world economy – and, specifically, reliable access to American markets and technology. The Chinese Communist Party's legitimacy depends on strong economic growth, and it will not risk this strategy for some 'authoritarian alliance' with Russia. Even within multilateral forums, the relationship between Russia and China is far from balanced. Given that China's economy is larger than the other four BRICS economies combined, the group's initiatives – including its new development bank – are likely to reflect a disproportionate Chinese influence. And though the Shanghai Cooperation Organisation has facilitated some diplomatic coordination, China and Russia remain locked in a struggle for influence in Central Asia."

It could hardly be more misleading, or more nonsensical. As noted before, historic reality shows that America never meant to "deter" the Soviet block, but only to destroy it. Second, Russia does not need a "tight military alliance" with China since both countries are perfectly capable of defending themselves on their own if needed. And if one compares the political systems of Russia and China, it is not hard to conclude which of the two is more "authoritarian". Moreover, the industry of Russia, including the military one, remains far superior to that of China, and so do the former other technical manufacturing sectors. But the financial clout of the People's Republic is indeed stronger. In this situation, advantages and shortcomings on both sides fit in perfectly well into a tandem which is bound to be of enormous benefit to Kyrgyzstan as well. This can be achieved by and large without America or even the EU. At the bottom of it all remains the question whether politics are supposed to be subordinate to economics or economics to politics. Washington seems to insist on the latter option, with nothing else in view than its own desire to rule the world by dividing it with the use of gunboat diplomacy and economic squeezes. With this in mind, Nixon indeed tried to use China as a wild card during CW I. It should not be allowed to do so in CW II. As for Kyrgyzstan (Kyrzbekistan according to the New York Times in one of its most recent blunders), since it is a strategic factor amidst current world developments, its main task is to develop a realistic high-grade diplomacy towards its powerful neighbours, not aimed at dividing them but to reinforce mutual consolidation for the sake of regional and indeed global stability.

2. Life after Ukraine: destination Kyrgyzstan

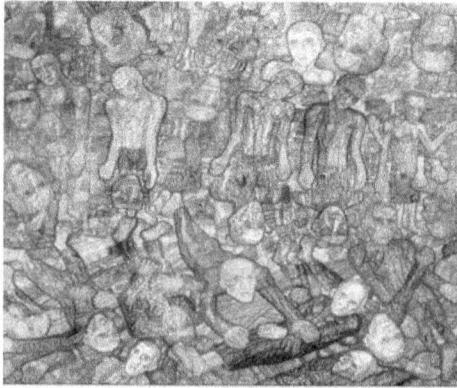

Pavel Filonov. Composition (A Raid). 1938(?). Oil on paper
71 x 86.8 cm. The Russian Museum, St. Petersburg, Russia

So where is there life after Ukraine? For western economic, political and economic blocks, the question involves survival. For the wider region to the east of the battleground centred around Kyrgyzstan, it rather means resurrection. Proof of the pudding is that media and other observers within the public domain in the eastern zone tend to remain pretty cool, shrugging of so-called sanctions and pointing at them as a golden opportunity to maintain life after the USA and its European puppets rather than seeing them as harmful. The "terrible blow to Russia's economy" and those of its allies simply fails to take place – as figures amply demonstrate. It merely consists of wishful thinking by those behind the device, echoed shamelessly by most western mass media in a part of the world where the press is nonetheless supposed to be independent and critical. These days, it is not.

One example is an article published in the yet rather prestigious-looking periodical The Diplomat in late September written under the illusive header

"Russia's chokehold on Kyrgyzstan" by a certain Casey Michel – "graduate student at Columbia's Harriman Institute, focusing on post-Soviet political development" in the subhead's words. Not only are these the obvious words of someone who has trouble distinguishing Kyrgyzstan from Kenya not unlike the way an overwhelming majority of US citizens appears to have trouble distinguishing Ukraine from Uruguay and who may never have set foot in Kyrgyzstan. It is most of all a sad example out of many that shows how so-called opinion makers sitting on quasi-academic pedestals prostrate and prostitute themselves to treacherous warmongers sitting behind hermetic security shields with little other aim than to destroy the world. 30)

At the heart of the avalanche of blurred outcries is Kyrgyzstan's entry into the EEU. "President Almazbek Atambayev said Kyrgyzstan will join the Eurasian Union by the end of the year," the author notes in his ragtag report. "Not only has Kyrgyzstan pushed back planned accession time and again, but Bishkek has also announced that it won't be ready to implement all requirements until 2020 – all while still weaning loan after undefined loan from Moscow. Moreover, Atambayev didn't actually say Kyrgyzstan will join the EEU by the end of the year; rather, he said he hoped they'd be able to. [...] Kyrgyzstan fits firmly in Russia's pocket, at least in the short-term. There should be little dispute around this, and all the more after the United States' summer departure from its largest foothold in the region. But this geopolitical pull isn't due to Rosneft's (nonexistent) purchase of a 51 percent stake in Rosneft *(sic)*, and is in fact hampered by Gazprom's role in the gas shutoff in Kyrgyzstan's south. [...] Assuming any nation will march obediently into the EEU's fold is a fool's errand. Bishkek does, indeed, remain firmly oriented toward Moscow. [...] And with Russia's declining economic appeal, China's increasing sway, and Kyrgyzstan's own agency, this direction looks increasingly impermanent."

Back to the classroom or a hopeless case? Sheer stupidity or deliberated false tracks? It could well be a sort of combination of both. It becomes clear here that "economic appeal" to the average Yankee-doodle comes down to sheer raping and reaping – something that should have been put to an end a long time ago. As for Kyrgyzstan's entry into the EEU, it has been put forward, not backward – as more accurately reported facts clearly explain. "In May 2014 Kyrgyzstan declared its desire to join the Customs and Eurasian Economic Union on January 1, 2015," an update report published by 24.kg on September 30 read. "Since then, the ministries and departments hastily make changes to laws and regulations to bring them in conformity with the Union. Generally changes should be done in 21 bills. The cabinet approved the entire package. In early September, the Parliament made the first batch of changes from 16 bills: 4 relate to customs regulations, 2 to technical ones, 6 to tariffs and non-customs control, and 1 to trade and finance."

So what is the real balance so far? Kyrgyzstan is seizing a unique opportunity to get the best out of its mostly idle but excellent industrial production capacity – which is something the west is loath to see happening. What is even most abhorrent for western interested parties is that it does not plan to complete that process under the thumb of western corporate manipulators, but in cooperation with other so-called emerging economies in the region – varying from Russia and Kazakhstan to China and India. Kyrgyzstan and Kazakhstan alone have what it all takes: energy resources, construction, metallic and food resources. And they are not part of the boycott imposed by US and EU warmongers on the Russian Federation. In early October 2014, at the oil and gas service and contracting exhibition in Almaty, I spoke to a European contractor selling safety and protection services and devices – asking him if this was the ideal venue for "sanction"-targeted companies such as Gazprom to come shopping. The reply: "They were here this morning"…

"As part of a working visit of the Gazprom delegation to the Kyrgyz Republic, a meeting between Gazprom's Management Committee Chairman Alexey Miller and Kyrgyz President Almazbek Atambayev took place in Bishkek today," a press release from Gazprom dated August 29 read. "The parties addressed the main cooperation issues in the oil and gas sector and noted that Gazprom's entry into the Kyrgyz gas market was a guarantee of uninterrupted gas supply to Kyrgyz consumers. In this regard, the meeting discussed Gazprom Kyrgyzstan's intentions to extensively develop and upgrade gas transmission facilities across the Republic. A focus was placed on the southern regions of Kyrgyzstan. The participants looked into Gazprom's plans to conduct exploration activities in the Kugart and Eastern Mailu-Suu IV blocks, as well as the Company's involvement in the development of the Kyrgyz wholesale and retail refined products market. Alexey Miller also met today with Kyrgyz Prime Minister Djoomart Otorbaev. The parties addressed, among other things, the issues related to the Republic's preparations for the forthcoming autumn/winter period." 31)

The story goes a long way back in time indeed. "In May 2003 Gazprom and the Kyrgyz Republic Government entered into the long-term Agreement of Cooperation in the gas industry for a period of 25 years," Gazprom documentation reads. "The Agreement provides for: exploration, development and operation of hydrocarbon fields in the Kyrgyz Republic; retrofitting, construction and operation of gas trunklines and other gas infrastructure facilities in the Kyrgyz Republic; gas transmission and supply as part of joint projects. The document also stipulates the joint reconstruction of compressor stations at the Maili-Suu UGS facility as well as procurement of necessary equipment for the Kyrgyz gas complex. The subsurface use licenses for geological exploration of the Kugart and the Eastern Mailisu IV areas were obtained in early 2008. In July 2008 a geological exploration program was approved for the Kugart and Eastern Mailisu IV areas, and in October 2008 a Memorandum of Understanding was signed to develop cooperation within the privatization of a part of the state-owned stake in Kyrgyzgaz. In December 2008 Gazprom worked out the geological exploration projects in these areas. In 2010 exploration activities in the Kyrgyz Republic were suspended as a result of political events in the country. In February 2011 Gazprom and the Kyrgyz Government signed two protocols to resume and promote the cooperation. With a view to streamline the geological exploration program and bring up to date the economic efficiency indicators of the project, updates were made in the feasibility study of geological survey of the Kugart and Eastern Mailisu IV oil and gas prospects in the Kyrgyz Republic as well as in the Stepwise Geological Exploration Program. The Program will continue according to the results obtained." 32)

"The proven natural gas reserves in the Kyrgyz Republic are estimated at 6 billion cubic metre. The development of gas fields is hindered by the geological peculiarities and insufficiently developed infrastructure. The domestic production of natural gas in the Republic averages 30 million cubic meters per year. Gas consumption makes up some 700 million cubic metre per year, 95 per cent of which is imported from Uzbekistan. The work is underway as part of the Action Plan to ensure Gazprom's participation in Kyrgyzgaz shares purchase/privatisation of December 24, 2012. With the assistance of an independent expert an adequate inspection of Kyrgyzgaz was carried out and the market value of its equity capital was assessed. A feasibility study is under development for Gazprom to acquire shares in Kyrgyzgaz. An Intergovernmental Agreement on the terms and conditions of shares purchase and further activities of Kyrgyzgaz is being prepared for signature." With Gazprom now at the helm of Kyrgyzstan's entire gas business, such long series of negotiations, protocols and other formalities are now considered unnecessary."

Complementary supplies from Kazakhstan also remain secured. "KazTransGas JSC (KTG) and Gazprom OAO say they will increase the capacity of the main gas pipeline passing into Kyrgyzstan," a news statement from the Kazakh firm posted by the local agency KazTag posted on March 3 2015 was to read. "In Astana a meeting was held with representatives from the companies of KazTransGas and Gazprom, which discussed increasing the capacity of the Kyrgyz section of the MGP (the main gas pipeline) the BGR-TBA (Bukhara gas region Tashkent-Bishkek-Almaty) for stable gas supply to consumers of the city of Almaty and Almaty Oblast," the statement was quoted as reading. "As the statement explained, at the moment the technical condition of the main gas pipeline and gas pumping units at the Sokuluk compressor station, located in Kyrgyzstan, limits the capacity of the MGP BGR-TBA," in the news report's words. "The capacity of the pipeline at this site is no more than 250 thousand cubic metre per hour, which does not satisfy the growing needs of rapidly developing Almaty and the Almaty Oblast, where gas demand during the peak period is about 450 thousand cm/h. The two sides have agreed to develop a list of activities and assign turnaround time to increase the capacity of MGP."

Armchair commentators on yonder side of the globe keep getting confused over a question which is vital for Kyrgyzstan's economic development: are cheap oil and gas prices good or bad for the country? Unfortunately or fortunately, observations made by such economic pundits are evidently as confused themselves as they are meant to confuse. A bizarre mix of economic, financial and political flavours making the end result tasteless is the usual result.

"Lower oil prices and a tottering Russian economy are multiplying headaches from Baku to Bishkek, a report posted by Foreign Policy on March 3 under the frivolous header Central Asia's Cheap Oil Double Whammy read. "But that could be a boost for China's Silk Road dreams. The prolonged slump in oil prices is causing plenty of wailing and gnashing of teeth from Oran to Ottawa. But for countries in the Caucasus and Central Asia, the oil swoon has been coupled with Russia's economic implosion to create a particularly ugly economic outlook. That raises concerns about the region's stability — even as it opens the door for a bigger role there for China. The 50 percent drop in crude prices since last summer alone would be enough to spell pain for countries such as Kazakhstan and Azerbaijan that rely heavily on fossil fuel exports for government revenues. Kazakhstan last week trimmed its budget — which had been based on oil at $80 a barrel — while Azerbaijan may have to revise downward similarly rosy spending plans later this summer. Azerbaijan already had to dip into its oil fund for the first time since it was created 15 years ago. Kazakhstan's sovereign wealth fund is looking to borrow fresh money due to the oil collapse." 33)

CHAPTER IV

NATO'S AGENTS IN KYRGYZSTAN AND KYRGYZ FIFTH COLUMNISTS IN EXILE

Pavel Filonov. Eleven Heads. 1938(?). Oil on canvas. 82 x 72 cm.
The Russian Museum, St. Petersburg, Russia

Making Kyrgyzstan feel sorry for its allegiance with the new Red Bear and the old Red Dragon and tempting it to enter the new great game once more is in vogue among so-called news media which were never established as such but for the sake of convenience serve as political agents for western agencies to destabilise the country and keep it isolated from the region's economic constellation. Fake "media" which in fact are not media but propaganda machineries have lately stepped up efforts to break up Kyrgyzstan's economic consolidation policy, using twisted interview quotes and false insinuations to get the country and its nation down the drain once more, with little other aim than to get it choked in institutional debts that force it to bow in front of global market sharks and be cut to the bone. Pablo Neruda will weap in his grave – but apparently to no avail.

"The slowdown of Russia's economy is inflicting pain across Central Asia. But impoverished Kyrgyzstan has no choice but to stay close to Moscow, Prime Minister Djoomart Otorbaev tells EurasiaNet.org," a copy of a report written by a pundit in the service of tycoon George Soros posted on what looked like a related news site in late 2014 was to read. The report was trumpeted as "an exclusive interview" with Soros' propaganda mouthpiece. In fact, bits and pieces of what he must have said looked very much indeed like having been completely taken out of context and made look as though he and the nation he represents were victims of "Russian neo-imperialism" suffering from pressure but in fact yearning for western salvation to keep the bear (along with the dragon to the southeast) at bay and starve in the process. Pathetic. 34)

So who are these "opponents?" Of course, in the article they are not identified because this would betray the authors' intention to spread a new wave of hysteria among the Kyrgyz people leading to the renewed rise of yet another US-conducted puppet regime in the Republic with little other aim than to "Moscow's increased pressure" only discloses the so-called information media's true identity. All such assumptions are false: Ukraine is divided between a majority not just located in the east of the country but throughout the country that wants to be independent but in friendly and fruitful relation with its thousand-plus-years-old partner Russia and a minority of irregular gangs seizing the opportunity of embracing western provocations dominated by American state and half-state agencies but with the EU represented by freewheeler Barroso who took his position in the European Commission enjoying legal immunity after allegations that he had been part of a group plundering the coffers of his political party in Portugal. But then, it would be inconvenient for the likes of Eurasia-whatever to mention such factors.

The plain truth is that there could hardly be more mystifying and misleading suggestion than what this kind of so-called reporting is suggesting. Facts are that an overwhelming majority in a democratically elected parliament and regularly carrsied out opinion polls by unbiased agencies among the population have convincingly affirmed widespread support. Otorbayev was known to be convinced of that, and his allegiance to the spirit of the nation in this and other regards, respecting the general view among the people and resisting minority extremism, was hardly less well known.

1. Kyrgyzstan's choice

Pavel Filonov. Formula of Spring. 1927-1929. The Russian Museum, St. Petersburg, Russia

The twist is found in the margins – as usual. "We are a news organization that operates **entirely thanks to volunteers and donations** to meet our operating costs," the site (vulgar English spelling and grammar maintained) reads. "We don't like to have popups like this here, but **your funding is essential** to making sure that **Eurasia Review** continues to operate. To ensure **Eurasia Review** continues to operate, **please click on the donate button below! We thank you in advance!**" So here is the knack. Within a longstanding tradition, news and opinion media offer quality information and background feed to their audiences in exchange for subscriptions and paid support by advertisers. Advocates of free market ideologies should support this assumption – even if grumbling. They do not. With dumbfounding brutality, mouthpieces of those forces in the west on behalf of those who want to see former Soviet nations subdued to ruthless neocolonial imperialism controlled by American multinationals exploiting and draining the Eurasian nations' economies. They have their own fifth column: swindlers, gangsters and other predators from the former USSR who, together with their multi-billion bounties, are protected from the course of justice by the same state agencies that have caused the civil war in Ukraine by sponsoring and encouraging mavericks and mobsters who are now in power in the near-bankrupt state. They would love to see the likes of Mikhail Khodorkovsky, Rakhat Aliyev, Mukhtar Ablyazov, Maxim Bakiyev and other one-time well-positioned racketeers to gain power in Russia and other parts of Central Asia. They would fit into the pattern marked by Batista, Mobutu, Suharto, Pinochet, Videla, Somoza and their likes. This is the choice Kyrgyzstan, together with Russia, Belarus and Kazakhstan, has made. It is the choice between remaining an impoverished banana republic far in the wild and a member of a powerful economic block which together can survive on its own without being plundered.

For those who want to judge for themselves, here is the complete "report" as posted by the organisation – with the urgent request to mind the bad linguistics, the inconsistency, the misinterpreted, incomplete and/or ignored factuality and not to believe a word of it before thinking it over: "The slowdown of Russia's economy is inflicting pain across Central Asia. But impoverished Kyrgyzstan has no choice but to stay close to Moscow, Prime Minister Djoomart Otorbaev tells EurasiaNet.org. In an exclusive interview in Bishkek, Otorbaev addressed criticism of Kyrgyzstan's decision to join the Russia-led Eurasian Economic Union, his country's energy crisis, and the inevitability of slower growth due to the downturn in sanctions-afflicted Russia, Kyrgyzstan's largest export market. If I said we are independent of the problems in our biggest market, I would be wrong. Russia is our biggest market, the biggest regional economy. Of course we are dependent on it, but we must prepare for the worst, Otorbaev said in the November 15 interview. " 35)

"On November 12, the International Monetary Fund projected that Kyrgyzstan's economic growth would fall from 10.5 per cent in 2013 to 3 percent in the following year, and the inflation rate would jump to around 10 per cent. The plummeting value of remittances from Russia sent by labour migrants and traders is adding to trade deficits across the region, the IMF said, and a weaker rouble contributes to inflation. A day before the IMF assessment, Kyrgyzstan's Finance Minister Olga Lavrova told Parliament that the country's foreign debt accounted for 53 percent of GDP at the end of October and was entering dangerous territory."

"The rouble's 30 percent slide against the dollar during the second half of 2014 is the major factor in the sharp decrease in transfers from Kyrgyz citizens working in Russia, both migrant laborers and traders who depend on Russian markets," a news report on the issue was to read. "That is putting pressure on the som. The National Bank has spent over $300 million so far this year to try to ease the som's slide. But, like Russia, Kyrgyzstan is moving toward a free-floating exchange rate. Pointing out that a weaker som helps exporters, Otorbaev, a mathematician with experience in Europe's private sector and in banking, said, "We are not prepared to keep the som strong. The intervention is just to ease the spikes. [...] Some have criticised Kyrgyzstan's move to join the Eurasian Economic Union – which promises the "free movement of capital, goods, services, and labour" among members. Bishkek plans to sign on to the Russia-led organization by the end of next month, after several years of apparent foot-dragging. Opponents, inside Kyrgyzstan and abroad, say the project is Vladimir Putin's attempt to reassert Russian power throughout the former Soviet Union. Since Russian-fueled unrest began in eastern Ukraine this spring, Moscow has seemed to increase pressure on its neighbors to join. In recent weeks, Kyrgyzstan's parliament has passed reams of legislation on membership in both the customs union and the EEU, which will come into being on January 1. Otorbaev insists Kyrgyzstan will formally join both in late December and that border controls with Kazakhstan was to be lifted by the middle of the next year." 36)

"Aside from issues of economic integration, one of Otorbaev's toughest tasks is to raise artificially low energy tariffs – a legacy that Kyrgyzstan inherited from the Soviet Union. Previous governments postponed the painful measure, which he says is now critical. The Kyrgyz population has for too long expected to pay below-market rates for electricity, Otorbaev said. And now, reform can no longer wait. This year's drought, increased demand and aging infrastructure left the country with a deficit of 2.4 billion kilowatt-hours this coming winter. We have crossed the Rubicon. All of a sudden we went from being an export-oriented country to import-oriented, he said. Kyrgyzstan plans to import 1.4 billion kWh from neighboring Kazakhstan, for which it will pay eight-times more per kWh. In the immediate future, Otorbaev's government will subsidize much of the purchase, but the expensive outlay will force him to implement major reforms. No government before us did this. We have to do it. This is a gamble my government must take, he said. An obstacle that Kyrgyzstan will have to contend with for years is its poor relations with foreign investors. While protracted spats have frightened away would-be investors, Otorbaev tried to accentuate the positive. Kyrgyzstan is considered by the outside world to be a country where we always have revolutions. But things are cooling down dramatically, Otorbaev, who in previous governments held a number of senior economic posts, said. He pointed to a successful tourist season at Lake Issyk-Kul as an indicator that Kyrgyzstan is entering a more stable era. Politicians seeking to score points still interfere in the crucial mining sector, he conceded. Such meddling can be expected to continue as next fall's parliamentary elections approach. The choice to enter the EEU could have profound ramifications for Kyrgyzstan's relations with its largest investor, China, by hiking tariffs on Chinese imports. Otorbaev pointed out, though, that his country's cheap labor, electricity and real estate will continue to be a boon for Chinese investors seeking to build factories within the Moscow-led trade bloc. I think they will come more. They want to sell things to the Russian market, Otorbaev said. This is a fantastic opportunity for producers."

2. Crossing the crossroads

Pavel Filonov. Magi (Wise Men). 1914. Watercolor, brown ink, Indian ink, feather, brush on paper. 37 x 39.2 cm. The Russian Museum, St. Petersburg, Russia

As for the man behind the mechanism of Eurasianet's dubious information provisions, the following paragraphs in the Free Encyclopedia speak for themselves: "Soros had been building a huge position in pounds sterling for months leading up to September 1992. Soros recognized the unfavorable position at which the United Kingdom joined the Exchange Rate Mechanism. For Soros, the rate at which the United Kingdom was brought into the Exchange Rate Mechanism was too high, their inflation was also much too high (triple the German rate), and British interest rates were hurting their asset prices. On September 16, 1992, Black Wednesday, Soros' fund sold short more than $10 billion in pounds, profiting from the UK government's reluctance to either raise its interest rates to levels comparable to those of other European Exchange Rate Mechanism countries or to float its currency. Finally, the UK withdrew from the European Exchange Rate Mechanism, devaluing the pound. Soros's profit on the bet was estimated at over $1 billion. He was dubbed "the man who broke the

Bank of England". In 1997, the UK Treasury estimated the cost of Black Wednesday at £3.4 billion." 37)

"In 1988, Soros was interested in purchasing shares in French companies. The Socialist party had lost its majority of seats in the Assembly, and the new government under Jacques Chirac had instituted an aggressive privatisation programme. Many people considered shares in the newly privatised companies undervalued. During this period, a French financier named Georges Pébereau contacted one of Soros' advisors in an effort to assemble a group of investors to purchase a large number of shares in Société Générale, a leading French bank that was part of the programme. The advisor reported to Soros that Pébereau's plan was ambiguous and included an implausible takeover plan, which later failed. On that advice, and without ever having met the financier, Soros decided against participating. Soros did, however, move forward with his strategy of accumulating shares in four French companies: Société Générale, as well as Suez, Paribas and the Compagnie Générale d'Électricité. In 1989, the Commission des Opérations de Bourse (the French stock exchange regulatory authority) conducted an investigation of whether Soros' transaction in Société Générale should be considered insider trading. Soros had received no information from the Société Générale, and had no insider knowledge of the business, but he did possess knowledge that a group of investors was planning a takeover attempt. The COB concluded that the statutes, regulations and case law relating to insider trading did not clearly establish that a crime had occurred, and that no charges should be brought against Soros. Several years later, a Paris-based prosecutor reopened the case against Soros and two other French businessmen, disregarding the COB's findings. This resulted in Soros' 2005 conviction for insider trading by the Court of Appeals (he was the only one of the three to receive a conviction). The French Supreme Court confirmed the conviction on June 14, 2006, but reduced the penalty to €940,000. Punitive damages were not sought because of the delay in bringing the case to trial. Soros denied any wrongdoing, saying news of the takeover was public knowledge and it was documented that his intent to acquire shares of the company predated his own awareness of the takeover. His insider trading conviction was upheld by the highest court in France on June 14, 2006. In December 2006, he appealed to the European Court of Human Rights on various grounds including that the 14-year delay in bringing the case to trial precluded a fair hearing. On the basis of Article 7 of the European Convention on Human Rights, stating that no person may be punished for an act that was not a criminal offense at the time that it was committed, the Court agreed to hear the appeal. In October 2011, the court rejected his appeal in a 4–3 decision, saying that Soros had been aware of the risk of breaking insider trading laws. Soros was also known to have backed Arab protests uprisings and revolutions in 1989 [questionable since there were no such events at the time but this is what Wikipedia reads – ChvdL] "Reflecting on the Arab revolutions, one very important factor is that people were willing to sacrifice their lives for a common cause," Mr. Soros said. "That is a memory, a historic event, that will change those countries forever. It is irreversible." — to appreciate how rich the reward could be." Though the time setting must be later, for whom and for whose personal cause, it appears to be clear that the so-called revolutions have been spelling disaster for the Islamic world including Central Asia – meaning in all that the likes of Mr. Soros may or may not be entirely evil. But they are not exactly representing the kind of company Kyrgyzstan is in need for...

In a fresh attack on Kyrgyzstan's self-determination, nothing less than the ever so cool and prestigious New York Times on October 6 2014 added to the ongoing smear campaign against Kyrgyzstan. It was placed on the opinion page, thereby falling on the editorial team's disclaimer – but still. The author was Masha Gessen, the author, most recently, of a monograph called "Words Will Break Cement: The Passion of Pussy Riot." The article refers to unnamed "activists from nongovernmental organisations" as claiming that they "...noticed a couple of years ago that Russian-language media got suddenly more robust, gaining a crop of new freelance writers who seemed to come from nowhere. The same people seem to be writing for a recently revived Russian-language website called Stan Radar, apparently addressed to the residents of the five post-Soviet 'stans': Kyrgyzstan, Kazakhstan, Uzbekistan, Tajikistan and Turkmenistan. Many of the stories on the site emphasize the importance of the Russian language in these countries, as well as the potential economic dangers of not joining the customs union initiated by Russia. The site contains no specific contact information or any other identifying details, and activists say their efforts to find out who owns it have been futile. They have established, though, that the server is located in Moscow. Another website, the name of which translates as 'Eurasians: The New Wave brims with articles warning that Kyrgyzstan may face the threat of a Ukrainian-style revolution or a Syrian-style radical Islamist takeover if it fails to form a tighter bond with Moscow. It reveals little about its identity, only that it belongs to a foundation started in Moscow in 2010 'to strengthen the ties between Russia and Kyrgyzstan' and that its 'partners' include an organisation called Rossotrudnichestvo, or 'Russian Cooperation', a federal agency founded in 2008 to foster connections between Russia and Russian speakers abroad. In 2012 Konstantin Kosachev, a high-level functionary of Russia's ruling party, United Russia, was appointed to lead the ministry that runs Rossotrudnichestvo, and since then it has really made its presence known in Kyrgyzstan and elsewhere. It organises cultural events and sponsors Russian-language educational programmes." 38)

The article fails to suggest whether or not its author has ever set foot in Kyrgyzstan. On top of that it also fails to explain if any laws have been broken under the Kyrgyz Constitution. It even fails to put up a single quote to illustrate how outrageous Rossotrudnichestvo's activities are. Of course: fostering friendship is a lot more outrageous than fostering treachery – at least that seems to be the view voiced by mouthpieces of American military and security services. The author's conclusions come close to hysteria: "One thing that is certain about the Russian World is that it is not confined to the borders of the Russian Federation. It is an expansionist project, and an opportunistic one. [...]. Kyrgyzstan is a perfect lab rat: It is small and poor and extremely susceptible to Russian pressure. It is also, unlike its neighbors and Russia itself, not an authoritarian state. Nor is it a functioning democracy: It is, rather like Ukraine, a country with a transitional state of government. It has seen two revolutions in the last decade and is now ruled by a multiparty coalition designed to prevent a return of autocracy. [...] But even 23 years after the collapse of the Soviet Union, the country's democratic gains are fragile and uncertain — and are at the mercy of the Russian World's inexorable advance." In other words: watch out cowboys – the red bear is here to devour you!

It is all too preposterous to conceive. Whoever looks around (something the author obviously never did) can clearly see that Kyrgyzstan is NOT a "perfect lab rat" and that it IS a functioning democracy – for all its shortcomings but those are by and large the shortcomings any democracy in the world is suffering from. And we are no "crop of new freelance writers who come from nowhere" – nor are our news sources. At stake here is the very difference between reporting and interpreting facts on one side and spitting gossip on the other. The Kyrgyz nation's history goes back over two-and-a-half thousand years in time – something which cannot be said about that of the USA. For all those centuries, the Kyrgyz have managed to choose their own allies in order to determine their own fate. For the future that is about what it takes. If maintaining this principle is "anti-western" something must be sadly wrong with western minds…

3. Beleaguering the EEU

*Pavel Filonov. The Feast of Kings. 1913. Oil on canvas. 175 x 215 cm.
The Russian Museum, St. Petersburg, Russia*

Official motivations and explanations look crystal-clear. In a lengthy and exhaustive statement published by the Kremlin on the occasion of the signature of the EEU treaty in Astana towards the end of 2014, Vladimir Putin frankly explains the new Union's advantages but also its limits and restrictions. "The Agreement we signed is a truly historical milestone that opens up broad prospects for the development of our economies and improving the well-being of our countries' citizens," the text reads. "Russia, Belarus and Kazakhstan are moving towards a completely new level of cooperation by creating a common space where goods, services, capital and work force can move freely. The three states will follow a coordinated policy in such key branches of the economy as energy, industry, agriculture and transport." 39)

The spectre of a "reborn USSR" on the rise, much-suggested by western political pressure groups and their media outlets is categorically wiped off the table by the EEU leaders and representatives. "A new economic organisation has appeared on the international arena, one that has full juridical personality and acts based on the principles of the World Trade Organisation," Putin stated. "It is important that the transfer of certain authority to supranational agencies of the Union is of no detriment to the sovereignty of our states. Mutual benefit from integration has already been demonstrated in practice. The economic ties between Russia, Belarus and Kazakhstan are expanding, their trade structure is improving, the share of high-tech goods in the overall trade structure is increasing and our countries are becoming ever more economically competitive in the world. In the past three years trade turnover within the Customs Union has gone up by 50 percent – that is by $23 billion (in 2013 it amounted to $66.2 billion). Belarus and Kazakhstan together come in third in the overall trade balance of the Russian Federation (after the EU and China)."

With the treaty and the start of its implementation as of January 1 2015, the EEC as seen in the run-up to it remained yet far from complete. Nevertheless, citizens were seen as due to experience benefits from the very beginning. "For the future, we have set ourselves the goal of creating a common financial market," the statement reads further down. "The absence of barriers in the flow of capital will make it possible to diversify risks and improve the quality, accessibility and reliability of financial services. Stage-by-stage harmonisation of the currency policy will serve to enhance the stability of the financial systems of the Union member states and will make the national money markets more predictable and better protected from exchange rate fluctuations, and will enhance our sovereignty as well. The citizens of our countries should be able to fully assess the benefits of Eurasian integration. They will receive the right to work freely in the three states without having to obtain any work permits." But (and this is possibly one of the things causing anxiety in western political circles, if not sheer hostility) the EEU, apart from seeking new members starting with Armenia and Kyrgyzstan, the union, the Union aims at spreading its wings – in particular to the south and the southeast – as well. "We agreed to step up our negotiations with Vietnam on creating a free trade zone, to strengthen cooperation with the People's Republic of China, specifically in the exchange of customs information on goods and services, and to form expert groups that would work out preferential trade regimes with Israel and India," Putin concluded. "I am convinced that through joint efforts we will be able to create favourable conditions for the development of our economies in order to maintain stability, security and prosperity in Eurasia."

But the yet clear message to the rest of the world has fallen on deaf ears in western media. "The EEU, which is due to come into force as of the beginning of the upcoming year, is set to be an intermediary stage between the Customs Union which unites Russia, Belarus and Kazakhstan which started working back in 2010, followed by the Single Economic Space which functioned since the beginning of 2012, and the Eurasian Economic Union aimed at for the future," a comment in the Frankfürter Allgemeine Zeitung which appeared after the treaty's signature was to read. « The latter, at least in Moscow's imagination, should lead to the political integration of the member states. Institutions are already in place : the Eurasian Economic Commission in Moscow and a court of law in Minsk. Pressing is, to put it frankly, the current authoritarian state structure, represented by the council of the [member states'] three presidents. » 40)

Similar insinuations contradicting Putin's reassurances can be found in an editorial comment in Spain's leading newspaper El País. "The accounts that Russia's President Vladimir Putin has managed to settle with his Kazakh and Belorussian neighbours do not let themselves be explained in figures," the article reads. "The EEU is not supposed to make a big difference for some economies in dire straits and among which the dominating exporter will rather impose itself than being complementary. [...] In spite of the pomp with which the signature was celebrated, the pending questions are piling up and their importance has not become any less. [...] Nor is it a coincidence that the signature was made hardly more than a week after the gas agreement with China." The latter agreement ensures Russia's gas sales for a period of 30 years, should Europe fail to purchase sufficient volumes due to US-dictated "sanctions". 41)

Across the Atlantic, the undertone of fact-twisting reporting on the EEC has been even harsher, sometimes smelling like blunt hysteria. "Sitting at a table with his two fellow leaders in front of their respective flags, Mr. Putin said that the group, formally known as the Eurasian Economic Union, had the potential to create a global transportation hub joining the trade flows of Europe and Asia," the New York Times wrote in a leading article on the issue. "While that may eventually prove to be the case, the alliance that comes into force on Jan. 1 will be a pale imitation of what the members first envisioned: an eastern version of the 28-member European Union. [...] The agreement coalesced with great fanfare — and quickly — with members changing trade laws in a matter of years, a process that required decades for the European Union. But in the end, it became less about promoting economic development than about providing Russia with a diplomatic victory, analysts said. Like the huge gas agreement Russia signed with China this month, the Eurasian Economic Union is a way for Moscow to show that it is pivoting to Asia, and that it can withstand Western sanctions and other pressures as it pursues its national interests, as in its annexation of Crimea from Ukraine." 42)

What followed was a brutal reversal of facts, coming down to accusing Russia of exactly what Washington was trying to do itself at the moment. "Russia adopted the idea of a Eurasian union for three main reasons," the article reads further down. "First, Mr. Putin wanted to create his own economic pole that would raise Russia to the status of other major global trading powers like the European Union, China and the United States. Second, the union would secure Moscow's influence over the economic development of its former republics, particularly in Central Asia, before they began to look elsewhere — to China, for example. Third, many analysts believe that Mr.

Putin came to see the Eurasian union as an almost physical manifestation of his budding ideology that Russia and its satellites represent the anti-West, a bastion of more conservative, traditional and religious values opposed to aspects of Western culture, like equal rights for gays, an independent news media and political activism. [...] The fundamental flaw, experts noted, is that all the governments involved in creating the union are run by authoritarian figures loath to share power within their own governments, much less with other states. Even the democracies of the European Union wrestle with power-sharing issues constantly. Some analysts suggest that the loss of Ukraine as a potential member was the death knell for the Eurasian Economic Union."

Yet another piece of dirty demagogy published by Business Week under the headline "Putin's Eurasian Union looks like a bad deal even for Russia" was to read: "Alas for Putin, the new bloc comes nowhere near the big leagues. Even after Armenia and Kyrgyzstan enter, its total gross domestic product—about $2.6 trillion—will be less than one-fifth that of the European Union or the US and less than one-third of China's. Russia will account for more than 80 percent of the bloc's GDP and a similar share of its roughly 178 million population. [...] Belarus, and Kyrgyzstan declined about 7 per cent last year. The Eurasian Union will encourage members to trade among themselves by raising tariffs on goods imported from outside. A glimpse of what that could mean can be seen in Kazakhstan, which has already raised import duties after joining a Russian-led customs union that preceded the new bloc. [...] Armenia and Kyrgyzstan, which are World Trade Organization members, are asking Russia to compensate them for the probable retaliation they'd suffer from joining the bloc; its tariff regime would likely put them in breach of WTO rules. Even Ukraine's pro-Russian former president, Viktor Yanukovych, never promised to join the Eurasian Union, although he favoured close trade relations with Russia." For all it matters, Belarus' GDP rose by a modest 0.9 per cent on-year in 2013, and that of Kyrgyzstan by a spectacular 10.5 per cent... 43)

One of the outrages under the provocative headline Les Républiques d'Asie Centrale vont-elles être une nouvelle Crimée? (Are the republics of Central Asia going to be a new Crimea ?) published in Le Monde in mid-April and written by « political scientist » Olga Alinda Spaiser. The author quotes an Almaty-based « independent newspaper » called Assandi Times as suggesting that « Kazakhstan [is] threatened by a Russian occupation from tomorrow on ». All very political – and very little scientific if at all : the paper (which was shut down on a court order less than a week after Le Monde's publication) belongs to no one less than Mukhtar Ablyazov, at present behind bars in France (!) awaiting his extradition for having defrauded Kazakhstan's Bank BTA at the time he controlled it for – at least - 8 billion greenbacks.

As noted before, Ablyazov had been convicted to 22 months in an English jail by an English court for having lied in court. And the lies do not stop there. « After Ukraine, it is Kazakhstan that harbours the largest Russian minority in the world, » Le Monde's article reads. « Russian populations are also present in the other Central Asian countries, namely Uzbekistan, Kyrgyzstan, Tajikistan and Turkmenistan. At the same time, Moscow maintains strategic military bases in this region. » And as though to add combustion to confusion, the author notes that Kazakhstan's 24 per cent Russian population « ...sees itself more and more marginalised » and going as far as suggesting that Central Asian would pay « too high a price for their good relations with Russia : their sovereignty ». 44)

But the absolute champion of such kinds of anti-Russian agitation (unsurprisingly) remains so-called Radio Free Europe/Radio Liberty, as mentioned before the relic from the Cold War aimed at spreading unrest in the Soviet Union's Central-European allies. Now, the "call for liberty" stretches all the way to the very gates of China. "Police in Astana have detained dozens of activists protesting Kazakhstan's entry into the Eurasian Economic Union (EEU)," the American broadcaster, originally founded and funded by the CIA and currently maintained by Congress, reported in a briefing on the day of the EEU treaty's solemn signature. "The activists gathered in downtown Astana on May 29 wearing surgical masks and holding posters saying: Protect Yourself from Russia's Imperial Virus!" But it looks as though there is some sort of overlap between the news and the newsbringer here. "On May 27, seven activists and three journalists, including RFE/RL correspondent Orken Zhoyamergen, were sentenced to up to four days in jail after they were detained while covering an anti-EEU gathering in a town near Astana," the news report reads further down. This strongly suggest that certain western media are not content with fact-twisting and incriminating reporting but do not hesitate to agitate among the public themselves... 45)

4. The road to China

*Pavel Filonov. Two Heads. 1925. Oil on paper. 58 x 54 cm. The
Russian Museum, St. Petersburg, Russia*

Into the year 2015, after losing a modest extra annual income from the
departing US military base, Kyrgyzstan was now in for some sacrifices, as
its participation in two regional security task forces, the larger of which
comprised both the Russian Federation and the People's Republic of
China, will be indispensable to secure enough safety for the landlocked
country to step up industrial and other economic activity. Of late, military
and paramilitary exercises under the umbrellas of the Collective Security
Treaty Organization (CSTO) and the Shanghai Cooperation Organisation
(SCO) had become more and more frequent and took place on an evern
larger scale. At stake is not just an overspill of the threatening chaos in
"post-American" Afghanistan, but rippled towards the east of the standoff
between east and west over the civil war in Ukraine are also on the horizon.
On the other hand, closer regional cooperation on a slightly longer term

opened perspectives for investors and traders as well, as closer security coordination was bound to go hand in hand with regional economic consolidation.

This particular trend continues in spite of persistent attacks and counter-propaganda aimed against it in what is starting to look more and more like a tit-for-tat exchange under the guise of analysis in mass media on both sides of the fence. "It has been a transformative year for Eurasian integration and its flagship project, the Eurasian Economic Union (EEU). What started off as a relatively simple customs union in early 2014 has been transformed by treaty into a single economic space that includes Belarus, Kazakhstan, and Russia and will soon include Armenia and Kyrgyzstan. In some ways, the last year was a triumph. But expansion has come at the cost of the union's coherence, and as Russia's economy spirals into crisis, the prognosis for 2015 is dire. More and more, the peripheral economies realize that they are bound to a drowning Russia," one article posted by a US newsreel called VICE (*sic*) on December 31 2014. And vicious it is indeed – starting with the tendentious header "Eurasian Disunion - Why the Union Might Not Survive 2015". What, for all it matters, the author apparently ignores is that the Customs Union dates from 2010. 46)

"The EEU's predecessor, the Eurasian Customs Union, had been distinctive in the former Soviet Union because, unlike so many other multilateral bodies there, it was following its written rules and developing as an institution," the text continues. "New customs controls and tariff limits shared among Belarus, Kazakhstan, and Russia were being enforced. Hundreds of young civil servants had been hired. And progress had been made toward creating a shared regulatory framework for everything from financial services to telecommunications to agriculture. Capital, labour, and goods would soon flow freely, and even more ambitious goals seemed achievable, thanks to the political commitment of the powerful leaders of Belarus, Kazakhstan, and Russia." So far, not too bad. Further down, however, the text gets more and more erroneous, suggesting that "Russia's subsequent annexation of Crimea and invasion of eastern Ukraine terrified Belarus and Kazakhstan, each with its own large Russian minority", and "Russia dramatically sped up the accession process for Armenia and Kyrgyzstan, two marginal economies with little to offer the union besides a photo opportunity. […] Kazakhstan's President Nursultan Nazarbayev—the most sincere believer in the original project—rebelled against the expansion because of fears that inclusion of two Russian client states would dilute Kazakhstan's influence." He never did so.

Similar insinuations have been echoed in media during Europe's financial slump in 2008-2010 varying from suggestions that Greece, Portugal and Spain might fall out from the European Union, or at least from the Eurozone, to claims that the entire EU might fall apart altogether. Nothing of any such kind ever happened, nor was the possibility ever on the agenda. The fiercest attack in the article is not aimed against Russia, but in particular targets Kyrgyzstan, which is dubbed "a notoriously weak state that has profited from its position as a member of the World Trade Organization that shares a border with China. It is an open secret that goods flowing into Kyrgyzstan from China have tariffs assessed by weight at a single rate (essentially, an importer pays the same tariff for one ton of computers as for one ton of cauliflower), in violation of the country's WTO agreement. Fully complying with the union would require Kyrgyzstan to impose much higher tariffs on Chinese imports, and the government has neither the capacity nor the will to do so. A recent statement from the Kyrgyzstani customs service indicates that any imposition of new tariffs on Chinese imports will be delayed until well after accession."

The last phrase includes a hyperlink to an article posted on December 1 on multi-billionaire George Soros' Eurasianet, in which such a "statement" is nowhere mentioned, let alone quoted. As for imported goods from China, duties will only be increased for those the end destination is within the EEU, and nothing will change for transit goods, duties of which always were, and will remain being determined by the country of their end destination if it is outside the EEU. Besides, free trade agreements between the EEU and more than 40 non-EEU countries including China are at an advanced stage of negotiation and bound to put an end to any disadvantages the momentary situation might impose. "Kyrgyzstan also lacks the capacity to ensure that its meat and dairy products meet union standards. Although Russia has offered hundreds of millions of dollars in transition support (and presumably might be willing to cut its junior partner some slack on standards), Kazakhstan controls Kyrgyzstan's land borders with the union and can easily use stringent interpretations of the rules to keep Kyrgyzstan from shipping to Russia. Kazakhstan's own domestic producers have been feuding with Russia over import restrictions this year, and so it is unlikely that they will welcome additional competition from Kyrgyzstan in the south." For those who want to know: customs posts on the border between Kyrgyzstan and Kazakhstan will be closed as of May 1 this year, quality control and labeling of Kyrgyz food products has already been standardised in line with EEU directives and there has been no "feuding" over the issue between Russia and Kazakhstan whatsoever. 47)

Passages of equally insinuative character can be read where monetary issues are concerned. "For economic as well as psychological reasons, the values of regional currencies are tied to the cratering ruble. Already in 2014, Kyrgyzstan's National Bank has sold $464 million in dollars (the equivalent of about 6.5 per cent of GDP) defending the Kyrgyz som, which has still lost more than 17 per cent of its value against the dollar. The National Bank is now threatening to close foreign currency exchange points in order to stem speculation." For what it is worth, the National Bank never made such a threat, and limits on exchange transactions were only imposed by a number of banks on their own initiative. As for the Kyrgyz som's volatility, it remained well within the margins set by the National Bank and there is no reason whatsoever to suggest that things were, or still are, getting out of hand, as the following figures from the National Bank would demonstrate:

EXCHANGE RATE FLUCTUATIONS OF THE KYRGYZ SOM AGAINST LEADING CURRENCIES			
date	US dollar	euro	Russian rouble
September 20	54.1816	69.7615	1.4105
December 27	58.9000	71.8109	1.1319

source: *National Bank of Kyrgyzstan*

Towards the end, the author seems to become the victim of hallucinations. "The Eurasian Economic Union is dead in all but name. It will survive as another hollow post-Soviet multilateral institution celebrated with presidential summits but producing no progress toward its stated goals. The EEU's crumbling is proof that Russia's capacity for influence is weakening," the article reads in conclusion. And: "A genuine economic and fiscal crisis starting in Russia and spreading across the former Soviet Union will amplify existing nationalism, separatism, and military adventurism, not only in Russia and on its borders but across the whole post-Soviet periphery. Once that process gains momentum, neither the West nor China will be willing or able to stop it." As for the (wild) "West" this would come as no surprise since in such a case, imaginary and impossible as it is, it would dismiss any blame for it. All this clearly reflects Washington's propaganda machinery's continuing campaigns to spread hysteria at home and abroad with the ultimate goal to cry "victory" in the "Second Cold War" against an enemy that only exists as such in its imagination but in fact subdue the rest of the world in order to exploit it ruthlessly. This clearly explains that Kyrgyzstan's choice, for this and nothing else is what it is, has not just been an obvious one but it has made it an easy one as well – thereby providing the nation with the happiest New Year it can possibly be wished.

5. The myth of cash and the devastating effect of monetarism

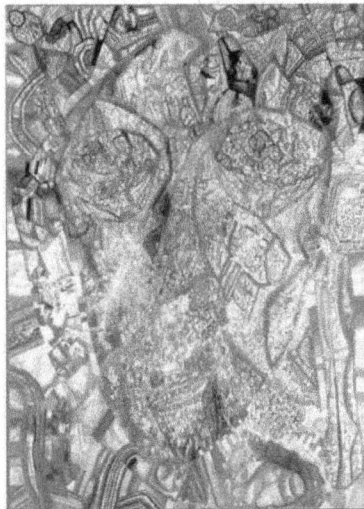

Pavel Filonov. Living Head. 1923. Oil on canvas. 85 x 78 cm.
The Russian Museum, St. Petersburg, Russia

When giant reptiles populated the earth, creatures big and small were deadly afraid of their fiercest specimen, the tyrannosaur. In the end, the bigger creates had all been devoured while the smaller creatures had become smart enough to run and hide. The last tyrannosaurs were thereby not slain but simply died of famine, the story goes. Since the Second World War, and especially since the moment America's President Richard Nixon dropped the gold standard, the US dollar has been gradually developed into such a tyrannosaur – devouring the world economy until it will drop dead and take the monetarism with it into its grave. Not all smaller creatures have full learnt how to survive. "On February 5 [2015], the National Bank of the Kyrgyz Republic sold $36.45 million in the foreign exchange market. Another rise in the dollar exchange rate forced the National Bank hold an intervention for the second day," the local independent news agency 24.kg reported the next morning. "During the day [the dollar] went up by 1.1 som from 60.4 to 61.5. However, the intervention slightly reduced the dollar by only 40 tyiyn. [...] Yesterday the National Bank held its first intervention in February, selling $11.9 million. However, is did not affect the dollar much." Earlier, in a report posted on January 28, the agency referred to the National Bank as noting that bank deposits' share in US dollar had gone up by 14.4 per cent through the year 2014 to a total of 58 per cent. 48)

On average, on every million greenbacks thus sold on the market against local currencies national banks lose within the range between $20,000 and $50,000 – depending on exchange rate fluctuations. That money is lost to national economies and simply disappears into the pockets of speculators. The alternative is to refrain from interventions and let the market decide how much national currencies are being valued. This is what the Central Bank of the Russian Federation did over the summer of 2014 – to certain limits, that is. Commodity prices are the key to where to put those limits. Into 2015, the price of oil represented less than half of its price a year earlier in dollars, but in roubles it had by and large remained the same. It was only when other base commodities such as grain and building materials started to rise in rouble denomination, that the Central Bank started acting on the currency market once more in order to prevent just that. Commodity prices over the last couple of years and through last year in particular have "lost" substantial "value" in the wordings of rusty commentators, with oil close to 60, metals in the order of 30 and cereals around 20 per cent on average. But have they really?

In terms of US dollars, quite so. But in Russian roubles, a barrel of oil cost about as much as it cost a year-and-a-half ago while other commodities have even become more expensive. It should therefore be considered quite natural if one thinks objectively for a moment using pure mathematics that a commodity producing and exporting country adapts its domestic currency's exchange value to sales prices against foreign currency with little other aim than to preserve as much of its domestic purchasing power and profits on domestic sales as possible. In this respect, the reaction of Belarus' President Alexander Lukashenko has been a true eye-opener. "You want to buy dollars?," he told the people in late 2014 during a lengthy open press conference. "Do so by all means, but if later you discover that you paid far too much for them, the state is not going to compensate you."

The policy pursued by the Russian government roughly consists of the following pattern: swallow losses in cash, compensate them by taking money from state reserves and use the opportunity to "de-dollarise" the national economy. "With the fall of the average price for oil from $100 to $50 per barrel in 2015, the budget revenues just from oil taxes could decrease by 2.1 trillion rouble [$31 billion] while a more serious fall in price, to an average of $40 [per barrel] for the year, could lead to a budget revenue decline of 3.1 trillion rouble [$46 billion]," Ilya Trunin, head of the Russian tax, customs and tariff department at the Russian Finance Ministry, wrote in an article posted by SputnikNews (former Novosti) posted on February 4. But he added that Russia has more than enough reserves to take care of the "losses" and can use the opportunity to make the state household book less dependent on a currency from the other side of the globe over which the local government has no control. Other former Soviet states are less consistent in their currency policies and at least in part cling to the dollar benchmark. In the end, they could lose a lot more in terms of national purchasing power than Russia does unless their governments grasp the overall idea. 49)

It all leads to two basic monetary scenarios for years to come. The first one consists of persistent, though fluctuating, undervaluation of commodities and overvaluation of cash, resulting in blowing bubbles on a regular basis which are bound to burst subsequently. To put it simply: a dead-end road leading from famine to feast and back to famine. The second scenario consists of a trend already visible and led by the Russian Federation and the People's Republic of China in particular, with most of southern Asia and Latin America following pace and even the European Union getting to its senses. The first step was the creation of currency baskets for national reserves, mainly consisting of US dollars, euros, yen, Swiss francs and Sterling but increasingly also of yuan. Logically, the next step should consist of a "demonetisation" of tangible goods markets – or to put it quaintly: let not cash value determine commodity value but the other way round. Interestingly, Central Asia with its rich variety in natural resources finds itself right in the middle of what could become the biggest economic and industrial revolution since the XVIII Century: a shift from a world economy based on greed to one based on need. The key to such a goal is realising or rather recalling what money actually is: a tool in the latter case and an aim in itself in the former one. It is here that economic problems are becoming profoundly mental – to the verge of philosophical. Each episode in the continuing cycle of economic and financial shakeups can be seen as "an artificial blow up of financial bubbles and craving for easy money, absence of proper responsibility of national financial institutions and the weakness of the global financial management" – at least in the words of Kazakhstan's President Nursultan Nazarbayev as he spoke at the opening of the VIth Astana Economic Forum back in late spring 2013. His opinion was later accompanied by that of Nobel laureate John Nash who simply observed on one of the panels he took part in that "money is a tool but has wrongly turned into a means in itself, an obsession".

"In fact, these and other fundamental causes of the global downturn have not been eliminated yet," the Kazakh head of state thundered in his address. "Hence, the world crisis cannot be considered as finished. Moreover, it seems to be transferring into a new stage to be accompanied by painful "bursts" of a number of local financial systems. [...] The deficiency of the global currency system is the main reason for the current global economic storm. Let me remind that I persistently urged to change the ways of global currency emission and circulation that do not meet the criteria of legitimacy, democracy, efficient controllability and responsibility. Yet to this day, there have been neither efficient global anti-crisis mechanisms, nor reliable global reserve currency or a group of regional currencies. No sufficient will and responsibility has been present to make radical decisions."

If asked today, Nazarbayev would indeed be most unlikely to have changed his opinion which is quite understandable since the country he is responsible for finds itself right in the middle of a crisis which is dominated by false images. Of late, the American periodical The Diplomat has developed itself into a core (though far from the only) outlet of such malicious attempt to fool the public. The overall undertone remains that Central Asian economies should dissociate themselves from that of the Russian Federation – using arguments varying from ridiculous to utterly false. "The rouble-to-dollar exchange rate has been on a catastrophic climb amid Russia's growing international isolation and the broader global collapse in oil prices," a fresh verbal attack posted on February 3 was to read. "At the time of this writing, the rouble sits at nearly 70 to the dollar. While the international media and economists have spent a considerable amount of time prognosticating about the future of the Russian economy, the rouble's moribund fortunes could absolutely devastate Central Asia's economies, many of which have little to no escape from their exposure to the Russian market. The most fundamental way in which the rouble's collapse will affect the economies of Central Asia is in terms of the effect it will have on the value of remittances — a crucial tool for transferring wealth from migrant workers in Russia back to their families in the former Soviet republics." 50)

"The rouble's collapse means that average consumer spending and wealth in the Central Asian states will drop precipitously. Even if Central Asian governments can tap into U.S. dollar reserves to keep their countries running, their citizens will immediately feel the effect of rising prices. Of course, the most worrisome long-term risk of Central Asia's current economic pain is widespread domestic political instability. The sharp increase in consumer prices could lead to widespread civil unrest and force governments to crack down violently. Kyrgyzstan, in particular, has already witnessed protests against electricity rate hikes during the winter. 2014 was a turbulent year for Kyrgyzstan with mass protests against the government of President Almazbek Atambayev, and though those protests were pacified as the year went on, rising inflation could reignite domestic tensions."

Really? Those who spent the year 2014 in Kyrgyzstan will no doubt testify that there have been no "mass protests against the government of President Almazbek Atambayev" (the author quoted here apparently fails to know that Kyrgyzstan has a parliamentary government) and there has been no "precipitous drop" in "average consumer spending and wealth" in the country – nor has there been such a thing in neighbouring states either. The article's author is either driven by personal wishful thinking or (more likely) by instructions from American state institutions to make readers imagine Kyrgyzstan and other Central-Asian states up in flames after the tragic example of Ukraine. Such desire becomes all the more clear in the article's "conclusion" which reads: Central Asia's economic pain will likely reduce popular support for Russian-led economic and political initiatives such as the Eurasian Economic Union. If anything, the rouble's collapse will be a wake-up call for a region that has done little to reduce its exposure to the Russian economy since the collapse of the Soviet Union. With China "marching west" and a United States eager to moderate Russian influence in the region, Central Asian governments would do well to diversify their economies and look away from Russia." The truth was that it appeared that this was simply not happening – thereby demonstrating that not the Russian Federation but America is finding itself more and more isolated in the world as its "monetary weapon of mass destruction" meaning a market-destructive use of the US dollar, is starting to get worn out.

By longstanding tradition, what is today commonly known as a banknote is in fact what is called *Wechsel* in German, Russian and a number of other languages alike: a signed and sealed piece of paper which entitles its holder to the amount of commodity indicated on it. Thus, an English one-pound Sterling note derives its name from the fact that he or she who presents it can change it into a pound of silver under Her Gracious Majesty's guarantee. Though in most of human history gold and silver were the denominations under which such notes were issued, the Chinese Empire used silk as a benchmark while ancient Egypt reputedly used grain for the purpose. It was Empress Catherine II who introduced the gold and silver standard in the Russian empire in the second half of the XVIII Century. By her decree the rouble's standard valuation was set to 4 *zolotnik* and 21 *dolya* (almost exactly equal to 18 gramme) of pure silver or 27 *dolya* (almost exactly equal to 1.2 gramme) of pure gold, with a ratio of 15:1 for the values of the two metals. In 1828, platinum coins were introduced with 1 ruble equal to 77⅔ *dolya* (3.451 gramme). On 17 December 1885, a new standard was adopted which did not change the silver rouble but reduced the gold content to 1.161 gramme, pegging the gold rouble to the French franc at a rate of 1 rouble against 4 francs. In the course of the French Revolution, the exchange rate changed in favour of the rouble, but the peg persisted until the rupture between Czar Alexander I and Napoleon. Almost worldwide, this type of halfhearted physiocratic trade value establishment (the true physiocratic method as defined by the XVIII Century French philosopher François Quesnay proposed a commodity basket) has been used until well after the Second World War. The beginning of the end came in 1944 with the so-called Bretton Wood accords between the Allied forces, later adhered to by the war's main losers Germany, Italy and Japan – but rejected by Stalin who refused to America's monetary hegemony over the Soviet Union's economy and halfheartedly adopted a policy China is more successfully implementing these days.

How justified Stalin's fears had been finally came out in 1971 when warmonger Richard Nixon dropped the dollar's valuation in gold. Under legislation signed after Nixon's disgrace by his successor Gerald Ford, the ancient principle was turned upside down: from there on, gold was to be denominated in dollars rather than dollars in gold. In other words: banknotes turned from a non-tangible valuable into a tangible one, from liability into an asset, while gold turned from a tangible valuable into a non-tangible one, or from an asset into a liability. In this manner, by deciding to print or not to print dollar bank notes, the Federal Bank of America got the entire world economy under its thumb. But it is becoming clear now that this is not going to last long. The coming of the European single currency has been a warning sign that the days of Bretton Wood and Nixon's subsequent detrimental move against the world economy could be counted. But the Central Bank of Europe lacked the powers doted to its US counterpart, and failed to procure a reversal from monetarism to a more physiocratic approach. At the moment, the dollar share in most countries' national reserves is on the decline while along with gold other currencies such as the euro, the Russian rouble and the Japanese yen are on the rise – proportionally that is. The ultimate goal of today's global monetary trends is to sluice cash out of countries' core economic assets altogether in favour of tangibles – meaning produce. And even then, other major so-called emerging economies such as Russia, India, Brazil and South Africa are likely to follow pace, thereby gradually annihilating demand for cash and consolidating that for commodities. This and little else is to change the map of the world economy in the most drastic and dramatic manner ever since rise of the European colonial empires.

CHAPTER V

THE "ISLAMIC" MENACE

Pavel Filonov. Animals. 1930. Oil on paper. 67.5 x 91 cm.
The Russian Museum, St. Petersburg, Russia

Sinister suggestions and even much more sinister realities surround the so-called Islamic State of Syria and the Levant, which according to Central-Asian state security officials and other observers currently harbours in the order of 3,000 "fighters" from Kazakhstan, Kyrgyzstan, Tajikistan, Uzbekistan and Turkmenistan. The number of mercenaries from the Russian Federation, mainly from the northern Caucasus but also from southwestern Siberia, is thought even to exceed that of the other Central Asian former Soviet republics. Numbers from China's northwestern autonomous region Xing-Yang are also believed to have joined the ISIL's ranks, but few details about them are known. The most immediate danger of the influx from Central Asia into the Middle East is that once those volunteers, well-drilled and well-indoctrinated, return home they could form a fifth column on behalf of the ISIL leadership.

Just a glance at the map shows that the only geopolitical buffers between the ISIL on one side and the Caucasus and Central Asia on the other are Iran and Azerbaijan – both dominated by shi'ite Muslims and therefore above suspicion to swear allegiance to ISIL which considers shi'ites as heretics due to be killed at random for it. This gives Iran in particular a valuable trump card in the eyes of both the former USSR's states and the west.

The group under whose control the ISIL is today was founded in 1999 by Abu Musab al-Zarqawi under the name Jamā'at al-Tawhid wa-al-Jihad (JTJ) – or "The Organisation of Monotheism and Jihad". Originally, the JTJ worked in allegiance with Osama bin-Laden's Al-Qaeda, but shortly after the attacks on America in 2001 they split up. On 29 June 2014 a rival JTJ leader by the name of Abu Bakr al-Baghdadi, known by his supporters as Amir al-Muminin, was elected as Caliph Ibrahim in the area occupied by the movement, which comprises about one-third of Syria's and Iraq's combined territory.

According to various sources, the occupied zone holds between 150,000 and a quarter million armed men (and women) entrenched. Local populations are held under sheer terror, with random killings, rapes, tortures, robberies and other misdeeds on a large scale being the order of the day. The ISIL leadership's current ideology is vague, contradictory and anachronistic. In all: a desperado would-be state reminding one of Bounty Island. But they still seem to have considerable amounts of cash at their disposition. Fingers have been pointed in that regard to Saudi Arabia, but also to the USA. It is known that far-right US politicians have huddled up in public with ISIL leaders – and there might be more to that story than meets the public eye.

1. "I will be the one who slaughters you"

Pavel Filonov. Beast (Wolf Cub). 1925. Oil on paper. 71 x 69 cm.
The Russian Museum, St. Petersburg, Russia

For Central Asia's secular governments, the situation hs been becoming more and more alarming indeed. On November 18, chairman of the Kazakh he National Security Committee (KNB) Nurtai Abykayev during a meeting with his peers from other former Soviet republics put the number of Kazakh "fighters" on ISIL territory at around 300, with the number of women among them up to about half, Central Asia Online reported the following day. "Abykayev revealed the figure at a November 5 session of the Council of Heads of Security Authorities and Special Services of the CIS, held in Astana," the news report read. "He based his estimate on a November 2013 jihadist video showing about 150 Kazakhstani militants, purportedly in Syria. The Kazakhstanis fighting there have formed their own combat unit, Abykayev added. Kazakhstan is alarmed that ISIL recruiters are radicalising young Kazakhstanis and sending them to fight in Syria and Iraq, Abykayev said."

The material compiled as evidence can be compelling. Thus, on November 23 an ISIL propaganda video was posted by a human rights reel called Al-Alam showing dozens of Kazakh children being drilled on ISIL-controlled territory in Syria. "The boys are shown sitting in a group and are all wearing matching camouflage fatigues," the accompanying text reads. "One of the boys shows off his ability to strip apart and reassemble a machine gun whilst the other boys watch on with little interest. The child soldiers are then shown carrying out gun manoeuvres and tactical formations. It also briefly shows shots of the boys working out in the gym and practicing martial arts. One of the Kazakh children, who gives his name as Abdullah, is asked in an interview what he is doing. The boy replies: 'I'm training in a camp.' When quizzed about what he will do in the future, Abdullah chillingly declares with a smile: 'I will be the one who slaughters you, O kuffar (non-believer)'." Similar signals have come from other Central Asian states. "Kyrgyz authorities say they are going after home-grown terrorists, domestic supporters of the Islamic State of Iraq and the Levant (ISIL), and citizens planning to fight outright for the Middle Eastern terrorist group," Central Asia Online reported on November 6. "The State Committee for National Security (GKNB) October 22 announced that it had arrested 36 suspected members of terrorist organisations during the past two years and charged them as extremists, [...] Kyrgyzstan has banned 17 extremist groups. [...] About 175 Kyrgyz are fighting in Syria, the government estimates." 51)

In the course of the winter of 2014/'15, things started to look really worrying as it appeared that though the Taliban in Afghanistan and northern Pakistan were in decline, they were less replaced by their countries' legitimate governments than by an even much worse nightmare. By weakening the ferocious hordes of the Taliban, accused of having been the brain tank behind the attacks on US targets back in 2001, by over a decade of raids and bombardments, along with numerous arrests and a large number of Taliban members surrendering themselves to the US-installed secular regime in

Kabul in exchange for pardon and rehabilitation, the US-led NATO forces now appeared to have only opened the doors in Afghanistan for an even more fearsome foe. It comes straight from the Middle East where Syrian and Iraqi forces are doing their best to constrain them but without decisive results.

At the time of writing, on combined Syrian and Iraqi territory, the ISIL occupied a slice of land of about the size of England, Wales and Scotland together. It also controlled parts of Libya. Now, ISIL forces, by taking control over Afghanistan using a tactic known from the Taliban – namely establishing a network of mid-size strongholds across the countryside encircling urban centres one by one with the aim to attack them from all sides – were a bigger threat to Central Asia than the Taliban ever had been. According to analysts, the next aim would be to occupy the Fergana Valley and its surrounding highlands, an area which is shared by Tajikistan, Kyrgyzstan and Uzbekistan. From there, ISIL troops could launch deadly attacks against those three states and even straight into nearby China. "Since the announcement of the Khorosan Province, covering modern day Pakistan, Afghanistan, India, Bangladesh, and part of neighboring central Asian countries, in January 2015, the ISIL had not only convinced commanders of Pakistani Taliban to declare their allegiance to Al-Baghdadi, the Group had also nominated the Pakistani Taliban commander Hafez Saeed Khan as the emir of Khorosan," one background report by Deedar R. Khudaidad, born in Afghanistan and a Bachelor in Politics and International Relations at the Edith Cowan University in West-Australia reads. "The allegiance of Hafez Saeed Khan and other Taliban commanders to Al-Baghdadi [the "caliph" of the ISIL – ChvdL] mean that the Pakistani Taliban is no longer under the command of Mullah Omar. [...] Around the country, the ISIL commanders recruited men from eastern provinces of Badakhshan, Nuristan and Nangarhar; South and Eastern provinces of Paktia, Logar, Ghazni, Helmand and Zabul; and Northern provinces of Jawzjan, Kunduz and Parwan. By expanding their presence in almost all major provinces of Afghanistan, today the ISIL is

117

not only considered a powerful rival against the Taliban, the group is also considered great threats to the stability and security of Afghanistan, Pakistan, and other neighboring countries." 52)

The three northern provinces mentioned border Tajikistan, Uzbekistan and Turkmenistan. Only Uzbekistan has a clearly marked and closely watched borderline whereas the other two have few official border posts and large numbers of unguarded unofficial ones that can be crossed without any hindrance. Hundreds of Kyrgyz and thousands of Uzbeks and Tajiks (no numbers are known regarding Turkmen and Uygur "fighters") have signed up to ISIL and slipped into Syria or Iraq to undergo training and obtain experience on the battleground. They were feared to be returning to Central Asia to serve as a fifth column within ISIL in its campaign to add the region to its global domain.

The scenario looked nightmarish indeed. An ISIL occupation of the Fergana Valley and surrounding areas, doubtlessly accompanied by huge massacres and subsequent savage oppression of the survivors, would not only expose the capitals of Uzbekistan, Tajikistan and Turkmenistan to subsequent attacks, but it would also allow the ISIL to take control over extensive oil and gas fields, metal deposits and processing facilities – including uranium which would enable them to fabricate atom bombs ready for use. As things looked into 2015, it could be less a question if but rather when a massive attack on Central Asia would be launched. Would the ISIL forces complete the sieges of Afghanistan's urban centres including the capital and subsequently take control over them first, or will they give priority to a surprise attack on the Fergana Valley? It did not look at all as though the remaining NATO forces in Afghanistan would be able to prevent either scenario. Nor were the armies of the Central Asian former Soviet republics expected to be able to wipe the ISIL forces out. They could hardly be considered a match for ISIL given the fact that the armies of Iraq and Syria also prove to be pretty ineffective in annihilating the ISIL…

Central Asia's ex-Soviet republics have sought support within the CSTO and the SCO, both regional multi-state security collectives engaged in anti-terror training and exercises. The second one includes China as well, while Iran, India and Pakistan are pushing for membership. The question remains whether secular governments with varying levels of democracy, will maintain enough popular support to stand firm against the advance of the ISIL and its regional counterparts and agents. And the worst thing is that the west, given their ambiguous role in Syria and Ukraine, cannot seem to be trusted in the eyes of most SCO members. In all: a geopolitical mess.

It may sound incredible, but at least in some respects including this one it looks indeed as though if Kyrgyzstan sneezes, the rest of the world panics at the thought of a global epidemic. The most popular microbe in this regard in vogue a bit everywhere in the world is the one related to Islamic extremism. The division between "east" and "west", though, result in lots of talk without anyone being able to deal a fatal blow either to the notorious "Islamic" state in the Near East which for Central Asia is the Near West, and their fifth columns in Central Asia in the form of the Taliban in Pakistan and Afghanistan, and several movements within the Central Asian former Soviet republics. Business consultants speak of "risks" for investments, stemming economic growth. And local authorities are most concerned by exactly that – hence the deadlock.

It was probably the first time English newspaper readers heard of the Al-Sarahsiy Mosque in a town called Kara-Suu with some 20,000 inhabitants in the central-west of a country called Kyrgyzstan – not to speak of a certain Rashot Kamalov, the mosque's "...charismatic imam, who is respected for criticising brutal and corrupt officials, society's moral decline and western pop culture," in the words of an article by The Guardian posted after the arrest. "However, on Friday 13 February, the two-story mosque near the Uzbekistan border was half-empty and surrounded by police. Government officials introduced a new imam. Kamalov had been arrested four days earlier for allegedly encouraging militants to fight alongside Islamic

State (Isis) in Syria and Iraq, charges his supporters say are intended to silence a prominent critic. 'The imam in custody has not just appealed for the creation of a caliphate but has also been telling believers about the war in Syria and making extremist statements,' Zhenish Ashirbaev, an Interior Ministry spokesman told Interfax on 10 February. Ashirbaev added that Kamalov is also suspected of belonging to Hizb-ut-Tahrir, an international Islamist group banned throughout the region which agitates for the creation of a state governed by its interpretation of Islamic law but officially disavows violence. Police "found extremist books and other materials at the suspect's house and in the mosque," Interfax quoted the spokesman as saying. In connection with Kamalov's arrest, Kyrgyz security forces have fanned out across southern Kyrgyzstan arresting dozens of alleged militants. Security officials say the raids have led to the recovery of illegal weapons and extremist literature, and have disrupted cells that were recruiting Kyrgyz citizens to join Isis." Kyrgyzstan's legislators have turned recruitment of "Islamic fighters" and joining Isis a criminal offence. 53) INTERSPACE "Kamalov, 36, is the son of Muhammadrafiq Kamalov, a prominent imam who was killed in August 2006 during a joint operation by the Kyrgyz and Uzbek security services," the article relates further down. "The details of the father's killing are still murky; Kyrgyz police said Muhammadrafiq Kamalov was a terrorist but presented no evidence to satisfy independent observers. The younger Kamalov began leading prayers at the Al-Sarahsiy Mosque after his father's death, though he was never approved by the Muftiate, the state-run Muslim board that appoints imams and ensures they toe the government line. Like his father, Kamalov reportedly permitted Hizb-ut-Tahrir members to worship at his mosque, but he publicly renounced links with the organisation and its aim of establishing an Islamic caliphate. [...] Kyrgyz officials say 200 Kyrgyz nationals have joined Isis, but it is thought that number may be exaggerated. In an interview weeks before his arrest, Kamalov said he had received death threats from Isis supporters for his criticism of the terrorist movement." Yet, Kyrgyzstan's attempts to prevent the formation of "Islamic" fifth columns within its borders bear little unique features or methods. "British counter-terrorism officials are monitoring 3,000 extremists in the UK who they fear could commit acts of domestic terror or become future 'Jihadi Johns', a report in the Financial Times dated February 17 2015 read. "Many will never have travelled abroad or been official members of terrorist organisations — underscoring the burgeoning problem facing intelligence and security agencies across Europe in trying to track radical communities of home-grown terrorists. The disclosure follows the unmasking of a Londoner, Mohammed Emwazi, this week as the hooded murderer — nicknamed Jihadi John by the press — responsible for some of the most barbaric killings perpetrated by the Islamic State of Iraq and the Levant (Isis). The figure of 3,000 is significantly higher than previous estimates. In late 2007, Jonathan Evans — now Lord Evans, and then director-general of Britain's domestic security service MI5 — said officers were monitoring 2,000 individuals. The number of subjects of interest ("SoIs"), as potentially violent extremists are known in MI5 parlance, had been stable until recent months. But the rise of Isis has greatly expanded their ranks. Senior Whitehall security officials, who specified the current number of extremists under watch on condition of anonymity, told the Financial Times that there was now real concern over the impact that social media were having on radical individuals in Britain and the new ability to magnify the effect and appeal of the eruption of jihadism across the Middle East. The Home Office declined to comment. The focus of counter-terrorism efforts in Europe until now has been on preventing citizens from travelling to Syria and Iraq to join terror groups. An estimated 3,000 Europeans have travelled to fight as jihadis there, including more than 500 Britons. But individuals who remain at home are increasingly being seen as high-priority targets for monitoring as the incidence of 'lone wolf' terror attacks grows and a legal crackdown on extremism across Europe raises tensions. They are becoming harder to track, too, say British officials, because they are less and less likely to be members of groups or well-connected networks. One senior security officer described the problem as like trying to follow the random Brownian Motion of particles in a teapot."

2. "Russia is in the same boat"

Pavel Filonov. The Gardener. 1912-1913. Watercolor, brown ink,
feather, brush, graphite pencil on paper. 49.1 x 50 cm.
The Russian Museum, St. Petersburg

From Britain, we zoom in on the Russian Federation - at odds with US-led western countries over two separatist provinces in Ukraine but facing similar problems and dilemmas. "The self-declared Islamic State isn't just a Western or Mideast problem, Russia's chief spy said today in Washington. It's a Russian problem, too – and in more serious ways," the Christian Science Monitor wrote in a report posted on February 20. "As many as 1,700 Russians are currently fighting in Iraq alongside the extremist group, Alexander Bortnikov, head of the FSB security service, told journalists after a security conference in the US capital, [adding that] this number almost doubled over the past year. Mr. Bortnikov, who was part of the Russian delegation to the Obama administration's Summit on Countering Violent Extremism, said it's time to create a special antiterrorism center under UN auspices and for intelligence services of all countries to pool their efforts. [...] His main point, as it has been in the past, is to stress that when it comes to the war on terrorism, Russia is in the same boat as Western countries, most of whom also have citizens who have gone off to join the jihad. Some 20,000 volunteers from 100 countries are currently fighting alongside IS, he said. The problem is arguably more worrisome for Russia than for much of the West, however. Bortnikov made no mention of Russia's seething North Caucasus region, where a low-level Islamist insurgency has been under way for almost two decades. Most of the purported Russian volunteers serving with ISIS would likely be from that region, or from the mainly Muslim central Russian republics of Tatarstan and Bashkortistan." 54)

Business lobbies, ever so careful to stress their "non-political" commitments, are nevertheless concerned about the lack of political determination to finish ISIS once and for all and the maintained strategy of everyone-for-himself where it comes to the spread of extremism and terrorism. One recent report by a Moscow-based business advisory firm called Minchenko Consulting tries to put an entrepreneurial view on the problem together without, however, coming to observations stretching much further than the known clichés. "Throughout 2014, the Eurasian macroregion was indirectly affected by the sanction war between Russia and the West," the report reads. "The consequences of this conflict were aggravated by economic problems, most notably by the falling commodity prices. The expansion of the so-called Islamic State of Iraq and Levant (ISIL) project is a potential risk for the Central Asian region as well. Geopolitical turbulence and unfavourable conditions in the global commodity markets negatively affect the region's investment attractiveness. As of early 2015, we are noting only a mild increase in the risk profile. The general trend is adverse, however, and the influence of negative factors is bound to keep growing. This is why the countries of the region need to establish individual anti-crisis policies in order to avoid investment outflow and to stabilise the economic situation. The countries' ability to mitigate adverse economic effects and to benefit from capital flight from unstable regions via its attraction to Central Asia is dependent on the success of this stabilisation. A reliance on Eurasian integration structures and unimpeded access to the Russian market may prove a crucial factor for several countries in overcoming negative trends." 55)

The assessment is wrong, though, in so far that the "sanctions war" was not "aggravated" by "economic problems, most notably by the falling commodity prices" but exactly the other way round. Investors, especially in the hydrocarbon and mining sectors, have never shown much hesitation to venture into the worst African hotbeds – including Congo, Angola and Nigeria just to name a few – and it is therefore that "lack of stability" is unlikely to keep them out of Kyrgyzstan. Low sales prices for their produce in the market place, by contrast, do keep them out. This plain fact is painfully missing in the consultants' report.

Instead, national economies of Central-Asian republics remain captives of the east-west controversy in the report's authors' view. "The side effects of sanctions and countersanctions are producing an impact on the macroeconomic prospects of Central Asian states owing to economic interdependence (in particular, that of Kazakhstan, Kyrgyzstan and Tajikistan as countries with closest economic ties to Russia)," the report continues. "Nevertheless, the countries of the region took a number of relevant risk mitigation measures. For instance, although the schedule of key milestones in the Eurasian integration process remained unchanged, Kazakhstan stayed true to its traditional multi-vector foreign policy. Kazakhstan's role as mediator in settling the Russian-Ukrainian conflict was received positively by the EU." Note: not by the USA...

3. Kyrgyzstan: "unstable rules of the game"

Pavel Filonov. The Workers. 1915-1916. Watercolor, brown ink, Indian ink, feather on paper. 52 x 50 cm. The Russian Museum, St. Petersburg, Russia.

Though confusing chickens and eggs, the report by the Moscow-based consultant does acknowledge the negative effects of the "ISIS epidemic" along with an arms raise amidst the existence of conflicts between Central-Asian former Soviet republics. "The key security risk for Central Asian countries is the concentration of various extremist guerilla groups on the northern Afghan borders, in particular those of Uzbek origin that are related to the Islamic Movement of Uzbekistan/Turkestan, Islamic Jihad Union and Al-Qaeda, which renders Tajikistan and Turkmenistan particularly vulnerable," in the text's words. "The handover of American military assets to Uzbekistan, Kazakhstan, Tajikistan and Kyrgyzstan presents another ambiguity, as it may, arguably, entail an increase in regional tensions." Concerning the "Islamic State threat", the report continues: "The region's countries are threatened not only by the very emergence of aggressive Islamic State on the Iraqi and Syrian territory, but also by the presence of a significant number of Central Asians among ISIS extremists, according to Kazakhstani and Uzbekistani security services."

Within this strange brew, the position of Kyrgyzstan is described as follows: "The republic partially solidified its position due to infrastructure development prospects at China's expense, new loans and grants from Russia and Kazakhstan, progress in rapprochement with the Customs Union and Eurasian Economic Union, and also thanks to the development of CASA-1000 energy export project. A high level of internal and external risks persists accompanied by a modest resource endowment. Positive effects from liberal business legislation are balanced by unstable rules of the game. Dispute over the Kumtor gold mine became not only protracted but also complicated by additional litigation. We do not expect an ease in tensions over property rights to the key national asset up until the 2015 parliamentary elections. Stabilisation in domestic politics could considerably improve Kyrgyzstan's standing, but current political institutions in the republic warrant little hope." For all it matters, the CASA 1000 project is an ill-conceived piece of propaganda paper advocating the construction of a power supply line from Kyrgyzstan and Tajikistan to export hydropower to Afghanistan and Pakistan, which is most likely to remain that way since the stations to generate that power will not be ready for years and regional demand (including China) is enough to make their investment worthwhile and it is a lot safer. As for the insulting disdain for the Kyrgyz authorities, the report joins a chorus resounding from Washington to Tokyo (though the Japanese usually have a milder tune-setting) and contributes little to a better understanding of Kyrgyzstan's position in the region.

In its little original conclusion, the report repeats earlier misjudgments and notes that "Central Asia remains a highly risky environment for capital investment. Key reasons include:

1. Authoritarian regimes and non-public politics, prone to both high corruption and abrupt strengthening of influence over the national leader wielded by external players and individual pressure groups or clans. This situation implies particularly high risks of constant revisions

in the "rules of the game" in favour of specific factions inside the elites in power. According to both our experts and reputable international and Russian indices, this type of investment risk is typical mainly for Turkmenistan and Uzbekistan. Kazakhstan's accession into the Common Economic Space has not yet affected the country's investment stability, as the Eurasian Union Court still has not created precedents for effective dispute resolution involving foreign investors.

2. Weak states teetering at the brink of becoming failed states. In the conditions described above a formally democratic system becomes quasidemocratic due to unstable political institutions and proves a major hindrance for foreign investment. According to many experts, the instability of institutional environment, often exacerbated by political rivals, is an even greater obstacle for successful foreign investment than opaque authoritarian regimes."

What the report fails to note, though, is that the "Eurasian superpowers" Russia, China and India are getting closer to a joint effort to police the region entangled between their national borders to cut off the spearhead piercing from the Near-East straight into the heart of Central Asia. Remarkably enough, the coalition, soon to be formalised with India's full membership of the Shanghai Cooperation Organisation, should find answers on the ground to stem both the "Islamic" threat and America's attempts to destabilise Central Asia through a steady advance of NATO into the region not just by joint security measures but evenly by economic cooperation with the aim to make Central Asia "economically resistant" to the likes of ISIS and Taliban and eliminate poverty that generates desperados. The SCO has a multi-billion development bank in the making, and business communities should indeed pay more attention to the opportunities the umbrella offers to secure enterprises' interests against eventual threats. "Russia, India and China today made a united pitch for bringing to justice 'perpetrators and sponsors' of terror acts as they sought an early conclusion of the India-moved resolution to combat international terrorism," the India Times wrote in a news report in its economic section posted on February 2 2015 following a summit between the three powers the importance of which has been heavily underestimated in western media. "Foreign Ministers of the three countries also agreed to enhance trilateral cooperation, including regional connectivity, during the 13th Russia-India-China (RIC) meeting here," in the article's words. "External Affairs Minister Sushma Swaraj represented India at the trilateral that was also attended by her Chinese and Russian counterparts Wang Yi and Sergey Lavrov respectively. The three countries also called for early conclusion of Comprehensive Convention on International Terrorism (CCIT), a resolution moved by India to address gaps in the international legal framework against terrorism. India circulated the draft CCIT at the UN General Assembly (UNGA) in 1996. The objective of the CCIT is to strengthen cooperation to combat international terrorism. Russia-India-China Foreign Ministers agree to enhance trilateral cooperation, Ministry of External Affairs spokesperson Syed Akbaruddin tweeted. Russia-India-China call to bring to justice perpetrators, organisers, financiers and sponsors of terrorist acts, he said in another tweet. China and Russia also voiced their support to India joining the Shanghai Cooperation Organisation (SCO) after completing all necessary processes. [...] The SCO, a six-member Eurasian political, economic and military grouping, was founded in 2001 in Shanghai by the leaders of China, Kazakhstan, Kyrgyzstan, Russia, Tajikistan, and Uzbekistan. India currently holds an observer's status in the bloc. The countries also welcomed India's participation in the Asia-Pacific Economic Cooperation (APEC). [...] The APEC is a forum for 21 Pacific Rim member economies that seeks to promote free trade and economic cooperation throughout the Asia-Pacific region." 56)

The comprehensive formula which links security to prosperity is something reminding one of Cold War I. It should be kept in mind that NATO was formed first and the Warsaw Pact only years later and in response to what was felt as a threat by NATO to undermine the communist block. While NATO, though, remained strictly military both in style and substance, the Warsaw Pact comprised a large number of economic and industrial elements which kept its framework together – until a gradual neglect of the economic side of the story in the end made it implode. That mistake could be avoided in the midst of CW II – thereby leaving the western powers either out of the game or inviting them to become team players rather than hegemonists. This is easier than before since though differences persist, the three SCO leaders maintain (limited but existing) free market and enterprise systems. Economic realities are being recognised and their basics no longer differ to crucial extents from those perceived in the west. In all: it may remain doubtful whether business is good for peace – but peace is definitely good for business, with the possible exception of the arms business...

4. Kyrgyzstan's hopes and where they could lie

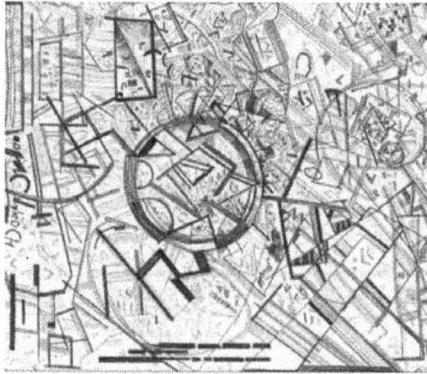

Pavel Filonov. Formula of the Universe. 1920-1928. Watercolor, Indian ink, feather on paper. 22 x 25 cm. The Russian Museum, St. Petersburg, Russia

So could Kyrgyzstan become a Central-Asian Switzerland? Such a scenario is hard to imagine indeed. Even in case Kyrgyzstan could revitalise its industries (including food and hardware manufacturing, banking and tourism) it would still lack the financial clout and culture to get anywhere near the profile that characterises Switzerland for generations – if ever. But apart from that and disregarding the economic factor, Kyrgyzstan is in a position to keep regional factors in balance which bears some resemblance to Switzerland. Located in the heart of Europe, the Swiss whose main state languages are French, German and Italian, holds a key position between the two most powerful economies of the European Union, namely France, Germany and Italy It does so by its own particular advantages and takes care to keep external forces, in particular the United States, out of its political arena. Looking at the map, one would be tempted to observe that Kyrgyzstan's geographical position between the Russian Federation and the

People's Republic of China bears some similarity with that of Switzerland. But that position will be undermined if instead of acting as a reliable partner towards its two powerful neighbours it would develop in the direction of a fifth column on behalf of a superpower on the other side of the globe without any mutual economic interests in common whatsoever.

Ironically, among the warning signs against Kyrgyzstan being absorbed in global conflicts threatening its regional position are pamphlets advocating such "dependent isolation" through US-led infiltration moves. Among those is the latest so-called decade-forecast, posted every five years by America's armchair propaganda tool (also dubbed shadow CIA) Stratfor. Ill-structured and full of contradictions and misconceptions, the report gives nonetheless a scaring picture of the way in which the world is supposed to take America's free hand where it comes to raping and reaping the globe for granted. "This is not a forecast rooted in patriotism or jingoism. It derives from our model that continues to view the United States as the pre-eminent power," the organisation claims in the opening observations of its report – meaning that "patriotism" and "jingoism" are what it is. So-called Jihadism, considered the main threat to Kyrgyzstan and surrounding areas today, is being downplayed – insinuating that "Islamic" extremism is not really on top of America's agenda. "We see the U.S.-jihadist war subsiding," in the report's words. "This does not mean that Islamist militancy will be eliminated. Attempts at attacks will continue, and some will succeed. However, the two major wars in the region will have dramatically subsided if not concluded by 2020. We also see the Iranian situation having been brought under control. Whether this will be by military action and isolation of Iran or by a political arrangement with the current or a successor regime is unclear but irrelevant to the broader geopolitical issue. Iran will be contained, as it simply does not have the underlying power to be a major player in the region beyond its immediate horizons." 61)

Rather than the Near-East, nothing less than the European Union finds itself under Stratfor's attack. "The diversity of systems and demographics that is

Europe will put the European Union's institutions under severe strain," the report reads further down. "We suspect the institutions will survive. We doubt that they will work very effectively. The main political tendency will be away from multinational solutions to a greater nationalism driven by divergent and diverging economic, social and cultural forces. The elites that have crafted the European Union will find themselves under increasing pressure from the broader population. The tension between economic interests and cultural stability will define Europe. Consequently, inter-European relations will be increasingly unpredictable and unstable." The irony of the report's twisted reasoning is that a similar fate must be believed to be in store for the Russian Federation. "Russia will spend the 2010s seeking to secure itself before the demographic decline really hits," the text continues. "It will do this by trying to move from raw commodity exports to process commodity exports, moving up the value chain to fortify its economy while its demographics still allow it. Russia will also seek to reintegrate the former Soviet republics into some coherent entity in order to delay its demographic problems, expand its market and above all reabsorb some territorial buffers. Russia sees itself as under the gun, and therefore is in a hurry. This will cause it to appear more aggressive and dangerous than it is in the long run. However, in the 2010s, Russia's actions will cause substantial anxiety in its neighbours, both in terms of national security and its rapidly shifting economic policies. The states most concerned — and affected — will be the former satellite states of Central Europe. Russia's primary concern remains the North European Plain, the traditional invasion route into Russia. This focus will magnify as Europe becomes more unpredictable politically. Russian pressure on Central Europe will not be overwhelming military pressure, but Central European psyches are finely tuned to threats."

What follows is simply hilarious: "We believe this constant and growing pressure will stimulate Central European economic, social and military development. China's economy, like the economies of Japan and other East Asian states before it, will reduce its rate of growth dramatically in order to calibrate growth with the rate of return on capital and to bring its financial system into balance. To do this, it will have to deal with the resulting social and political tensions.From the American point of view, the 2010s will continue the long-term increase in economic and military power that began more than a century ago. The United States remains the overwhelming — but not omnipotent — military power in the world, and produces 25 percent of the world's wealth each year." It is here where the danger for the rest of the world lies. "The United States will continue to be the major economic, political and military power in the world but will be less engaged than in the past," the report tries to argue further down ignoring the contradictions and lack of economic understanding it displays. "Its low rate of exports, its increasing energy self-reliance and its experiences over the last decade will cause it to be increasingly cautious about economic and military involvement in the world. It has learned what happens to heavy exporters when customers cannot or will not buy their products. It has learned the limits of power in trying to pacify hostile countries. It has learned that North America is an arena in which it can prosper with selective engagements elsewhere. It will face major strategic threats with proportional power, but it will not serve the role of first responder as it has in recent years. It will be a disorderly world, with a changing of the guard in many regions. The one constant will be the continued and maturing power of the United States — a power that will be much less visible and that will be utilized far less in the next decade."

From there on, it goes from worse to worst. "Considered with the rise of Euroskeptic parties on the right and left, the growing delegitimation of mainstream parties and the surging popularity of separatist parties within European countries, the fragmentation and nationalism that we forecast in 2005, and before, is clearly evident," the report tries to suggest. "These trends will continue. The European Union might survive in some sense, but European economic, political and military relations will be governed primarily by bilateral or limited multilateral relationships that will be small in scope and not binding. Some states might maintain a residual membership in a highly modified European Union, but this will not define Europe. What will define Europe in the next decade is the re-emergence of the nation-state as the primary political vehicle of the continent. Indeed the number of nation-states will likely increase as various movements favouring secession, or the dissolution of states into constituent parts, increase their power. This will be particularly noticeable during the next few years, as economic and political pressures intensify amid Europe's crisis. Germany has emerged from this mass of nation-states as the most economically and politically influential. Yet Germany is also extremely vulnerable. It is the world's fourth-largest economic power, but it has achieved that status by depending on exports. Export powers have a built-in vulnerability: They depend on their customers' desire and ability to buy their products. In other words, Germany's economy is hostage to the economic well-being and competitive environment in which it operates. [...] Our forecast is that Germany will begin an extended economic decline that will lead to a domestic social and political crisis and that will reduce Germany's influence in Europe during the next 10 years."

By detabilising the EU's core area in western Europe, Stratfor imagines the rise of Central Europe as America's main base on the Continent to crush the former USSR. "At the center of economic growth and increasing political influence will be Poland," the report reads further down. "Poland has maintained one of the most impressive growth profiles outside of Germany and Austria. In addition, though its population is likely to contract, the contraction will most probably be far less than in other European countries. As Germany undergoes wrenching shifts in economy and population, Poland will diversify its own trade relationships to emerge as the dominant power on the strategic Northern European Plain. Moreover, we expect Poland to be the leader of an anti-Russia coalition that would, significantly, include Romania during the first half of this decade. In the second half of the decade, this alliance will play a major role in reshaping the Russian borderlands and retrieving lost territories through informal and formal means. Eventually as Moscow weakens, this alliance will become the dominant influence not only in Belarus and Ukraine, but also farther east. This will further enhance Poland's and its allies' economic and political position. Poland will benefit from having a strategic partnership with the United States. Whenever a leading global power enters into a relationship with a strategic partner, it is in the global power's interest to make the partner as economically vigorous as possible, both to stabilize its society and to make it capable of building a military force. Poland will be in that position with the United States, as will Romania. Washington has made its interest in the region obvious."

5. "Central Asia will destabilise" - "Washington is the only power"

Pavel Filonov. Formula of the Cosmos. 1918-1919.
The Russian Museum, St. Petersburg, Russia.

And so the authors swagger on in the constant idée-fixe of imagining Washington's would-be puppets in Central Europe pushing east in moves to destroy Russia from within, by fabricating more and more "revolutions" as witnessed in Georgia, Ukraine and Kyrgyzstan before. "It is unlikely that the Russian Federation will survive in its current form," the report daydreams. "Russia's failure to transform its energy revenue into a self-sustaining economy makes it vulnerable to price fluctuations. It has no defense against these market forces. Given the organization of the federation, with revenue flowing to Moscow before being distributed directly or via regional governments, the flow of resources will also vary dramatically. This will lead to a repeat of the Soviet Union's experience in the 1980s and Russia's in the 1990s, in which Moscow's ability to support the national infrastructure declined. In this case, it will cause regions to fend for themselves by forming informal and formal autonomous entities. The economic ties binding the Russian periphery to Moscow will fray."

Washington's scheme to dismantle Russia and plunder its remains pushes all the way through to Kyrgyzstan and its periphery. "To Russia's west, Poland, Hungary and Romania will seek to recover regions lost to the Russians at various points," the report continues to hallucinate. "They will work to bring Belarus and Ukraine into this fold. In the south, the Russians' ability to continue controlling the North Caucasus will evaporate, and Central Asia will destabilise. In the northwest, the Karelian region will seek to rejoin Finland. In the Far East, the maritime regions more closely linked to China, Japan and the United States than to Moscow will move independently. Other areas outside of Moscow will not necessarily seek autonomy but will have it thrust upon them. This is the point: There will not be an uprising against Moscow, but Moscow's withering ability to support and control the Russian Federation will leave a vacuum. What will exist in this vacuum will be the individual fragments of the Russian Federation. This will create the greatest crisis of the next decade."

After this, comes the twist – with the suggestion that America can lay its hands on Russia's military arsenal and use it to keep the entire megacontinent of Eurasia under its thumb. "Russia is the site of a massive nuclear strike force distributed throughout the hinterlands," the text reads further down. "The decline of Moscow's power will open the question of who controls those missiles and how their non-use can be guaranteed. This will be a major test for the United States. Washington is the only power able to address the issue, but it will not be able to seize control of the vast numbers of sites militarily and guarantee that no missile is fired in the process. The United States will either have to invent a military solution that is difficult to conceive of now, accept the threat of rogue launches, or try to create a stable and economically viable government in the regions involved to neutralise the missiles over time. It is difficult to imagine how this problem will play out. However, given our forecast on the fragmentation of Russia, it follows that this issue will have to be addressed, likely in the next decade." In all – an open exhortation to stage more "revolutions" in Kyrgyzstan and the rest of Central Asia, including parts of Russia. So what would this nightmare scenario mean for Kyrgyzstan. Following the "logic" imagined by Stratfor, it should start with proxy attacks, e.g. against the Russian military bases at Kant in the central north of the country and on Lake Issyk-Kul, hydroelectric installations and other targets, for which "terrorists" can be blamed and even used, or directly conducted by US terror squads infiltrating into the region. This should destabilise Kyrgyzstan's fragile political and economic composition and lead to one more "revolution", bringing down the country's political institutions and replace them by an African-style military dictatorship, opening the country up for America's mining and agro-corporations to get natural resources under control. Would Russia and/ or China be able and willing to defend Kyrgyzstan against such a threat? If not, there is no hope for the Kyrgyz people.

So what could save the day and allow Kyrgyzstan to continue its laborious economic build-up undisturbed? The answer to that is twofold: first of all, America's boldness in pursuing its global hegemony undermines those attempts by overestimating its capacities to achieve them. A second element is America's internal weakness in the form of sociopolitical escalations in various parts of the USA which imposes increasing threats to the country's unity. In other words: while getting too big for its boots elsewhere in the world, Washington ignores that what it hopes to be in store for the Russian Federation is actually brewing in its own domain. "Over the past 50 years the US and European powers have engaged in countless imperial wars throughout the world. The drive for world supremacy has been clothed in the rhetoric of 'world leadership', the consequences have been devastating for the peoples targeted. The biggest, longest and most numerous wars have been carried out by the United States. Presidents from both parties direct and preside over this quest for world power. The ideology which informs imperialism varies from "anti-communism" in the past to "anti-terrorism" today," another report posted in the course of 2014 by Global Research looking at the dark side of Washington's present-day aspirations read. "Washington's drive for world domination has used and combined many forms of warfare, including military invasions and occupations; proxy mercenary armies and military coups; financing political parties, NGO's and street mobs to overthrow duly constituted governments. The driving forces in the imperial state, behind the quest for world power, vary with the geographic location and social economic composition of the targeted countries." 57)

"What is clear from an analysis of US empire building over the last half century is the relative decline of economic interests, and the rise of politico-military considerations. In part this is because of the demise of the collectivist regimes (the USSR and Eastern Europe) and the conversion of China and the leftist Asian, African and Latin American regimes to capitalism. The decline of economic forces as the driving force of imperialism is a result of the advent of global neoliberalism. [...] The greatest impetus to successful US imperial expansion did not take place via proxy wars or military invasions. Rather, the US empire achieved its greatest growth and conquest, with the aid of client political leaders, organisations and vassal states throughout the USSR, Eastern Europe, the Baltic States the Balkans and the Caucuses. Long term, large scale US and EU political penetration and funding succeeded in overthrowing the hegemonic collectivist regimes in Russia and the USSR, and installing vassal states. They would soon serve NATO and be incorporated in the European Union." At an early stage, this seemed to be happening indeed. But as noted, the glorious capitalist conquerors were soon (though too late) to discover that they were somewhat less than welcome among the "former communist" nations.

"The very rapid and extensive imperial expansion, between 1989-1999, the easy conquests and the accompanying plunder, created the conditions for the decline of the US empire," the report reads further down. "The pillage and impoverishment of Russia led to the rise of a new leadership under President Putin intent on reconstructing the state and economy and ending vassalage. The Chinese leadership harnessed its dependence on the West for capital investments and technology, into instruments for creating a powerful export economy and the growth of a dynamic national public-private manufacturing comulplex. The imperial centers of finance which flourished under lax regulation crashed. The domestic foundations of empire were severely strained. The imperial war machine competed with the financial sector for federal budgetary expenditures and subsidies. The easy growth of empire, led to its over-extension. Multiple areas of conflict, reflected world-wide resentment and hostility at the destruction wrought by bombings and invasions. Collaborative imperial client rulers were weakened. The world-wide empire exceeded the capacity of the US to successfully police its new vassal states. The colonial outposts demanded new infusions of troops, arms and funds at a time when countervailing domestic pressures were demanding retrenchment and retreat. All the recent conquests – outside of Europe – were costly. The sense of invincibility and impunity led imperial planners to overestimate their capacity to expand, retain, control and contain the inevitable anti-imperialist resistance." A perfect example is represented by the five-year rule of the Bakiyev clan and the accompanying plunder of state assets and financials under the very nose of US military. The "client regime" was eventually removed much to the displeasure of Washington, and it can safely be assumed that the exiled figureheads are looking at the USA in the hope to be restored to power.

The most hopeful place to prevent that from happening is not Kyrgyzstan but America itself. The economic vacuum resulting from that resulted in deconsolidation of Europe's delicate economic framework – viewed as an obstacle to global hegemony in particular since the introduction of the euro threatening America's control over global markets. But though in a different format, America itself shows increasing signs that it is not immune to internal implosion either. Apart from Alaska and Hawaii, which are permitted to seek independence under the UN Charter, separatist parties seeking secession from the USA are on the move in a number of states including Vermont, Texas, Florida and California. In the northwest, there is the movement seeking for a new independent territory dubbed Cascadia which is comprising the US states of Oregon and Washington together with British Columbia on the other side of the border with Canada. Movements meaning to revive the confederal state that triggered the Civil War in the XIX Century exist throughout the south. In some states (e.g. Florida) separatist political parties are the third-largest political formation after the Democrats and the Republicans.

On top of geopolitical fragmentation and in at least some cases closely related with it are social and racial antagonisms which are reaching the surface of US society to increasing proportions as well. "Many states have varying bands of hate groups, but for their map, the SPLC qualified them into eight categories: black separatist, neo-confederate, Christian identity, racist skinhead, white nationalist, neo-Nazi, Ku Klux Klan and general hate," in the words of an article in the Daily Mail posted on March 3 2014 referring to the Southern Poverty Law Centre (SPLC), an NGO which monitors sociopolitical frictions in the USA. "The California-based American Freedom Party that was originally founded by racist skinheads group in Southern California is one of the top two groups that the SPLC have flagged up as particularly threatening. They have stepped up their rhetoric against immigrants and in support of 'the interests of white Americans. The other group that has been cited as a cause for concern is Crew 41 which started online. They take aim at sex offenders and members of a South Carolina outpost allegedly shot and stabbed a middle aged couple after finding out that the husband was a registered sex offender. The trail of hate then returns to the south with Georgia, which has 50 known groups. From there the next portion of the list is found in the Northeast, with 44 groups in New Jersey, 42 in New York and 41 in Pennsylvania. The geographic composition of the map also shows how the groups tend to be found in or around cities. For instance, all but nine of New York's 42 hate groups are found in and around New York City." The lesson looks clear – at least as seen from the outside: instead of pushing Kyrgyzstan, Russia and other former Soviet republics into chaos with the aim to seize their military assets and natural resources, America's government would do better to have a thought about what could happen if such "hate groups" should consolidate into a major political force, win lower-level and eventually federal level elections – laying their hands on American mlitary installations in the process... 58)

CHAPTER VI

UNDERMINING THE EURASIAN ECONOMIC UNION

Pavel Filonov. After the Raid. 1938. Oil on paper. 74 x 64 cm.
The Russian Museum, St. Petersburg, Russia

In his short musical *Die sieben Sünden des Kleinbürgers* (The seven petty citizen's sins) Berthold Brecht gives seven "weaknesses" of the individual leading to a degrading society: inertia, arrogance, rage, indulgence, lust, greed and envy. The piece ends with one of the main characters (one of two sisters) having experience all "sins" overcomes and abjures them. In other words: the solution to "corruption" is a strong character knowing what good and bad is and defying all "bad habits" for the sake of principle. The lesson to be learnt here could be that from a social awareness point of view, Kyrgyzstan's choice, namely to adhere to a concept of order, gives a convincing impression to be the right one.

Debates in Kyrgyzstan can easily get heated and sometimes overheated, as the nation's history during the last two decades demonstrates. Observers at home and abroad have therefore long speculated on fresh confrontations in the process of Kyrgyzstan's entry into the Eurasian Economic Union virtually all year long. The imaginary scenario, for all it matters, reminds one of the attacks on the European Economic Community during the 1960s, in the USA but also in the UK before it finally applied for membership, that the EEC was doomed to become the arena of a new confrontation between France and Germany, Europe's largest economies. Such "euroskeptics" persist up to this day, especially in Britain and in Scandinavia, but lately also in Central Europe where people feel, rightly or wrongly, that their countries' hasty adhesion to the EU has brought less gains than expected. Especially American and English media have echoed the spectre of a "collapse of the Eurozone" more than once over the last half decade. In both cases, nothing of the kind has happened, tough. In line with this, not a single trace of the imagined "EU-Maidan" *à-la-kyrgyzienne* has occurred anywhere in Kyrgyzstan. Exchanges of thoughts between Parliament (including opposition factions), the government and the head of state on the issue have been unusually courteous, and virtually every player in the country's political arena has openly declared that this is not a time to walk with one's head in the clouds but to face the realities of life in the most advantageous possible manner. For once, the Kyrgyz nation has shown rare unanimity – which for all it matters raised high hopes that parliamentary elections in fall 2015 and presidential ones the following year would proceed in an orderly manner as well and result in the continuation of Kyrgyzstan's development into a parliamentary democracy without reversals. In all: an overwhelmingly vast majority within the Kyrgyz nation has apparently begun to realise that in the quest for a better life, economics prevail over politics.

Let it be clear: neither membership of the European Union nor that of its Eurasian counterpart means a free ticket to prosperity. It means an opportunity for each member state's nation to pick some fruits from its productivity without too much of a burden – but it can only be so if there is productivity which fully depends on each member nation's own efforts. Membership also obliges nations to keep their household books in order, and to put an end to forms of so-called free entrepreneurship which are a bit all too free in terms of economic order and social decency. In Kyrgyzstan, a number of such malpractices, most of which are already in violation of Kyrgyz laws, will have to be combatted, including the relabeling of imported goods from China "made in Kyrgyzstan". A number of cases, involving clothing and gadgets, were already signalled in the course of this year, but little seems to have been done to bring culprits to justice. Overall, smuggling and counterfeit rings, believed to be large, well-organised and prone to violence if under threat, on Kyrgyzstan's domestic economy will have to be rigorously marginalised. Since all EEU economies suffer from the same phenomenon, policing it is poised to become easier since the number of boundaries across which forgers and their goods' traders can escape will have diminished.

Generally speaking, the EEU member states are obliged to respect private property and private entrepreneurship rights, as much as they will be obliged to see to it that entrepreneurs, both public and private, operate strictly under the law. These could well be obstacles to prospective candidate members Uzbekistan and Turkmenistan, where private entrepreneurship is subject to severe restrictions and state entrepreneurship enjoys substantial arbitrary privileges, and Tajikistan where law enforcement on entrepreneurship remains weak and rudimentary. Progress in both regards made by Kyrgyzstan partly explains its timely entry into the EEU.

1. "Equal rights and duties" - Putin

Pavel Filonov. The Hog. 1912-1913. Oil on paper. 38 x 43 cm.
The Russian Museum, St. Petersburg, Rus

On the whole, Kyrgyz mass media, whether loyalist or "critical", have been reporting on the EEU issue with similar serenity to that displayed in the political arena. "22 documents, including on the accession of the Kyrgyz Republic to the Eurasian Economic Union were signed in Moscow after a meeting of the Collective Security Council of the Collective Security Treaty (CSTO Collective Security Council) in the Grand Kremlin Palace," a report posted by 24.kg posted over summer in 2014 was to read. "The meeting was attended by Presidents of Russia Vladimir Putin and the KR Almazbek Atambayev, and the heads of Belarus Alexander Lukashenko, Kazakhstan's Nursultan Nazarbayev, Tajikistan's Emomali Rahmon and Armenia's Serzh Sargsyan, and CSTO Secretary General Nikolai Bordyuzha. According to Russian media, the Russian president said that the Eurasian Economic Union is open to work with all its neighbours: for partners in the east and the west. The head of the Russian Federation noted that participation of Kyrgyzstan in the union will contribute to the development of our country. [...] Putin also said that the Eurasian Economic Union's participants have equal rights and duties, as well as equally represented in its governance structure, and integration is based on mutual benefit, mutual respect and consideration of each other's views. As noted, the leaders of the Eurasian Economic Union adopted a number of documents aimed at the development of trade and investment ties." 59)

Some sideliners have tried to identify the two remarkably distinguished trends between factual and aggressive reporting on the issue for some time now. "It would be simplistic to reduce the nascent EEU to a toy in the hands of the Russian president. When it comes into force, on 1 January 2015, it will be the most advanced organisation for regional cooperation the former Soviet bloc has seen, an achievement preceded by many false starts," The Guardian wrote as early as October 28. "In fact, the EEU already exists. It has a headquarters – a glass building near Paveletsky railway station in Moscow – and officials who would not look out of place in Brussels. Its member states have already lifted some internal customs barriers and harmonised others for the outside world." The newspaper describes this as the "real" EEU – "a trading alliance slated to guarantee free circulation of goods, services and assets, but not hydrocarbons". "The other Eurasian Union is imaginary, the brainchild of Putin, first mentioned in October 2011. As he sees it, this organisation will be the equal of the EU and other major regional entities, a powerful bloc that will matter on the world stage. Its official formation is also intended to show the world that Russia has fully recovered, while crowning Putin's efforts to pull together the states making up the post-Soviet sphere of influence. Those who deride the scheme see it as an attempt to restore the empire." 60)

In attempts by the latter to convince the world of their imagined scenario, no moral boundaries seem to exist. Defenders of the would-be Russian conspiracy tend to display an attitude accusing all who try to argue against their views as "pro-Russian". Campaigns against the EEU also try to imagine "enemies within" the block. "Kazakh President Nursultan Nazarbaev suggested Russia's isolation from the West over the Ukraine crisis is creating tensions between Moscow and its closest partners," one report by Radio Free Europe/Radio Liberty read – quoting the Kazakh head of state as declaring: "The instability of world markets, the policy of sanctions, the deterioration of trust between the leading world powers, the threat of aggravating the military and political situation -- all of this will impact the processes for building the Eurasian Economic Union." 61)

Some other commentators have tended to push even further and harder for the clash and following implosion of the EEU they wish to see. Thus, one more attack by The Diplomat in its December 2014 edition reads as follows: "After months of awkward delays and thinly disguised aversion, Kyrgyzstan has officially signed on to the Russia-led Eurasian Economic Union (EEU). Joining Russia, Kazakhstan, Armenia, and Belarus, Kyrgyzstan's agreement will enter into full force by May 9. This agreement should put to bed rumors that Kyrgyzstan had pulled out of the arrangement, but nonetheless came with the distinct lack of enthusiasm recently seen in Bishkek's rhetoric. With this expansion has come a raft of questions that continue to poke holes in the Kremlin's notion of the EEU as a group centered on equality, rather than a vehicle for Russia's neo-imperial ambitions. Not only has Kyrgyzstan announced that it would not achieve all of the union's regulations until 2020, but it remains wholly possible that the new customs requirements that would otherwise cut off Kyrgyzstan's lucrative re-export trade from China may not be as rigorously enforced as otherwise demanded. Much like the new customs realities surrounding the Armenian-held enclave of Nagorno-Karabakh – which has recently seen at least one official come out vociferously against the EEU – these customs requirements may yet exist primarily on paper, without being translated to the reality on the ground. While the lack of enforcement may help tamp Kyrgyzstan's looming unemployment crisis, it won't exactly inspire confidence in the EEU's efficacy." Following a sum-up of ill-argued suggestions scrapped together from various newsreels (without mentioning sources for most of them), the article concludes: "The EEU may not quite be dead on arrival during its official unveiling in January, but there's little to indicate it will be worth more than the paper it's written on for the foreseeable future." Such suggestions, whatever one should think of them, do perfectly fit into The Guardian's "imaginary" view on the EEU. The method used to advocate them is clearly driven by malevolent wishful thinking. Rather than comparing all arguments in order to draw a conclusion, the conclusion has been fixed on forehand after which the author desperately looks for suggestions, mostly taken out of their context, Thus, Nazarbayev's observation on factors that "impact the processes for building the Eurasian Economic Union" obviously refers to the necessity to act together in response to provocations and look for substantial and constructive solutions instead. This is a red line that can be recognised in all of Nazarbayev's numerous and often lengthy statements since the beginning of the new century. As for Kyrgyzstan, there never was any "looming unemployment crisis" to begin with. 62)

Reading more exhaustive references to the Kazakh President's observations should open one's eyes in this regard. "The year 2015 will go down in history as the beginning of the new stage of Eurasian integration. The Treaty on the Eurasian Economic Union that incorporates Kazakhstan, Russia, Belarus, Armenia and Kyrgyzstan, will come into force on January 1. For the first time in history, an economic union with a powerful natural and resource potential, strategically important in terms of global and regional transport, energy and technology systems is being created on the vast expanses of Eurasia on a voluntary, equal and mutually beneficial basis," Nazarbayev was quoted by the Kazakh independent newsreel Tengrinews as publicly declaring on the occasion. "We have combined our economic potentials in response to the challenges of the XXI century," the Kazakh head of state continued. "The Eurasian Economic Union is created primarily for the ordinary people and their vital interests. On the vast territory stretching from the Baltic to the Pacific, from the Arctic to the Tien Shan mountains, more than 180 million citizens of the member states are gaining equal opportunities for business, free trade and employment, use of communications, expansion of interregional cooperation and humanitarian cooperation. Today, we are defining a powerful long-term vector of peace, harmony, mutual support and benefits for our countries. And at the same time, integrating economically, all member states shall strengthen the immutable principles of political sovereignty and independence, cultural and linguistic uniqueness of our peoples. Of course, volatility of the world markets, sanctions, failing trust between the major powers of the world, threats, aggravation of military and political situations – all this will affect the processes of formation of the Eurasian Economic Union. We are taking these challenges into account." 63)

Many western observers, including high representatives from the UN, the OSCE and the EU have been praising Kyrgyzstan as an "island of democracy" in a region seen as dominated by more authoritarian rule so far into the current decade. But they tend to overlook that the country also remains an island of poverty, and that the much-despised EEU is the only chance to develop a stable economy in a place where abandoned mining sites and idle factories dominate the scene, along with large and disorderly makeshift market places. Reversing this trend is the only for all Kyrgyz citizens not just for the sake of their living standards but for their dignity as well. And a little less flattering from overpaid diplomats is well worth the effort. As for the investment climate, none of Kyrgyzstan's EEU partners will put any barriers on investments' inflow nor on their conditions. And even should a rift occur, neither America nor Europe has a monopoly on funding. The EEU not just opens doors to Russia, Belarus and Kazakhstan. China, India and Latin America have already declared their readiness to open privileged trade and finance links with the new block and on recent occasions similar messages have even been voiced from the European Union – and if there is one place that occupies a most strategic geographic position within that constellation it is indeed Kyrgyzstan. Missing such an opportunity is a fatal step on the road to nowhere, and sustains lawlessness and other scourges usually dubbed "corruption" though consisting of various types of misbehaviour.

2.   "The lesser of two evils"

Pavel Filonov. Heads. 1910. Oil on cardboard. 28.5 x 47.5 cm.
The Russian Museum, St. Petersburg, Russia

In all – false alarm: Kazakhstan and Kyrgyzstan are NOT going to be included in Russia's political agenda through their membership of the Eurasian Economic Union, taking off as of January 1 2015, the Chinese People's Republic is NOT going to lose its export market for manufactured goods either in member- or in non-member states of Central Asia, and there are NO threats of internal political turmoil in sight either in Kazakhstan or Kyrgyzstan as a result of their EEU membership. Over summer 2014, deputies in the Kyrgyz Lower House of Parliament representing well over three-quarters of the voters had approved the first package of new legislation and amendments in existing laws which facilitate the country's entry into the Eurasian Economic Union due for January 1. In contrast to many insinuations by western media, Kyrgyzstan has made its decision without any pressure to speak of from any of its future partners. Nor has it been under any pressure from third parties, in particular China, to stall its entry into the EEU. In October, gathered at a CIS summit in Minsk, the three heads of state of the current Customs Union, due to be transformed and expanded in the form of the Eurasian Economic Union as of January 1 2015, have formally accepted Kyrgyzstan's "roadmap" for its due entry, thereby clearing the way for it to happen in a timely manner. The final treaty formalising Kyrgyzstan's entry was due to be signed on December 23. The roadmap is based on the Treaty on the establishment of the Eurasian Economic Union, signed on May 29 2014 between the three CU members, free movement of goods, services, capital and workforce and conducting coordinated policies in key sectors of the economy, such as energy, industry, agriculture and transport.

The Treaty on the Eurasian Economic Union stipulates customs and technical regulation, foreign trade policies and measures to protect the internal market. The agreement also envisages the transition to common customs tariffs. The EEU is now set to unite the Russian Federation, Belarus, Kazakhstan, Kyrgyzstan and Armenia, thereby creating a block of close to 200 million consumers. A vast majority of deputies and their voters (which a number of opinion polls have shown) consider access a painful process but also, on a slightly longer term, a unique opportunity for Kyrgyzstan to develop itself from a community of peddlers into an industrialised nation. Taking after the example of Kazakhstan, the government of Kyrgyzstan has implemented a number of measures to allow local and foreign investors and entrepreneurs to revamp exiting, but idle industries and create new ones. Clothing, meat, vegetable and fruit products, furniture and chemicals are high on the agenda. But new oil refineries under construction and to be completed before the end of the upcoming year will also grant surplus capacity in oil products output, which would perfectly fit in to Kazakhstan's shortage of refining capacity. Finally, from 2016 on Kyrgyzstan will have boosted its power generation capacity to extents that enable it to export well over half of its generated electricity.

The main difference is that whereas Kazakhstan has more than sufficient financial resources to make up for a significant part (though far from entirely) of the required funding, Kyrgyzstan can only hope that the financial integration of the EEU members' capital markets will allow it to attract Russian and other EEU funds to boost its industrial productivity. Chinese investors are unlikely to be discouraged by Kyrgyzstan's entry into the EEU – quite the opposite can be expected. So where does all this leave the rest of Central Asia, and in particular China? Kyrgyzstan's imports from the People's Republic are hard to calculate, since most of it slips through the border without registration let alone duties. Local manufacturers complain that the inflow of cheap and low-quality produce from China is spoiling the local market. But this is due to change. China is working hard on quality improvement – which in turn is bound to mean higher sales prices – anyway. And trade relations with Kyrgyzstan and other EEU members are already privileged and in for further regulation through the Shanghai Cooperation Organisation. The SCO unites China, Kazakhstan, Kyrgyzstan, Russia, Tajikistan and Uzbekistan, which as of end-2013 stood for combined economic output worth the equivalent of over 11 trillion US dollar – representing 14.9 per cent of the global total.

Still, provocations have staunchly persisted. "Kyrgyzstan's re-export trade with China, a built-in advantage through the country's World Trade Organisation membership, has already seen a significant hit, which only looks set to continue following Kyrgyzstan's membership. (So long as all extant regulations are enforced – which remains another question entirely). As Bishkek moves closer to joining the EEU, Kyrgyzstan's leadership has allowed its distinct lack of enthusiasm slip into its public discourse," an article in The Diplomat posted on November 21 2014 reads, adding two quotes from PM Joomart Otorbayev and President Atambayev respectively, with the former mentioning "no alternative" to the EEU option and the latter speaking of "the lesser of two evils". For all it matters, the quotes have been largely taken out of their original context. There is a broad consensus in Kyrgyzstan concerning both the EEU and the SCO. Earlier, similar insinuations suggested that Kazakhstan "opposed" alleged attempts by the Russian government to develop the EEU into a "political" block out of even more alleged fears that Kazakhstan's northern provinces with their large ethnic

Russian populations might be tempted to follow the Crimea's example and seek incorporation into the Russian Federation. All this is blowing smoke. The EEU is going to be an economic entity, with the possibility that probably through the SCO it might consolidate into a monetary block dominated in terms of sheer volumes by Russia and China, but to the full advantage of other member states which remain fully equal in terms of content. 64)

In the case of Armenia, the motive to team up with the EEU looks clear. The landlocked country has hostile neighbours, namely Azerbaijan and Turkey to its east and west respectively, while relations with Iran to its south and Georgia to its north are lukewarm at best. Immediate economic effects, though, are likely to remain limited since Armenia lacks access to open seas and has no direct border with any other EEU member state. Transit traffic overland through Turkey and Azerbaijan is excluded, while Georgia might object to it because of its hostility towards the Russian Federation. With Kyrgyzstan, though, the situation is different. Opponents to its EEU membership claim that trade with China is set to plummet due to it, since import duties from the People's Republic are due to go up. They also tend to argue that its industrial capacity is insufficient to serve a market exceeding 180 million souls (including Kyrgyzstan and Armenia). The opposite seems to be true, though: both Russia and Kazakhstan also share borders with China and trade across them remains on the rise. Moreover, the EEU is bound to come to a collective mutual trade agreement with China sooner rather than later which in turn will put Kyrgyzstan in a strategic position between China and non-EEU members.

Ever since Kazakhstan became a member of the Customs Union, trade turnover of Kazakhstan with the Union's other two members increased by 88 per cent, the state news agency Kazinform reported in the autumn of 2014 referring to the chairman of the Statistics Agency Alikhan Smailov. Export to the other states grew by 63 per cent and import by 98 per cent. But it is not just intensivation of internal trade and communication that matters for the Customs Union and imminent Eurasian Economic Union. "Initially, the idea of economic integration was based on the fact that we are creating a broader and more representative and attractive market. Its capacity today exceeds 170 million consumers.," the Kazakhstanskaya Pravda in the winter of 2014/'15 quoted Eurasian Economic Commission member Andrei Slepnev, responsible for trade, as stating in an interview. "Now we see concrete positive effects, especially on the example of Kazakhstan, which today is actively involved in the processes of development within the Common Economic Space. [...] The common market opens completely different opportunities in the service sector. If we speak about Kazakhstan, it is primarily connected with the transit potential of the country as a key area of the New Silk Road from China to Europe. With intensification of trade, the sphere of transport is expanding, as well as the scope of services for traffic flows. And this is a significant segment of economy." As for Kyrgyzstan's industry, membership should be seen as an incentive rather than a hindrance for its development. The notion of returns-oriented community-based investment resources as a key funding tool in an economy is in place in all three current CU member states (and China as well) and is high on Kyrgyzstan's agenda as well, and joining up should speed up its implementation.

The idea is in fact centuries old, and was already clearly defined by the economic school of the French determinists some two hundred years back in time and put into practice under Louis XIV almost a century earlier. The policy has become known under the name mercantilism, and also under that of colbertism after the surname of Louis' cabinet minister Jean-Baptiste Colbert who put it in place. The system mutually integrates investment and trade and keeps both of them alive and kicking. The result was that France, up till then little more than a trade hub within Europe's economic constellation and caught with no assets to speak of amidst fast-growing industrial powers such as Prussia, The Netherlands and Britain, started to catch up. Shipyards and factories (including Saint-Gobain and Les Gobelins which exist up to this day), as well as other facilities were built at high speed. State guarantees for industrial investments sent the previously virtually inexistent banking and finance industry booming. It all looks like a perfect roadmap in response to the dilemma Kyrgyzstan is facing today. There is definitely an end to gold-digging and sooner or later even untouched reserves in subsoil treasures will be depleted. With modest tax rates and average wages hardly surpassing the equivalent of 200 US dollar a month, (compared to close to $800 in Russia), Kyrgyzstan can keep industrial production costs low even if it doubles its salaries overnight. It will create jobs, which are a much sounder basis for economic development than cross-border petty trade.

3. The EEU and the China syndrome

Pavel Filonov. Two Men. 1938. Oil on paper. 82 x 69 cm.
The Russian Museum, St. Petersburg, Russia

As on May 29 2014 the heads of state of Kazakhstan, Russia and Belarus pushed through with the signature of the treaty uniting them into the Eurasian Economic Union, as a follow-up to the existing Customs Union, and with the outlook of Kyrgyzstan and Armenia teaming up during the upcoming winter, the new economic block had already been under threat for years. Apart from the shadow hanging over it all due to Ukraine, which in the words of Belarus' President Lukashenko "got lost on the way", a storm of verbal aggression has blown from the west against the EEU on the occasion. "A new geo-economic reality of the 21st century is being born today," media quoted Kazakhstan's President Nursultan Nazarbayev as declaring at the event. "The deal, 20 years in the making, was "a hard-won achievement". Nazarbayev was quoted by Kazinform as saying that the signed document "...covers all the basic aspects inherent in international organisations, enshrines the principles of sovereign equality, territorial integrity, and respect for the particularities of the political systems of the members of the union. The important point is that decision-making at all levels of the organization is based on the principle of consensus [...] A new economic organisation has appeared on the international arena, one that has full juridical personality and acts based on the principles of the World Trade Organisation," the official statement by Russia's head of state Vladimir Putin read. "It is important that the transfer of certain authority to supranational agencies of the Union is of no detriment to the sovereignty of our states. Mutual benefit from integration has already been demonstrated in practice."

So far, so clear. But the way western media, in particular those across the Atlantic, have reacted comes down to a distorted caricature of a perfectly serene event. Friend and foe have been embarrassed by the demagogic and otherwise misleading manner in which western media have echoed, to Washington's whistle, suggestions of horror and threat represented by the signature of the tripartite treaty on the formation of the Eurasian Economic Union. "Sitting at a table with his two fellow leaders in front of their respective flags, Mr. Putin said that the group, formally known as the Eurasian Economic Union, had the potential to create a global transportation hub joining the trade flows of Europe and Asia," the New York Times wrote in a leading article. "[...] The agreement coalesced with great fanfare — and quickly — with members changing trade laws in a matter of years, a process that required decades for the European Union. But in the end, it became less about promoting economic development than about providing Russia with a diplomatic victory." 65)

Yet another piece of dirty demagogy published by Business Week under the headline "Putin's Eurasian Union looks like a bad deal even for Russia" "Alas for Putin, the new bloc comes nowhere near the big leagues. Even after Armenia and Kyrgyzstan enter, its total gross domestic product—about

$2.6 trillion—will be less than one-fifth that of the European Union or the US and less than one-third of China's. Russia will account for more than 80 percent of the bloc's GDP and a similar share of its roughly 178 million population. [...] Belarus, and Kyrgyzstan declined about 7 percent last year." For all it matters: Belarus' GDP increased by 0.9 per cent on-year in 2013 and Kyrgyzstan's by 10.7 per cent.

In the midst of all this, China remains in a unique position within today's global economic constellation. Awash with cash, and keen on keeping on track with the most spectacular large-scale economic development the world has ever seen, China has been investing around the world as far as South-America ever since the break-up of the USSR. Hoarding commodities, varying from oil to metals (including gold) and from metals to cereals, it is putting François Quesnay's good old physiocracy into practice once more: hedging cash reserves in tangible assets. Though the dragon spreads its wings a bit everywhere in the world, neighbouring Central Asia remains on top of the agenda. "China's president, Xi Jin-ping, swept through Central Asia, gobbling up energy deals and promising billions in investment," The Economist wrote in September 2013 on the occasion. "His tour left no doubts as to the region's new economic superpower. In Turkmenistan, already China's largest foreign supplier of natural gas, Mr Xi inaugurated production at the world's second-biggest gasfield, Galkynysh. It will help triple Chinese imports from the country. In Kazakhstan $30 billion of announced deals included a stake in Kashagan, the world's largest oil discovery in recent decades. In Uzbekistan Mr Xi and his host, President Islam Karimov, unveiled $15 billion in oil, gas and uranium deals, though details in this opaque country were few." China was already a partner in three major oil areas in Kazakhstan: Mangistau in the southwest, Aktobe in the north and Shymkent in the central south. "China is the biggest trading partner of four of the region's five countries (the exception being Uzbekistan)," The Economist noted in its article. "During Mr Xi's trip, Chinese state media reported that trade volumes with Central Asia topped $46 billion last year, up 100-fold since the countries' independence from the Soviet Union two decades ago." 66)

"Kazakh crude oil exports to China totalled 11,036,400 tonne in 2011, worth $8.602 billion, accounting for 52.8 per cent of exports to China during the whole year," an article published in last year's December issue of China International Studies by an analyst named Li Xia-yu read. "Petroleum and oil extracted from bitumen, sulfur and other byproducts from oil and gas processing totaled 3,414,800 tonne, worth $1.261 billion, accounting for 7.5 per cent of exports to China in that year. The volume of natural uranium and uranium compounds totaled 10,900 tonne, worth $1.288 billion, accounting for 7.9 % of the exports. The above statistics show that the energy resources for 68.2 per cent of Kazakhstan's total exports to China. Other resources, such as refined copper, metal products and iron ore, totaled 9,850,800 tonne, worth $3.783 billion, and accounting for 27.9 per cent of total exports." 67)

But China's interests stretch further than oil and gas. Power including wind, solar and hydro-energy and infrastructure are also on the agenda. An agreement for the joint construction of the Dostyk Hydro facility on the Khorgos River was signed between Kazakhstan and China on November 13, 2010. The new hydropower station's location is on the Khorgos river 24.5 kilometre from the Khorgos border checkpoint. A new road and rail link from Almaty to the border point is under construction, also financed with Chinese funds. In Kyrgyzstan, China is the largest foreign investor, engaged, among other things, in the refurbishment of the Kara Balta oil refinery, a new motorway linking the western towns of Jalalabad Osh with Naryn in the Kyrgyz heartlands to its east, where it links up with the road from Balykchy on the shore of Lake Issyk-Kul to the Chinese border in the south. The total costs for the project amount to the equivalent of 800 million US dollar. Elsewhere in the country, Chinese capital is engaged in the refurbishment of several former Soviet factories, lying idle ever since.

So what is the secret behind China's investment expansion boom? To trace it leads from Washington all the way to Peking. To put it simply: there are far too many greenbacks in circulation worldwide and in China in particular, and at the same time there is far too little in hard assets to buy with it within China's own borders. As of early 2015, Chinese currency reserves were worth the equivalent of 5 trillion US dollar, 2/3 of which consist of greenbacks and the rest of other currencies. At the time, the dollar share was on the decline while other currencies such as the euro, the Russian rouble and the Japanese yen were on the rise – proportionally that is. But that is not the end of the story. For the ultimate goal is to sluice cash out of the country's core economic assets altogether in favour of tangibles – meaning produce. And even then, other major so-called emerging economies such as Russia, India, Brazil and South Africa are likely to follow pace, thereby gradually annihilating demand for cash and consolidating that for commodities. This and little else is to change the map of the world economy in the most drastic and dramatic manner ever since the decline and fall of the European colonial empires.

4. The EU and the EEU: waiting for a wakeup call

Pavel Filonov. Faces. 1940. Oil on cardboard. The Russian Museum, St. Petersburg, Russia

The "West" – meaning the USA and under its pressure the European Union – may well grind its teeth and try to convince the world through its mass media that it is not happening, feeding on the experience of the 1960s. But the world has changed. Manipulating and blocking information has become all but impossible and credibility can only be based on facts these days rather than on suggestions, since the public at large is perfectly capable of verifying each and every inch politicians and so-called experts hold up in front of it. Arguments and facts have become inseparable. It is thereby that the war drums dominating the public domain at the start-off of Cold War II are increasingly drowned out by voices of reason. Take Federica Mogherini, the *EU* "foreign policy coordinator" under Italy's current chairmanship of the Union – who recently in a paper upset some of the EU governments and most of Washington's war-trumpeters by simply saying what most people in Europe are thinking. "Eurasian integration is a major foreign policy initiative and a priority of Russia, but also has a direct impact on the scope of the EU's economic relations with Russia's integration partners, such as Kazakhstan, Belarus and Armenia, her paper posted recently by the Financial Times read. "Geopolitical and other considerations also need to be taken into account, including the non-negotiable principle of free choice for all partners in the common neighbourhood. While recalling the EU's and Russia's shared objective of creating a common economic space 'from Lisbon tu Vladivostok' the question arises how best to promote such a vision, whether through the establishment of ties between the EU and the EEU or a set of other bilateral and multilateral arrangements." The paper calls for a "study analysing options and limitations with Russia and the wider region, taking into account their political and economic implications, including an assessment of the implications of a possible establishment of relations with the EEU". The paper concludes with the observation: "Moving beyond the short- and medium-term approach will require further reflection, including on the desirability and feasibility of a new framework for EU-Russia relations, [...including] resumption of EU-Russia summits." 68)

This is quite a different language from the one used by former European Commission chair Barroso – who became the virtual architect of the ongoing Ukraine crisis by confronting the latter with the threat to downgrade its relations with the EU should it join the EEU. By not giving in to such blackmail, the Ukrainian government fell into a trap that would lead to its downfall. The irony is that Mogherini's recent observations reflect not wishful thinking in falsely noting "divisions" within the fledgling EEU as well as between the Russian Federation and the People's Republic of China, but instead a deeply divided Europe – with the pendulum steadily shifting from the side of the attackers to those who see the advantages of both the EEU and its improving relations with China. For what the former ignore (deliberately or not) and the latter appear to realise is that Russia and China are no longer the "anti-capitalist" fortresses they once used to be. Both countries have free trade economies, private commercial enterprises, stock markets, currency exchanges and all other equipment working according to market principle and practices. State authorities' influence over mass media may still exist but it does not represent the absolute power over information and opinion expression they used to wield. The EEU member states have elected heads of state and parliaments. In all, they have more in common with EU member states than in difference with them. And China is, though following a different process, also heading for a situation in which the state is more and more acting as a partner than as a power with the country's citizens.

The conclusion, as observed by a growing number of opinion leaders, that looking for ideological motives on the side of the Eurasian domain is based on fantasy and make-believe. "The Russian Federation and the People's Republic of China have recently increased the level of their cooperation and partnership at a time when a series of political, economic and security crises in Europe, Asia and Africa have been changing the nature of world politics. The respective countries have entered a new period of rapprochement with the advent of the new millennium, in which bilateral security cooperation, political dialogue and booming economic relations have come to the fore as a counterbalance to Western supremacy in world affairs," one article by an international expert **from the University of Upsala named** Eşref Yalinkiliçli posted on January 29 2015 was to read. "[...] At a political level, Beijing has taken a neutral stance on the crisis in Ukraine by underlining diplomatic solutions to the issue, and Chinese authorities have condemned Western economic sanctions on Moscow. However, China has chosen to side with Russia at the U.N. Security Council meetings regarding the conflict in Syria and the Bashar Assad regime, together with Iran's hotly-debated nuclear negotiations." 69) INTERSPACE Both sides' motivations for their mutual approach, however, appear to be far less political than practical. "After Western sanctions targeted Russia's energy, finance and security sectors, the Russian leadership decided to enhance commercial and economic ties with China," the report read further down. "These soon-to-be-established commercial ties are also expected to move bilateral relations further toward a strategic partnership at a time when the Euro-Atlantic community continues its military and economic pressures on Moscow. The fundamental common ground in the Russia-China partnership may be the profit-maximised economic relations from which both parties benefit within a win-win situation. Over the past several years, China has become a major commercial partner for Russia as the trade volume increased by 17 per cent in 2013. Meanwhile, Russia is also among the top countries for Chinese foreign trade, with the trade volume reaching almost $90 billion at the end of the same year. For Russia, China constitutes a stable market with its insatiable demand for energy resources. On the other hand, China gets cheaper energy supplies securely, while avoiding the hurdles of energy geopolitics which affect deals between Europe and Moscow. Hence, both Russia and China appear to be becoming increasingly interdependent."

What appears to be true for the renewed tandem of Russia and China, appears to be even more important regarding the formation of the EEU. "In this context, Russia's enhanced ties with China, most notably in the economic sector, renders the newly-born Eurasian Economic Union (EEU) more significant in terms of a prospective geo-economic shift in the global economic system," the article reads yet further down. "First proposed by Kazakh President Nursultan Nazarbayev as a blueprint for the post-Soviet space in 1994 and, later becoming Putin's flagship in foreign policy, the long anticipated EEU was officially inaugurated on Jan. 1 2015. Signed by the leaders of the ex-Soviet trio of Russia, Belarus and Kazakhstan in Astana, the Kazakh capital, on May 29, 2014, the EEU Treaty has allowed Moscow to succeed in the creation of a single-market community. With the formal participation of Armenia and Kyrgyzstan early in 2015, the EEU will bring almost 183 million people together within a regional market of $4.5 trillion gross domestic product. The E.U.-like EEU will function as a customs union and regulate financial, agricultural and industrial policies between its member states. At first glance, the EEU does not appear formidable in terms of industrial size and attractiveness of its feeble, post-communist transition economies in comparison to the Eurozone or the North American Free Trade Agreement (NAFTA). However, Russia's flourishing economic partnership with China draws attention due to its promising future. In other words, a China-Russia economic partnership might facilitate the creation of a prospective center of gravity regarding the integration of regional economies in the newly-formed EEU."

It is this very observation that seems to virtually kill the voices of aggression. "In the wake of Western economic sanctions, declining oil prices and historic drop of its national currency, the rouble lost almost 45 per cent of its value against the dollar and euro last year," in the report's words. "As a result, the Russian economy has been in recession since the last quarter of 2014. Under these circumstances, China has appeared as an economic panacea, enabling Russia to take a breath when Western pressures have increased on its economy. Moreover, the parties have recently agreed on using the national currencies, the ruble and yuan, in their commercial exchange - another significant monetary move that will certainly accelerate the de-dollarisation of Eurasian transactions by further integrating regional economies with Moscow and Beijing. Therefore, one might say that the current financial-economic trends in Russia-China relations have the potential to reverse Western economic supremacy in the long run. In this sense, the EEU presents a challenge from within a region where the fastest growing economies in the world, such as China and India, together with sanctions-hit and long-isolated Iran, and even Turkey, are eager to cooperate with Russia, Central Asia and the Caucasus. That is to say, the newly-formed EEU could come to prominence given the fact that the region's countries have already been collaborating militarily and politically since the Shanghai Cooperation Organization (SCO) agreement was signed in 2001. For the Central Asian republics, the new economic union with Russia seems attractive, as they aim to break their landlocked isolation in trade and access to Western markets. Kazakhstan, in this particular, has long been the champion of such a customs union with Russia, and Kyrgyzstan returned to favoring this path after Almazbek Atambayev won the presidency in 2011. Both Nazarbayev and Atambayev have expressed several times that they have no option other than to integrate economically with Moscow. But the respective leaders have also stressed that the EEU would only serve as an economic cooperation and must avoid the rhetoric of a political union with Russia." Here, for all it matters, the otherwise by and large correct observations tend to get astray. If one reads the EEU charter, it is clearly and explicitly prescribed that EEU decisions can only be made by consensus – meaning that each member state big or small has a blocking vote.

Certainly, the voices of reason can hardly be expected to silence those advocating blind confrontation. Thus, an article written by two authors by the names of Bayram Balci and Ekaterina Kassimova posted on January 24 by Silk Road Reporters once more tries to push readers to ignore the facts and let ill-conceived arguments prevail. In the authors' words, the EEU "... was created to bring together most of post-Soviet countries of Europe, the Caucasus and Central Asia but it appeals works differently for each of them. The regimes in Central Asia can't make a decision between bitter resignation and fierce hostility, as Moscow tries to impose the project on them. [...] The Russian political and strategic ambitions of the whole Eurasian project contradict those of its partners in Central Asia, whatever their status." Where Kyrgyzstan (misspelt in the article) is concerned, the authors show themselves particularly erroneous. "Theoretically, except for a reversal of the situation, Kirghizstan should be the next to join the EEU," the text reads further down. "This little economically vulnerable and politically unstable country, which depends very much on its cooperation with Russia especially in the field of workers' migration, is not so enthusiastic about the idea of swearing allegiance to Moscow again. However, economic and security issues, linked to the growing Chinese economic supremacy, have led the public and elites to believe that renouncing some of its sovereignty to Russia and the EEU benefit is not such a bad alternative to total absorption by China." 70)

And so it goes on and on: "Now the Russian annexation of Crimea and support from Russian separatists in Ukraine hang over all post-Soviet countries as more potential threats of reprisal in the event they wouldn't be ready to follow Moscow's choices. Although Russia is momentarily weakened by the financial crisis affecting the rouble and by the European economic sanctions against its military intervention in Ukraine, it still has leverage against post-Soviet countries, but these means differ very much in efficiency and scope according to internal resistance factors and potential external reactions from the international community." Yet further down, the authors repeat and extend their aggressive bias against Kyrgyzstan (this time spelt correctly): "Kyrgyzstan is extremely vulnerable and its economy remains largely dependent on Russia, especially in terms of labour migrations. The lack of official data to quantify the importance of seasonal labour migrants shows how informal the phenomenon is. It is estimated that almost a million Kyrgyz are currently employed in Russia. Without the income they're sending home, the whole of the Kyrgyz society would not make ends meet. The country is on a drip-feed and close to bankruptcy. Worrying social unrest remains and raises concerns about a potential third revolution in less than a decade. President Askar Akayev was toppled in 2005, as was President Kurmanbek Bakiyev in 2010 by an angry population. The Kyrgyz vulnerability to Russian pressure has also a military dimension. The Russians still operate the base in Kant, outside the capital city of Bishkek and the Russian minority in the country still counts for 12 per cent of the population. Both give considerable leverage to Moscow. On the other side, Kyrgyzstan is under the aggressive economic pressure of China and the government of Almazbek Atambayev seems now more resigned than ever to joining the EEU with a better-known Russian leadership. In December 2014, there was rumour in Kyrgyzstan that the Russian financial crisis will convince the Kyrgyz parliament to veto joining the Eurasian Union scheduled in May of 2015. However, there is little Kyrgyzstan can actually do to oppose Russia and resist the EEU. Threats, like a simple ban on seasonal work from Kyrgyzstan, military maneuvers in Kant or media propaganda against Kyrgyz economic and political choices, make Kyrgyzstan a vassal to Moscow against an unfavourable public opinion and a skeptical Eurasian parliament." Once more: neither Atambayev, nor the government, nor Parliament ever "resigned" to join the EEU but explicitly requested it to its three, initially reluctant, original members. The "rumour" referred to never appeared anywhere in the public domain and is thereby a mere invention by the authors – as is the "unfavourable public opinion" and a "Eurasian parliament" which does not exist.

The good news of it all is that of late the war-cries that have dominated so-called news reports and so-called "analytical" items in the public domain for most of the year 2014 and into the following year, have been more and more pushed towards the margin, both on would-be academic and political levels. It may well leave the European Union divided into hawks, doves and chameleons and America isolated. But at least there will be no yankee doodle flotilla sailing through the Bosphorus to bomb and occupy the Crimea and the two self-proclaimed republics in Ukraine proper. And the world economy, now under (limited) pressure by the tit-for-tat measures between the USA and the Russian Federation, with the EU caught in the middle, might get a chance to recover if trade and enterprise are given back their capability to function as such, rather than serve as tools in gunboat diplomacy between states and political factions.

CHAPTER VII

US "DIPLOMACY": PEDDLERS AND MEDDLERS IN CENTRAL ASIA

Pavel Filonov. The Narva Gates. 1929. Oil on paper. 88 x 62 cm.
The Russian Museum, St. Petersburg, Russia

In an article posted by 24.kg on February 9 2015, one of the agency's most brilliant news interpreters and staff journalist Darya Podolskaya gave what she called "a slight hitch" regarding the appointment of a new American ambassador – not the one expected but a high-flying diplomatic old-timer with a controversial reputation. "The sudden reshuffle is confusing," the article reads. "The US Embassy in Kyrgyzstan, for all it matters, prefers to remain silent on this case and doesn't comment on why Washington changed candidates. After the former US Ambassador to Kyrgyzstan Pamela Spratlen left for Uzbekistan, it was expected that the diplomatic mission would be headed by Sheila Gwaltney. Back in August, US President Barack Obama personally recommended senators to approve [the appointment of] Gwaltney, an experienced diplomat, as ambassador to Bishkek. This was written by foreign media with reference to its sources in the White House. But then 78-year-old Miles, who was on pension, suddenly received an appointment to Kyrgyzstan." Follows a neutral-looking overview of Miles' backgrounds: "Ambassador Miles has received many awards and certificates, including those for special services and reporting performance. In 2004 he won the prize of US State Department for the peaceful conflict resolution." 70)

One could easily imagine some possible answers to Darya Podolskaya's question which she asks in her headline "What is the purpose of your visit, Mr. Miles?" "Peaceful conflict resolution"? Doubtful – since at present there are no conflicts in Kyrgyzstan heading for violent resolution (except imaginary ones but we shall come to that later on). "Special services"? Doubtless – but that takes a bit more to elaborate on. Take the view of Seth Ferris, American "investigative journalist and political scientist and expert on Middle Eastern affairs" in the words of a biographical note under the recent publication of one of his articles in the online magazine New Eastern. "Richard Miles was a top intelligence officer in the Navy and close to a key professor at the Patterson School of Diplomacy, long since proven to be a major recruiting ground for the CIA as well as the US State Department," the article's paragraph on the new US "interim ambassador" reads. "He has held several posts, but perhaps the most prominent was as chief of mission to Yugoslavia between 1996 and 1999. In 1997 Miles brought in and led a large group of consultants, PR companies, pollsters and 'democracy promotion' organisations which nevertheless failed to ensure the election of the favoured US candidate. The following year [Miles] led the observer teams which oversaw the implementation of the ceasefire in Kosovo, later revealed by the BBC to be fronts for gathering information which could be used to trigger war against the Serbs, not stop conflicts as they might be presumed to be doing. In 2000 the Yugoslav elections were rigged,

American-backed protestors refused to accept the results and Slobodan Milosevic was overthrown, which was the plan all along. The war in Kosovo had all been part of the plan, engineered by Miles in his official capacity, to destroy a country, install US-friendly governments in the remaining fragments and, by coincidence, establish bases there. Miles was gone, but his handiwork remained." 71)

1. "Need revolution send Miles"

Pavel Filonov. Formula of the Revolution. 1920s. Watercolor on paper.
73 x 84.3 cm. The Russian Museum, St. Petersburg, Russia

But Miles in his zeal to help recreate the Cold War pushed him ever further east. "In 2002 [Miles] was in Eduard Shevardnadze's Georgia," the paper reads further down. "The Western powers had always supported this man, despite his total lack of support within Georgia, because he spoke their own dirty language. But by this time they had finally realised this was because he was more unprincipled and venal than they were, so he had to go. The same crowd of characters used in Serbia entered Georgia. Mikhail Saakashvili was installed in the Rose Revolution as the new pro-Western leader. Misha's behaviour soon breached any Western norm of conduct and most Third World ones, but that was OK as long as the US could fulfill its objectives. Then Zurab Zhvania, the Prime Minister of Georgia who knew too much, started complaining. He was found dead. No one ever believed the official version about being poisoned in his flat by a faulty Iranian gas heater. Now this death is being reinvestigated and it has been demonstrated that a FBI agent, Bryan Paarmann, was involved in covering up the murder and destroying evidence about it with the help of the US Embassy. These things don't happen without approval from the top. Miles was the ambassador at the time. He is best known in the Foreign Service for making revolutions happen, 'need revolution send Miles'. Miles represents doing anything which suits US purposes in other countries, including death, destruction, murder and mass repression."

Miles goes indeed miles back a long time into post-Soviet history from its very earliest stages – as noted among many other sources by Mark Ames in a background report posted by a newsreel named The eXile – a "Moscow-Based Alternative Newspaper" as it dubs itself in late 2011. "Miles was named U.S. Ambassador to Georgia in March of 2002. Roughly ten years earlier, he had been named ambassador to Azerbaijan [being] the first leg of the Caspian Sea oil pipeline, and he served there long enough to watch approvingly as Haidar Aliyev established his decidedly anti-democratic dynasty. Miles was named ambassador to Georgia last year at a crucial moment. America had just introduced its first units of Special Forces ostensibly to train special Georgian battalions to rid the Pankisi Gorge of supposed Al Qaeda terrorists. It caused an uproar in Russia and was one of the key moves which drastically cooled relations between Russia and America. The Al Qaeda rumors were generally recognized as a bogus excuse to introduce American forces, thereby pulling Georgia deeper into America's grip. Not that the Georgians minded most welcomed the arrival of the American Green Berets, naively believing that they would protect Georgia from the Russians and reconquer lost territory. This move backfired and the Russians now have more control over Georgia than any time since the collapse of the Soviet Union' but more on that later. In his Senate confirmation hearings in Washington that year, Miles began his statement, "President Shevardnadze will retire in 2005. As you well know, three years is the blink of an eye in the world of politics. A top priority of U.S. policy on Georgia during this critical period will be to help Georgian political leaders and Georgian society to prepare for a peaceful and democratic transition of power in 2005." Sounds nice on the surface, but what it means in the local context is this: America is not only going to make sure that this 'transition of power' takes place, but how and to whom." 72)

Miles in Ferris' report appears to be part of a closely related American diplomats whose activities in recent decades have including somewhat less than diplomatic ones. One of his closest peers Richard Norland, Miles' successor in Georgia, is described as having "...worked in some even more sensitive places – Ireland, where he handled negotiations with the IRA in Northern Ireland, Afghanistan and Georgia itself during the civil war period. He also states in his official biography that he undertook 'business trips' to Chechnya, probably because it isn't recognised by the US and therefore doesn't have diplomatic relations with it. One of the principal funders and weapons suppliers of the Provisional IRA was NORAID, which US courts have publicly recognised as a front for arms supply. Yet this organisation continues to operate legally in the US, despite being declared by its courts to be illegally supplying weapons to a terrorist organisation. The Georgian civil war came about because the US provided material support for the violent overthrow of the legal president."

"John Bass, who happened to be Miles' predecessor in Georgia, has left colourful traces in occupied Iraq as well. Bass's reconstruction team in Baghdad was a USAID project, Ferris relates. "His role was to act as link man between USAID, the State Department, KBR, Halliburton and Blackwater. These major engineering, oil and security companies all have significant financial interests in Georgia, but as defence contractors, as Georgia does not have a domestic oil industry. Bass also has longstanding links with two other defence contractors who have long-term interests in Georgia, Cubic and Archangel. Of course, the US has a defence relationship with Georgia. But is that all? Both countries reckon they have a broad strategic partnership. An ambassador with such close ties to defence contractors is unlikely to be there to promote artistic exchanges or tourism, particularly when he has been sent there from securing a US-funded regime change in Baghdad. Bass has also worked for the Bush White House. His boss there was Dick Cheney. He was supposed to be behind the plane which flew illegal arms supplies, amongst other things, to the unrecognised republic of Nagorno-Karabakh. It was registered in Batumi, Georgia, while Bass was the ambassador."

The most alarming link exposed here is beyond doubt Blackwater. The man behind the organisation, which has carried out much of Washington's "dirty wars" abroad, including Iraq, Afghanistan and Ukraine (and possibly Kyrgyzstan – see below) has been Erik Prince, "the would-be mercenary king of America [whose] resume reads like a laundry list of contemporary armed conflict and geopolitical disaster," in the words of a lengthy essay on the man and his business written by Jeffrey Cavanaugh and posted on December 31 2014. He also dubs the culprit "America's Harbinger Of Death And Democracy". "The Blackwater founder's movements can be read like tea leaves: Wherever he goes, tragedy and death surely follow, trailed by tens of millions of dollars," in Cavanaugh's words. 73)

"Prince is a former Navy SEAL and right-wing, Christian fundamentalist millionaire who inherited his money and made it his life's mission to wield force, for a price, for the United States or, as it turns out, anyone else willing to pay him," the document relates. "He first appeared on the scene in 1997, when he and fellow Navy SEAL Al Clark formed Blackwater USA, a private security firm that billed itself as a provider of training and expertise for the complex security environment of the post-Cold War world. Like much of the rest of the "End of History" rhetoric bandied about in those days, Blackwater USA — currently known as Academi — came to be seen as a "faster, better cheaper" solution to the problem of armed intervention abroad. Like every road to hell, the impetus for the formation of Blackwater was a good intention: providing a "middle way" for democratic powers like the U.S. to wield power in places where terrible things were occurring, but where a raw calculation of political interest didn't point to sending in the Marines."

As could have been expected from the very beginning, it all went terribly wrong. "Instead of being the adjunct of democracy that Prince had envisioned, employment of Blackwater personnel became a way for America's pro-war elite to avoid accountability in an increasingly confusing, shadowy war that few could justify as time went on," the paper continues. "Yet Prince and Blackwater still managed to finagle nearly $1.6 billion from the U.S. government between the formation of his company in 1997 and its sale to a group of private investors in 2010. Of that, $600 million came in the form of clandestine CIA and military contracts, and the U.S. State Department made Blackwater the biggest provider of security to department personnel in Iraq until the company's ouster from the country in the wake of a 2007 massacre of civilians in Baghdad's Nisour Square. The shooting led to the deaths of 17 people. Several Blackwater employees were eventually sentenced to lengthy prison terms in the U.S. for their role in the incident, and the Iraqi government banned the company from its territory. This isn't the only example of company malfeasance in Iraq, of course. Prior to the massacre U.S. government investigators looking into the company had been threatened with death by company officials, and the military had long accused Blackwater of cowboy operations that endangered U.S. personnel."

"By the time the company had been tossed out of Iraq the political winds had shifted in the U.S., and Prince and his company, once seen as saviors by the conservative establishment, were no longer viewed so kindly. With the Iraq War winding down and with the right wing out of power in Washington, the time must have seemed appropriate to sell. So, in 2010, Prince did, walking away from his company and netting a cool $200 million in the process. After moving on from serving as Uncle Sam's cat's paw, he found himself in Abu Dhabi in 2011, where he began working with the United Arab Emirates to build, in the words of The New York Times, an 800-man 'secret American-led mercenary army', capable of 'conducting special operations [and] missions inside and outside the country, defending oil pipelines and skyscrapers from terrorist attacks and putting down internal revolts'.

That last observation brings the story straight home to the streets of Bishkek, in that fateful month of April 2010. As soon as late May the same year, a devastating report written by F. William Engdahl on what had really happened through the last half decade appeared. "The protests again the US-backed Bakiyev began in March over allegations of extreme corruption on the part of the President and his family members," in the document's words. "In 2009, Bakiyev began amending an article in the country's constitution regulating presidential succession in case of death or unexpected resignation, a move widely seen as an attempt to introduce a 'dynastical system' of power transfer in the country, one factor which fuelled the recent nationwide protests in Kyrgyzstan. He placed his son and other relatives in key posts where they raked in huge sums for the US airbase rights at Manas – reportedly as much as $80 million a year – and other enterprises. Kyrgyzstan is one of the poorest countries in Central Asia with more than 40 per cent living below the official poverty line. Bakiyev named his son, Maxim – who also managed to find time and funds to buy part ownership of a UK football club – to be head of the country's Central Agency for Development, Investment and Innovation, where he gained control over the country's richest assets, including the Kumtor gold mine." 74)

The Kumtor mine was originally a joint venture between the state of Kyrgyzstan through its public enterprise Kyrgyzaltyn and Canada's Cameco mining company, until the latter's share was taken over by a split-off through a management buy-out called Centerra Gold. During Bakiyev's rule, the Kyrgyz share in the joint venture was swapped against stock in Centerra – no doubt with the aim for the Bakiyevs to stack income from it on private offshore accounts. Under the new government, parties tried to reverse the situation to the original formula. After this had failed, the government of Kyrgyzstan, supported by its parliamentary majority, changed its plan again and sticking to the existing situation, tried to increase control over Centerra's board.

2. "Thoroughness and sophistication"

Pavel Filonov. Bourgeois in a Carriage. 1912-13. Oil on cardboard.
The Russian Museum, St. Petersburg, Russia

The beginning of the end of the Bakiyev regime is still fresh on the mind of the average Kyrgyz citizen. "Bakiyev government security forces, reportedly including Special Forces sharpshooters on rooftops, killed some 81 opposition demonstrators, leading to a dramatic escalation of the protests in the first week of April," Engdahl relates. "What is remarkable about the events and suggests that there is more going on behind the curtains, is the fact that the full-blown popular uprising exploded onto the scene with little pre-warning in the international media. There had been protest demonstrations repeatedly since Bakiyev took control in the Washington-financed 2005 Tulip Revolution. That Washington-financed regime change of 2005 had involved the usual list of US NGO's including Freedom House, The Albert Einstein Institution, The National Endowment for Democracy and USAID. None of the previous protests until this April, however, had the obvious thoroughness and sophistication of the latest one. Events seem to have caught everyone by surprise, not the least the corrupt Bakiyev family and his Washington backers. [...] On April 7, as Bakiyev was losing control, he reportedly rushed to the Americans, but as they saw the blood on the streets caused by Bakiyev's sharpshooters and the growing fury of the crowds against the government, they reportedly whisked the President and his family to his hometown of Osh, apparently hoping to bring him back after events had calmed. That never happened. Following the resignation of his entire government, including the heads of the army and national police and border guard, Bakiyev resigned on April 16 and fled to neighbouring Kazakhstan."

Only months after the end of the long-lasting trials against father and son Bakiyev, resulting in long-term prison sentences for both, questions remained which were far from being regardless of what could happen next – and with whose assistance. Early reports referred to snipers operating from the roofs of buildings surrounding the square in Bishkek where protests took place. Later forensic reports strongly suggested that a majority of the dead and wounded had not been shot from above but from short distance on the ground – which, if compared to the bloodbaths Blackwater had committed only months earlier in Iraq and were later to commit in Kiev and Odessa, bears its signature. Then came indeed Kiev, late 2013. Here, evidence of Blackwater (under whatever name) having directly been involved in "action" including atrocities committed in the capital and later in Odessa appeared to be more tangible than in Kyrgyzstan. After all, being "capable of conducting special operations" in order to "put down internal revolts" also means being capable of "conducting special operations" with the aim to make them happen. And it has not finished. "Longtime *Die Zeit* correspondent and advisor to German government agencies on Islamic extremism Michael Luders told Phoenix TV on January 20 this year," a report posted in early 2014 by the Executive intelligence Review was to read. "The Ukraine government is determined to solve the problem militarily ... and one must presume that it didn't make this decision alone," as the government is bankrupt and has no financial or military resources of its own for an offensive. "The Europeans are not excited about this development." There have been contacts between the regime in Kiev with Washington, and in Ukraine "there are 500 mercenaries of the Blackwater organisation which has been renamed in the meantime," – in the report's words. Dozens if not hundreds independent reports have already confirmed Blackwater's involvement – thereby spelling doom for countries like Kyrgyzstan in the near future. 75)

"The resumption of open conflict in Ukraine (which never truly 'ceased' in the first place) looks to be the first 'new' war of the year, and it's entirely Washington-backed," one report posted by Sputnik News on January 19 2015 was to read. "The US has been using Ukraine as a proxy against Russia ever since the EuroMaidan Colour Revolutionaries seized power last February, so it's not surprising that it would have an interest in the current hostilities. In fact, Congress even voted to send weapons to the country last month in a move that was guaranteed to destabilise the situation sooner or later. On the 'non-governmental' front, Blackwater has taken to training an 'experimental battalion' of 550 soldiers for Kiev. Mixed together, the combination of US support and Blackwater training is a surefire recipe for disaster in any country of the world." It has been reported on numerous occasions that shortly before Bakiyev's downfall, a similar "experiment" was at an advanced stage of preparation in the district of Batken – the sensitive area where the borders of Kyrgyzstan, Uzbekistan and Tajikistan come together and where all evils in the world poke around… 76)

It takes but little to look through the official propaganda which tries to justify the "West"'s policies and its undermining goals – evoking dreams of a new breed of Mobutus. Suhartos and Pinochets for Central Asia. "The United States has finalised a review of its strategy for Central Asia, a region facing economic and political uncertainty tied to Russia's flagging economy amid the Ukraine conflict and the murky succession plans of aging regional autocrats. Experts say that while Russia's military interference in Ukraine last year was not the sole factor prompting the review, the reassessment shows the Kremlin's actions continue to cause ripple effects across U.S. foreign policy," a report posted in early spring 2015 by Radio Free Europe/Radio

Liberty was to read. "U.S. President Barack Obama's administration 'recently completed an interagency policy review, which reaffirmed our enduring commitment to the people and governments of Central Asia', a U.S. State Department spokesperson told RFE/RL. The State Department, which spearheaded the policy review, declined to disclose details of the assessment or when they would be available. People familiar with the matter said they expect conclusions of the review to be made public in the coming weeks. A congressional staffer told RFE/RL that the strategy would likely be made public in the form of a document that would 'lay out goals and objectives for the region'. The State Department spokesperson said that United States 'will continue to work' with Central Asian governments 'to uphold regional security, increase economic integration with regional and global markets, demonstrate respect for human rights and democratic governance, and promote other bilateral and regional issues of mutual interest'." 77)

The report is just one out of a myriad of examples of NATO's pseudo-journalism, putting forward often anonymous "experts" to give propagandistic content an air of objectivity. The list of names, though short, however, says enough. "Recent statements from senior U.S. officials indicate the updated policy will not differ radically from Washington's previous Central Asia strategy, which includes the New Silk Road initiative aimed at boosting regional trade to promote stability following the departure of U.S. and NATO troops from Afghanistan. While the pace of the New Silk Road plan has been sluggish, Richard Hoagland, the U.S. principal deputy assistant secretary of state for South and Central Asian affairs, said in a March 18 speech in Washington that the initiative 'is our long-term strategy to make Central Asia, including Afghanistan, once again a crossroads of global commerce'. 'Progress is happening. Since 2009, intraregional trade in Central Asia has increased by 49 percent, and since 2011 the cost of moving goods across regional borders has decreased by 15 percent," Hoagland said, adding that 'still much remains to be done'. Experts on Central Asia say Washington's New Silk Road strategy is being trumped by China's aggressive push to build its own "Silk Road" trade routes through Central Asia, details of which Beijing is expected to release this month. U.S. officials say U.S. and Chinese efforts in the region are not mutually exclusive and can complement one another." Richard Hoagland is a former US ambassador to Kazakhstan, and a long list of Wikileaks has demonstrated how throughout his job he blundered to his host country's echelons, little hindered by knowledge...

3. "A threat of violent repression"

Pavel Filonov. At the Table. 1912-13. The Russian Museum,
St. Petersburg, Russia

Further down, the meaning of it all becomes clearer: "Russia, meanwhile, has secured oil-rich Kazakhstan, the region's largest economy, as a member of the Kremlin-led Eurasian Economic Union, which another Central Asian republic, Kyrgyzstan, is set to join in May. While the Central Asia policy review was not 'strictly' prompted by Russia's military incursion into Ukraine and subsequent annexation of Crimea in March 2014, Russia's role in the conflict 'certainly was on the minds of people who were putting that policy together,' says Paul Stronski, a former director for Russia and Central Asia on Obama's National Security Council staff. Senior U.S. officials discussing Central Asia in recent months have repeatedly said that Moscow has no right to force its agenda on governments in the region. 'We recognise that the countries of Central Asia have close political, economic, security, and people-to-people ties with Russia,' Hoagland said on March 18. 'But we also maintain that no country has the right to unilaterally determine the political and economic orientation of another country.' He added that 'what Russia is doing in Ukraine is cause for concern for the countries of Central Asia' and accused Moscow of 'blanketing' the region with 'propaganda' that presents 'a skewed and anti-American/anti-European interpretation of events'. Russia has defended the annexation by claiming that Crimeans faced a threat of violent repression after Ukrainian President Viktor Yanukovych fled Kyiv amid street protests in February 2014, an argument Kremlin critics and Western governments dismiss as false. Russia has also denied accusations by Kyiv and the West that it has provided arms and personnel to pro-Moscow separatists in eastern Ukraine."

What follows is all but a literal copy of old Cold War propaganda and points at not just gunpoint hegemony but the economic supremacy eyed by the USA for itself in the world alongside. "John Herbst, a former U.S. ambassador to Uzbekistan, says the events in Ukraine present a 'specific twist' to the larger issue facing Central Asian states, namely how to 'get along' surrounded by large powers who may not have 'their best interests at heart'. He noted comments by Russian President Vladimir Putin, who said in August that "the Kazakhs never had any statehood" and that it would be beneficial for the Kazakh people to "remain in the greater Russian world." 'Putin basically threw down a marker...when he called Kazakhstan an artificial country,' Herbst told RFE/RL. Both Stronski and Herbst say security threats, including the potential for Islamic extremism, remain serious in Central Asia as U.S. and NATO forces withdraw from Afghanistan. But while earlier U.S. policy in the region was focused largely on security issues, the updated U.S. policy needs to address 'economic issues and some of the political modernisation issues' in the region, Stronski told RFE/RL. Central Asian governments have been hit hard by Russian financial troubles stemming from plummeting oil prices and Western sanctions. The falling rouble has dented remittances from millions of Central Asian migrants working in Russia and pressured local producers forced to compete against cheaper Russian goods. Furthermore, the governments in the region -- most notably in Kazakhstan and Uzbekistan -- face uncertain political futures. Kazakh President Nursultan Nazarbaev and Uzbek President Islam Karimov, both in their 70s, have announced plans to seek reelection this year in ballots almost certain to see them remain in power. 'We have countries that are very much still based on sort of personality-based politics and not institutional-based politics, and so this does create problems in the long term, particularly as you get some very old leaders,' Stronski said."

Central Asia's "weak spot" namely poorly-observed human rights obligations remains a top hit in the displays put up by the likes of "Radio Liberty". "Financial industry players have voiced similar concerns as well," the article's conclusion reads. "Future policy choices are difficult to predict in the medium term because of uncertainty surrounding the eventual succession of Mr. Nazarbaev, who is 74 years old, the Standard & Poor's ratings agency noted this month. Emomali Rahmon and Gurbanguly Berdymukhammedov, the respective strongmen presidents of Tajikistan and gas-rich Turkmenistan, are comparably entrenched atop their respective states with no clear successors. Each of these leaders' governments has faced criticism from rights watchdogs and Western officials for alleged rights abuses. Senior U.S. officials insist they are raising these issues with Central Asian governments while saying a balanced approach is needed, a position some rights advocates criticise as a Faustian bargain to secure cooperation on counterterrorism and other security matters. Fielding a question about a 'new' U.S. strategy in Central Asia, Daniel Rosenblum, U.S. deputy assistant secretary of state for Central Asia, told Voice of America's Uzbek Service in January that the strategy addressed 'political reforms' and 'respect for human rights'. 'We have robust engagement with Uzbekistan on those issues, on issues of democracy and human rights, and on security, and we think it is possible to pursue both and try to maintain that balance in the relationship,' Rosenblum said."

In concrete terms, all this, including the crocodile's tears over human rights (it would not be a bad idea, for the sake of comparison, to read the chapter on the USA in Amnesty International's annual report) the picture of what is in store the upcoming winter for counties like Kyrgyzstan, Kazakhstan, Russia and other former Soviet republics becomes chrystal-clear. Low oil and other commodity prices are hitting the west, and the USA in particular, just as hard as more commodity-based economies in the world. Most of America's own resources have become uneconomical because of high production costs and low sales prices – which is why hunger for cheap resources outside is already rumbling once more in Uncle Sam's stomach. The breed of suspect diplomats pouring into the region is more than just illustrative for such a trend. "It can be certain that the arrival of the 'Male Nuland' to Kyrgyzstan, freshly forced out of retirement to take on this pivotal role, portends the Central Asian anti-Russian equivalent of what Nuland unleashed in Eastern Europe over a year ago with EuroMaidan," one report posted on March 18 under the header "The Coming Colour Revolution Chaos in Kyrgyzstan" on Russia Insider and written by Andrew Korybko, a political analyst from Cleveland, Ohio, on Russian international relations and a specialist on Middle Eastern politics, Central Asia, and Eastern Europe studying at the Moscow State Institute of International Relations (MGIMO) was to read. "Zeroing in on Kyrgyzstan and Richard Miles' 'temporary' appointment as the de-facto ambassador there, it's likely that the general course of Colour Revolutionary chaos will take on a relatively predetermined path. Parliamentary elections are scheduled for October, and will likely serve as 'the event' needed to 'justify' a Colour Revolution. This is a very opportune time for the destabilisation to commence, since Kyrgyzstan would have already joined the Eurasian Union, and 'opposition' candidates and/or activists can attempt to manipulate this into a campaign issue (either within the country or in front of the foreign media)." The author dubs Miles a "Male Nuland" after the notorious hawkish far-right-minded American state official Victoria Nuland. 78)

Should this occur, part of the scenario is a split-up of Kyrgyzstan into "North" and "South" with western parts being annexed by Uzbekistan as a result of ethnic conflicts. "Also, October represents the tail end of fall and the beginning of winter, which in Kyrgyzstan, leads to a de-facto months-long division between the North and the South owing to the blocking of critical mountain passes connecting the two," the report reads further down. "With the country having almost split during the last spate of externally driven instability in 2010, the prospects remain for it to do so once more if there's a repeat of similar violence. This is because the North-South Kyrgyzstan rivalry hasn't gone away in the years since, but only went underground and outside of the international public's attention. The emergence of 'South Kyrgyzstan' in fact or in form could become an epicenter of future conflicts and easily follow the Afghan model of drug trafficking and terrorism. These fears could create the conditions needed to force Russia and the CSTO into a Reverse Brzezinski intervention, made even more difficult by the mountainous terrain that favours insurgency over counter-guerrilla operations."

A nightmare scenario which (hopefully) will not materialise? It is up to Kyrgyzstan and its neighbours to take care of that – but do not let them count on America to do so. "Left to its own, 'South Kyrgyzstan's' black hole of destabilisation could combine with a renewed Taliban threat in Afghanistan to existentially endanger Tajikistan, which aside from further pressuring Russia to intervene and crush the fledgling 'Central Asian Islamic State', could raise fears in China that Uighur terrorists will exploit the disorder to establish bases for carrying out attacks in Xinjiang," the author warns. "The entire dynamic would be complicated by the re-eruption of ethnic violence in Kyrgyzstan's portion of the Fergana Valley, where the ethnic Uzbeks' grievances and the tensions between them and ethnic Kyrgyz were simply swept under the rug for the past few years in the same way that the North-South Kyrgyzstan rivalry was. In the event that Miles succeeds in initiating any type of Colour Revolution disorder in the country (which given its existing instability, isn't that difficult to do), it's expected that the 2010 ethnic chaos will return, when about 300,000 Uzbeks were displaced and 100,000 fled to Uzbekistan. This time, however, instead of Uzbekistan sitting on the sidelines and reacting to the crisis, it's forecasted that it will directly intervene in the country, which is the tripwire that will irrevocably break Uzbek-Russian bilateral relations and herald in Tashkent's role as the US' Lead From Behind partner in Central Asia."

Prevention measures on the spot enabling authorities to stop any subversion attempt short should be taken in advance rather than when it is too late, Korybko opines, and they should be thoroughly coordinated. "If the Kyrgyz authorities and their Eurasian Union and SCO allies aren't successful in quickly containing and extinguishing Miles' planned Colour Revolutionary violence, then the prospects for foreign military intervention dramatically increase, due to all actors' fears that the situation will rapidly spiral out of control if left unattended," the article continues. "While it's never known exactly how any campaign can play out in advance, if the oncoming crisis in Kyrgyzstan even remotely mirrors that which the country experienced in 2010, then the following is the most likely way that events could play out: Russia retains an air base in Kant, located on the outskirts of Bishkek, and it's forecasted that this would form the nucleus of any stabilisation force deployed to Kyrgyzstan. As previously mentioned, Russia will try its best not to get trapped in the Kyrgyz cauldron, meaning that it would likely limit any boots on the ground to Northern Kyrgyzstan, where they can more easily assist in restoring peace and order in cooperation with their legitimate counterparts there. This intervention only becomes possible if the Kyrgyz security forces begin to lose control of the capital and other major cities in the north straddling the Kazakh border, and specifically request external assistance in restoring governance there. Even then, the Russians could always take a 'wait-and-see' approach to avoid being drawn into a Reverse Brzezinski, but if the violence becomes uncontrollable, they'll be forced to intervene, especially if the Kant Air Base is threatened. On the other hand, unlike in 2010 when Russia refused to conventionally intervene in support of the friendly revolutionary government, in 2015, the situation may be that the friendly legitimate authorities request Moscow's help in order to beat back violent anti-Russian mobs trying to seize control of the state a la the EuroMaidan model."

4. A Cyprus-scenario

Pavel Filonov. Execution (After 1905). 1913. The Russian Museum,
St. Petersburg, Russia

The provocation of Russia in this scenario is huge, and might lead to an intervention giving NATO one more excuse to vilify "aggressive Russia" in the way it used to do so in Soviet times and continues to do today. "In such a situation, it may be hard for Russia to say no, understanding that failure to shore up stability in Kyrgyzstan could either create the black hole of chaos that it's been dreading or lead to the establishment of a radical pro-Western government obsessed with pursuing a Russophobic foreign policy," in Korybko's words. "Not only that, but a serious crisis of that nature sprouting up inside the Eurasian Union could destabilize the entire organization and increase pressure on Russia and the other members (all of which are part of the CSTO) to actively respond. In any case, it is highly unlikely that Russia and its partners will intervene in Fergana Valley, because just like in 2010, they don't want to dangerously get caught between two warring ethnicities and/or create the impression (which would be obviously manipulated by the hypocritical Western media) that they're waging a 'war on Islam' by 'occupying' conservative Muslim strongholds there. As for Southern Kyrgyzstan, it will most probably remain a 'no-go' zone for all foreign military parties due to the forthcoming winter snow (if the destabilization commences in October as predicted) that would hinder all but the most essential military operations in that mountainous and sparsely populated area. Seeing as how the Fergana Valley isn't anticipated to have any Russian or CSTO military intervention in the event of any forthcoming Kyrgyz destabilisation, this leaves Uzbekistan as the only probable actor that can flex its muscles in that area. At this moment, one needs to recall the first part of this article dealing with the US' strategy towards Uzbekistan, Ambassador Pamela Spratlen, and Washington's desire to see the country become the pro-Western Lead From Behind proxy for Central Asia. It should also not be forgotten that Uzbekistan and Russia appear to be on the cusp of a minor renaissance of relations, and that the US has a vested interest in tearing Tashkent and Moscow apart just it did Kiev and Moscow after EuroMaidan. Keeping this in mind, it becomes understandable why the US would press for an Uzbek 'humanitarian intervention'."

But even if the "internal scheme" in Kyrgyzstan fails, there is always the possibility for the USA to provoke cross-border conflict in particular with Uzbekistan "…in the foreseeable event that ethnic clashes resume between Uzbeks and Kyrgyz there amidst a statewide meltdown," in the report's words. "Considering that this would amount to Uzbekistan invading a CSTO-member state (Kyrgyzstan), such an action would certainly bring Uzbek-Russian relations to a crisis level, which is exactly what the US wants. In fact, Pamela Spratlen's ultimate strategic objective is to convince Uzbekistan to perform a 'media Crimea' in the Fergana Valley in order to lay the seeds for prolonged tension between it and Russia for the years to come. By this, it is meant that Uzbekistan actually perform in the Fergana Valley what the Western media falsely stated that Russia had done in Crimea, which is a military invasion and subsequent annexation of its neighbor's territory on the grounds of protecting one's ethnic compatriots. Russia never did any of this, but it doesn't matter, since it's still guilty of these 'crimes' in the eyes of the Western media, and the international audience is now largely attuned to understanding what the fake 'Crimea precedent' means. Thus, if Uzbekistan stages a 'media Crimea' and invades and annexes Kyrgyzstan's Uzbek-populated parts in the Fergana Valley (perhaps even spreading to include all or parts of Osh and Jalal-Abad, Kyrgyzstan's most important cities in the area), then this would not come as a surprise, and ironically, would actually be cheered on by the West. Other than precipitating a major crisis between Uzbekistan and Russia/CSTO (which would automatically make Tashkent turn to the West), it would also be a way to 'stick it to Russia' by using the fake 'Crimea precedent' as a weapon to harm its interests, which could then be touted as an informational victory in its own right (despite not having any real connection to Russia's actual actions vis-à-vis Crimea). If Uzbekistan balks at Spratlen's initial 'suggestion' of a 'media Crimea', then she could always turn up the heat by utilising existing Colour Revolution infrastructure within the country to launch a massive 'grassroots' campaign to pressure the authorities to accede to her demands. This could realistically be coupled with Western governments 'guilting' Uzbekistan for its failure to intervene next door, much as they attempted to do with Turkey over Ayn al-Arab (Kobani in Kurdish). If the Uzbek authorities continue to refuse Spratlen's 'suggestion', then the 'grassroots' movement for a 'media Crimea' in the Kyrgyz Fergana Valley can morph into an actual Colour Revolution attempt against the government, which might just be the straw that breaks the state's back."

Such a "Cyprus-scenario" would be bound to divide Central Asia in to blocks, one backed by Russia and the other by NATO. America, according to the author, hopes in this context to revive the so-called Nixon doctrine, meaning charming China with the aim to isolate Russia. "Throughout all of this, China's mediation role is assured due to its strategic interests in all three actors," the text reads further down. "The Russian-Chinese Strategic Partnership guarantees that Moscow and Beijing have no intention of ever butting heads over something as relatively minor to their bilateral relationship as Uzbekistan, while China's hefty energy investments and pivotal pipeline transit through Uzbekistan makes it so that Beijing will not turn a blind eye towards Tashkent's interests as well. While China may publicly chastise Uzbekistan through the SCO format for its 'media Crimea' in Fergana, it will by no means support a Russian/CSTO military counter-measure against it (which is unlikely anyhow) because it believes that such a move could further destabilise the country and endanger its pipeline security. Russia is not expected to behave unilaterally and/or militarily respond to Uzbekistan, and in any case, it will not risk jeopardising the Russian-Chinese Strategic Partnership after Beijing warns it not to do so. The Strategic Partnership is thus that it is fully dependent on trust between Moscow and Beijing, and that if either one violates this understanding and begins behaving in a manner that is seen as counter to the other's interests, a classic security dilemma can emerge that could speedily lead to the dismantlement of the 'gentleman's agreement' and a possible Sino-Russian split. Both sides are acutely aware of this and know that the US fantasizes about such a scenario, hence why they will not risk a falling out over something as relatively trivial to them (in the global perspective) as Uzbekistan."

It should be admitted that Andrew Korybko's view on Kyrgyzstan's near future looks a bit far-fetched – but this does by no means make it needless to heed. "Concerning Kyrgyzstan, China is currently involved in an anti-terror campaign in Xinjiang against militant Uighur separatists, and it fears that a destabilised Kyrgyzstan abutting the province could serve as a terrorist rear base. Thus, it is in Beijing's interests to see overall stability returned to Kyrgyzstan if it becomes wracked with violence after another US-directed Colour Revolution, but due to its tradition of non-interference, it will stop short of committing its troops to any operation on its territory. Instead, it will likely fortify the border as much as it can and take the diplomatic lead in helping all parties in the country reach a negotiated settlement in order to restore peace as soon as possible. Once this is achieved, albeit even partially, then all the countries can begin to (jointly?) tackle the shared problem of

Southern Kyrgyzstan. Amidst turbulence in Northern Kyrgyzstan and possible Uzbek annexation in the Fergana Valley, Southern Kyrgyzstan will be largely forgotten until these two issues are first dealt with. As was discussed earlier, October (the time of the Parliamentary elections, the suspected Colour Revolution onset event) is very close to the beginning of winter, and if the period of destabilisation described above is not resolved soon enough, then the inclement weather may de-facto intervene to divide the country by cutting off the few mountain passages linking the north and south. This would have the effect of incubating Southern Kyrgyzstan's drug and terrorism threats and preventing all but the most serious and determined external interventions from eradicating them before they spread throughout the region. Of course, the mountainous population of this portion of Kyrgyzstan (minus the Fergana Valley, of course) is very small, but still, the area it covers is large enough to present a critical non-state actor threat that can directly affect Uzbekistan, Tajikistan, and China's Xinjiang Province. Indirectly, but no less important, the problems festering in Southern Kyrgyzstan can quickly make their way north into the Eurasian Union and further afield into Russia proper, thereby compelling Moscow into some type of action to stem this virus before it becomes uncontrollable (to say nothing of the immediate danger it presents for Russian forces in Tajikistan). Some type of foreign action would have to be taken to resolve this issue, but it's impossible to know what it will look like. The only thing that can be ascertained is that it would involve the Kyrgyz authorities and potentially a multilateral force incorporating Tajik and/or Russian elements, with Uzbekistan and China notably not taking part (the former due to tensions over the 'media Crimea' and the latter due to its policy of non-interference)."

So what should Kyrgyzstan's authorities do to prevent their country's orchestrated collapse? "Richard Miles' return from retirement in order to staff the US Embassy in Bishkek is more than just a random event," Andrew Korybko warns his readers in conclusion. "The Colour Revolution specialist was ordered to Kyrgyzstan not to gently shuffle papers, but to forcibly shuffle the composition of the government. This is in accordance with the 21st-century Reagan Doctrine that Hillary Clinton publicly unveiled in December 2012, whereby it was decreed that the US will do whatever it can to roll back Russian influence in the Near Abroad. In conjunction with the US-inspired destabilization that is projected to hit the country around the October Parliamentary elections, Washington also envisions pulling Tashkent away from its flirtation with Moscow through coaxing it into a 'media Crimea' in the Kyrgyz Fergana Valley. Dividing Uzbekistan from Russia in the same manner that Ukraine was separated from it a year prior is the ultimate strategic goal of the US in the region, since it would create a long-term Lead From Behind proxy to challenge Russian influence in Central Asia. Kyrgyzstan's role, or more precisely, that of Southern Kyrgyzstan, is intended as nothing more than a permanently failed state abutting the Eurasian Union, Uzbekistan, and China, in order to continuously inflict destabilising pressure on them. No matter which shape the oncoming chaos takes, it can be certain that the arrival of the 'Male Nuland' to Kyrgyzstan, freshly forced out of retirement to take on this pivotal role, portends the Central Asian anti-Russian equivalent of what Nuland unleashed in Eastern Europe over a year ago with EuroMaidan."

An even more devastating attack on Washington's war scene directors came on March 20 in an article under the header "Russia Under Attack" written by Paul Craig Roberts, former Assistant Secretary of the US Treasury for Economic Policy in the Reagan Administration, as well as one-time associate editor and columnist with the Wall Street Journal, columnist for Business Week and the Scripps Howard News Service. His article tries to unravel what goes on in the higher echelons of the Pentagon and NATO behind the scenes on the ground. "While Washington works assiduously to undermine the Minsk agreement that German chancellor Merkel and French president Hollande achieved in order to halt the military conflict in Ukraine, Washington has sent Victoria Nuland to Armenia to organise a 'colour revolution' or coup there, has sent Richard Miles as ambassador to

Kyrgyzstan to do the same there, and has sent Pamela Spratlen as ambassador to Uzbekistan to purchase that government's allegiance away from Russia," the text reads. "The result would be to break up the Collective Security Treaty Organisation and present Russia and China with destabilisation where they can least afford it." 79)

In other words: the present-day status quo in Central Asia in general and in Kyrgyzstan in particular may not be ideal, but it is becoming clear that all other possible situations can only be a lot worse for everybody on the ground. "Russia faces the renewal of conflict in Ukraine simultaneously with three more Ukraine-type situations along its Asian border," the article elaborates further down. "And this is only the beginning of the pressure that Washington is mounting on Russia. On March 18, the Secretary General of NATO denounced the peace settlement between Russia and Georgia that ended Georgia's military assault on South Ossetia. The NATO Secretary General said that NATO rejects the settlement because it 'hampers ongoing efforts by the international community to strengthen security and stability in the region'. Look closely at this statement. It defines the 'international community' as Washington's NATO puppet states, and it defines strengthening security and stability as removing buffers between Russia and Georgia so that Washington can position military bases in Georgia directly on Russia's border. In Poland and the Baltic states, Washington and NATO lies about a pending Russian invasion are being used to justify provocative war games on Russia's borders and to build up US forces in NATO military bases on Russia's borders. We have crazed US generals on national television calling for 'killing Russians'. The EU leadership has agreed to launch a propaganda war against Russia, broadcasting Washington's lies inside Russia in an effort to undermine the Russian people's support of their government."

In conclusion, Roberts tries to place current developments in a historical and broader context – by explaining that the real target of America is not Kyrgyzstan, not China and not even Russia – but nothing less than

Europe. The introduction of the euro was seen as an attempt to undermine America's market monopoly. By adding Central-European former Warsaw Pact member states jut just to the EU but first and foremost to NATO, Washington has beleaguered Western Europe including some of its NATO-skeptics such as France. "All of this is being done in order to coerce Russia into handing over Crimea and its Black Sea naval base to Washington and accepting vassalage under Washington's suzerainty. If Saddam Hussein, Gaddafi, Assad, and the Taliban would not fold to Washington's threats, why do the fools in Washington think Putin, who holds in his hands the largest nuclear arsenal in the world, will fold? European governments, apparently, are incapable of any thought. Washington has set London and the capitals of every European country, as well as every American city, for destruction by Russian nuclear weapons. The stupid Europeans rush to destroy themselves in service to their Washington master. Human intelligence has gone missing if after 14 years of US military aggression against eight countries, the world does not understand that Washington is lost in arrogance and hubris and imagines itself the ruler of the universe who will tolerate no dissent from its will. We know that the American, British, and European media are whores well paid to lie for their master. We know that the NATO commander and secretary general, if not the member countries, are lusting for war. We know that the American Dr. Strangeloves in the Pentagon and armaments industry cannot wait to test their ABMs and new weapons systems in which they always place excessive confidence. We know that the prime minister of Britain is a total cipher. But are the chancellor of Germany and the president of France ready for the destruction of their countries and of Europe? If the EU is of such value, why is the very existence of its populations put at risk in order to bow down and accept leadership from an insane Washington whose megalomania will destroy life on earth?"

5. No power to the people

Pavel Filonov. They Who Have Nothing to Lose. 1912-12. Oil on paper. 96.5 x 76.2 cm. The Russian Museum, St. Petersburg, Russia

So does all this eventually mean that America's long arm could eventually stretch to the very gates of China, by holding Central Asia's fledgling economies in its claws? This is the main question that is sizzling through the public domain and in public debates throughout Central Asia. The answer is not just political – but first and foremost economic. The strange conclusion looking at what happens in war-torn Ukraine is that the more cash you attract, the poorer you will become in the end. As in particular Kyrgyzstan has experienced and other Central Asian nations are all too well aware of, so-called austerity does not go unpunished and can trigger revolutions and other forms of violence. The EEU is based on preventing just that rather than provoking it. This cannot be said, though, of Ukraine's "generous" loan sharks.

There is a third party, though, that both politicians and businessmen tend to overlook: the overall population – meaning consumers and voters. "Ukraine is expected to receive a total of $27 billion from international donors including the International Monetary Fund (IMF), the World Bank, the United States and the European Union," Novosti's international branch Sputnik News reported on September 2 2014. "More than half of the amount is expected to be paid this year. In May, the IMF approved a $17 billion loan to Ukraine in the form of a two-year stabilization program. The first tranche of the IMF loan of $3.16 billion was sent to Ukraine in early May. On Monday, Ukraine received the second installment of financial aid, totaling $1.4 billion. To receive the IMF funds in full, Ukraine agreed to a severe austerity program that includes shedding 24,000 government jobs, raising taxes, selling off state assets and withdrawing subsidies on natural gas." This should make it clear for all to see how Ukraine's self-styled government is pushing the nation towards the abyss. In all, the country has an estimated cash shortfall equivalent to up to a staggering 53 billion greenbacks – almost twice the amount which it should receive if indeed it manages to squeeze the population's purchasing power and let the bulk of the people plunge into poverty. Cracks over this policy have already appeared within the EU and the IMF with the Czech Republic and Brazil standing up as dissenters. Nevertheless, the lesson for Central Asia is to keep a sound distance from such "generous" fund providers and survive on the region's own resources.

In the course of summer 2015, it would appear that Russia's and Belarus' economies were in for another winter of stagnation, while friend and foe predicted a default for Ukraine, whether or not a few extra billions were pumped into its bottomless pit. That left Kazakhstan, hit harder than any other ex-Soviet state (with the possible exception of Azerbaijan) by continuing downward pressure on oil prices. It therefore needed Russia to stand by more than ever – something that was clearly understood in the Kremlin. "Kazakhstan is Russia's closest strategic ally and partner," Putin was quoted as stating during a youth forum by Russia Today in late summer 2014. "Kazakhstan is ten-fold smaller than Russia in terms of population, but it is still a big country. And I am confident that a majority of its population supports development of close ties with Russia. [...] Philosophers (historically) track the development of the Eurasianism idea in Russia. The

Kazakhs have picked it up. It is good for development of their economy and for staying part of the large Russian world that is part of the global civilization in terms of industry and advanced technologies. I am confident that that is the way things are going to be in the mid and long run."

In response, Nursultan Nazarbayev told Itar-Tass that all suggestions from western officials and mass media echoing them pointing at Russia to "dominate" as much of the world as it possibly could are pointless and misleading public opinion. "On August 25, President Nursultan Nazarbayev in an interview with Khabar state TV channel said 'if membership in the Eurasian Economic Union would threaten Kazakhstan's sovereignty, the republic will be ready to leave the Union'. 'The Union is not about Russian dominance, but consensus,' assured Nazarbayev noting all the sides have equal rights. He stressed the Union is a purely economic union. Three representatives from each member country of the EEC make the Eurasian Economic Commission, and therefore Nazarbayev thinks it is necessary to use these opportunities of cooperation with the neighboring countries." 80)

But modern politicians do look at the business side of the story as well – as illustrated by Russia's cool response to western "sanctions" and the way it responds to them. "We are working with other foreign producers, with Latin America - Brazil, Argentina, Chile, with China and other countries," Putin was quoted as saying in an interview with Channel 1. "It is strange to hear European colleagues calling these countries not to supply their goods to Russia (...) it is hard to imagine businessmen who would willingly waste such an opportunity to enter our market. (...) This holds some danger for our traditional suppliers (Europeans and Americans), because when some or other companies settle firmly in a market, we are talking about the Russian market in this case, it is hard to push them out of this market afterwards, practically impossible. I think that European companies, not politicians but businessmen, understand this, and they are disappointed with the policies of their governments."

So is America poised to become, and remain for some time, Central Asia's bully or will it one day be ready to take up a position as a team player amidst the rise of an ever-consolidating block of rival economic powers? The answer is not to be found in the former USSR, the Islamic world or the Far East – but in the USA itself. In the eyes of an overwhelming majority of nations in the world, the "ugly American" is back again. To solve that problem, not just Washington's policy must change but its final goals as well – something only Americans can do. Criticism in the USA is growing, but critics lack the political tools to make decision makers think twice. The only solution lies in political reforms… in America. For like it or not: America's strive for a "unipolar world" following the break-up of the Soviet Union appears to be faltering. The "Eurasian superpowers" Russia, China and India are getting closer to a joint effort to police the region entangled between their national borders to cut off the spearhead piercing from the western side straight into the heart of Central Asia. Remarkably enough, the coalition, to be formalised this year with India's full membership of the Shanghai Cooperation Organisation, should find answers on the ground to stem all attempts to destabilise Central Asia – by whomever, that is. The most important dimension of the process is that security and economy are wings of a single bird. The "Eurasian integration process" is marked not just by joint security measures but evenly by economic cooperation with the aim to make Central Asia "economically resistant" and eliminate poverty that generates desperados. The SCO has a multi-billion development bank in the making, and business communities should indeed pay more attention to the opportunities the umbrella offers to secure enterprises' interests against eventual threats. All those measures are of a purely economic nature. As mentioned before, SCO members are maintaining private enterprise, stock markets, commercial banks and every other tool that serves a "capitalist" state. Ideology is no longer an argument. This dimension is what, with whatever motive, the USA and NATO are categorically overlooking. And not for the first time. Crackdowns have been carried out without thinking of the consequences ever since the US intervention in Vietnam. "Imperialism by invitation" hosted by the vassal

Yeltsin regime, easily appropriated Russian wealth. US imperial conquest of the East, created a "unipolar world" in which Washington decision-makers and strategists believed that, as the world's supreme power, they could intervene in every region with impunity. The scope and depth of the US world empire was enhanced by China's embrace of capitalism and its ruler's invitation to US and EU [multinationals] to enter and exploit cheap Chinese labour," in the words of an article posted by Global Research, which has a lead in voicing opinions coming from America's critics at home.

Exaggerated? Perhaps – but the turning point in that trend which happened to coincide with the turn of the millennium can hardly be denied. "The pillage and impoverishment of Russia led to the rise of a new leadership under President Putin intent on reconstructing the state and economy and ending vassalage. The Chinese leadership harnessed its dependence on the West for capital investments and technology, into instruments for creating a powerful export economy and the growth of a dynamic national public-private manufacturing complex," the article reads further down. It should not be overlooked that such signals come from within US society. And calls for a fundamental change in Washington's hegemonic policy are getting louder. "China is an Asian power with global ambitions. Russia has historically defined itself as a European power, although it recently started its own pivot toward Asia. The two nations share a bitter and bloody history. After the Cold War, though, they seemed to find new chemistry in defending against U.S. hegemony. China and Russia established a strategic partnership in the late 1990s while the U.S. was extending its unipolar system," a remarkable article which appeared in the normally fiercely pro-Cold War II periodical The Diplomat over summer 2014, written by Huiyun Feng, senior researcher at the Danish Institute for International Studies and Associate Professor of Political Science at Utah State University, read. "As always, power politics is still the major game in town. Another chapter in the rise and fall of the great powers – this time played by the United States, China, and Russia – has just opened. [...] Despite the positive trends, the bilateral relationship still lacks a solid foundation of mutual trust and common identity. Only a strong common threat from the West could push China and Russia to move closer economically and militarily. This is in the hands of U.S. policymakers. Continue to prod Xi and Putin and they may indeed see a military alliance or at least a close partnership between Beijing and Moscow. [...] Although furious competition among the United States, China and Russia is probably inevitable, a delicate balance of power is the essence of diplomacy." 81)

Even though the article tends to overlook India's increasing clout, the message, made in USA, is clear: there is no future in the way USA and (to lesser extents) the EU tries to bully Central Asia to maintain a political spearhead in an area that finds itself at the heart of the Russia-China-India triangle. In the eyes of hawkish parties in the USA, that spearhead should consist of Ukraine, the southern Caucasus and from there straight across the Caspian to the very gates of China. But the more Washington hangs on to that illusion and fails to heed its critics at home, the stronger resistance on the ground against it is bound to become. The trouble seems to be that the target of American criticism stretches all over the two Democrat and Republican mainstreams, both dominated by reactionary elements leaving serious opposition without political clout and ever on the losing end of the "democratic" system. As long as the absence of a political pendulum in that system persists, so will the illusion, leaving little hope for the return of a friendly rather than an ugly American in Central Asia.

Over the winter of 2014/'15, official Washington more than once announced a thorough update dna upgrade of "US policy concerning Central Asia. At the time of writing, no major official document on the issue had been publicised. What could be expected, though, was reflected in a speech by Antony J. Blinken, Deputy Secretary of State, held at the Brookings Institute in Washington DC on March 31. Referring to what he (quite rightly so for all it matters) dubbed "the sometimes Byzantine regional politics of Eurasia and Central Asia, not to mention the sometimes

Byzantine policy-making process here in Washington", the official, however, used lots of words to say pretty little the better thinking part of the world had not been aware of for some time. The speech started rather unusually smoothly, almost diplomatic: "Our security is tied to a stable Central Asia, and at the same time we see a region of enormous potential, a region that could act as an economic bridge from Istanbul to Shanghai and provide opportunities for our own businesses, technologies, and innovations to take root; a region that could offer goods and energy to the booming economies of South and East Asia; and a region that could serve as a stabilizing force for Afghanistan's transition and an indispensable partner in the fight against narco-trafficking, terrorism, and extremism. To help unleash this dynamic potential, the United States stands committed to investing in the region's people and its political and economic stability. So what I want to do today is lay out a little bit of the vision for our policy in Central Asia that's founded on two distinct ideas: First, that our own security is enhanced by a more stable, secure Central Asia that contributes to global efforts to combat terrorism and violent extremism; and second, that stability can best be achieved if the nations of Central Asia are sovereign and independent countries, fully capable of securing their borders, connected with each another and with the emerging economies of Asia, and benefitting from governments that are accountable to their citizens. The United States wants to broaden and deepen our bilateral relationships with each of the states in Central Asia. At the same time, we do not see these relationships in the region as exclusive, or zero-sum, in any way. The nations of Central Asia need healthy, mutually beneficial relations with all of their neighbours. And it is their right as sovereign nations to develop those relations as they see fit, free from pressure or intimidation. It is their choice -- not ours, not anyone else's. Our engagement is animated by the vision that at a time of unique challenge and opportunity alike, Central Asia can reassert its historic role as a vital hub of global commerce, ideas, and culture. It can seize on a model for growth and governance that actually delivers for its citizens and connects them to the dividends of progress." 82)

Reading between the lines, it will be clear for all to see that with "anyone else" Russia is meant. Nevertheless, the expression "not ours, not anyone else's" does signify a change of tone in the verbal ammunition used by Washington's officials. Further down, the avalanche of words points in a similar direction: "Ultimately, for Central Asia to fully reap the benefits of shared prosperity, it has some choices to make between the political and economic practices of the past that offered limited potential for long-term, diversified growth, and the possibilities of the future – the surge of innovation and energy that comes from building more open societies at home and joining a dynamic, just, and rules-based global marketplace. These rules are not designed to assert the authority of one nation over another. They serve to protect and benefit us all. To give businesses the confidence they need to invest – drawing on skills of young, educated populations, and building a growing market for entrepreneurial talent. Now, I know that destination may seem distant as we gather here today, but it promises what nothing else can: the opportunity for Central Asians themselves to enjoy in the fruits of their prosperity."

What "fruits"? What "prosperity"? If such terms come from Washington's power brokers regarding anyone else than themselves and their cronies, something should be wrong – which there is. It is towards the end of the whirlwind of words that the pattern of the US official's brainwash becomes clear, as honey makes place for vinegar: "From its position at the heart of Asia, the region looks out to China and its growing economic influence; it supports Afghanistan's cautiously hopeful transition; and it hedges against Russia's renewed aggression; and it warily guards against the growing pull of extremist ideology among its youth. China looms large in the region with its ambitious plans to advance Asian connectivity through overland and maritime routes. It's committed tens of billions of dollars to building roads and rails to better connect its factories and markets in Asia and Europe. And we support these efforts to connect the region, but we also urge that they advance trade in all directions and adhere to international norms. We don't see China's involvement in Central Asia in zero-sum terms. Its development of infrastructure in Central Asia can be fully complementary to our own efforts. And in particular, we see an important role for China in supporting the transition in Afghanistan and advancing its own integration into the broader Asia region. On the other hand, Russia's actions on its periphery, including its violation of the territorial integrity and sovereignty of Ukraine, threaten the very foundation of international order – not only in the region, not only in Europe, but beyond and around the world. As Russia and the separatists that it backs continue to destabilise eastern Ukraine, they're doing more than violating the borders of one country. They are threatening the fundamental principles that we all have a stake in defending in Europe and, indeed, around the world: the principle that the borders and territorial integrity of a democratic state cannot be changed by force; that it is the inherent right of citizens in a democracy to make their own decisions about their country's future; that linguistic nationalism, something we thought was confined to the dustbin of history, cannot be allowed to be resurrected; and that all members of the international community, especially its leading members, are bound by common rules and should face costs if they don't live up to the solemn commitments that they make. [...] So there is a lot at stake in Russia's actions in Ukraine that we need to continue to stand up for. Now there are obviously costs to the pressure that we're exerting on Russia for its actions in Ukraine, and we know these costs reverberate around the region. And while the nations of Central Asia understand the dangers posed by Russia better than most, they're also feeling the impact of Russia's economic weakness more than most. We understand that anxiety and we're committed to leveraging our own economic tools to help Central Asia diversify their economies and interlink their markets. We do not ask any country to choose ties with the U.S. to the exclusion of anyone else. We reject the false choices imposed by anyone else. We fully support the aspirations of Central Asian states to pursue a multi-vector foreign and economic policy."

6. The economic dimension: back to basics

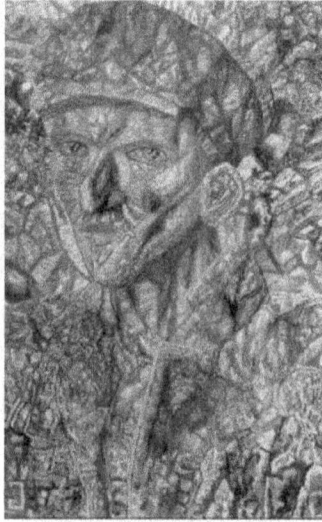

Pavel Filonov. Worker in a Cap. 1930s. Oil on cardboard.
58.5 x 37.5 cm. The Russian Museum, St. Petersburg, Russia.

So what does this basically mean? The real answer to that question is the terrifying spectre of usurpers governing, terrorising and abusing those who make humanity feed on the earth forever. Global "economic order" – global slavery. No escape from the golden mafia keeping the world population drugged with monetary narcotics: money which means nothing to the Pantagruels cracking the whips but everything to those exposed to them. It is time for a global revolution – not a "coloured" one but a rainbow full of colours which evicts the colourless tyranny distorting the world economy and imposing fake values on helpless populations. The "democratic state" of Ukraine has not been "violated" by Russia – it has been torn apart by America and cronies and what is left of it is being usurped and terrorised by local scavengers pocketing billion after billion under the benevolent eye of global loan sharks keen on making the population bleed for it. Similar scenarios are in store for Central Asia with no other purpose than to submit populations to an American-conducted "world economic order" in comparison to which Stalin's state structure came close to a holiday resort if one looks behind the velvet veil.

Taking this into account, on the ground, what could the mid-term outcome of the American-led campaign be? Looking at the overall geopolitical situation, there are two basic scenarios for the region comprising the former USSR. Either it becomes another Central America, subsaharian Africa or southeast Asia, fragmented, with each economy drowning in debts caused not by lack of productivity but by monetary manipulations. But that is only a tool and not an end in itself. The main target for the USA and its crooked elites is to destroy the European Union. In the case of Ukraine, they did so by hiring fifth-columnists in Brussels, mainly Barroso who according to Wiki information had reputedly plundered the coffers of his political party in Portugal and was all too happy to find legal immunity from the authorities by seeking refuge as chair of the European Commission. The damage done to the USA by so-called economic sanctions has been practically zero while the EU has suffered multi-dozen-billion euro in loss of trade and investments because of them.

The second option is a broad coalition between non-US nations, including the EU, forcing the USA to become a team player rather than a dictator in world politics. But as observed more than once before, this requires a revolution – in the true sense of the word and namely in the USA. It may sound revolutionary, but the only cause the global political and economic (the two of them being heavily intertwined as ever but also more heavily intertwined than ever) deadlock lies in the USA wherefore the only solution lies in an all-American revolution. Occupying Wall Street was a gesture in the right direction: occupying Capitol Hill and the White House seems an appropriate move to make the world a place worth living in – from Oklahoma to Vladivostok via Brussels

Since economic issues are really all there is where it comes to global geopolitical games and schemes, the last word in this roundabout through the margins of gun smoke should be presented in the form of an article posted in the middle of May 2015 by the (Russian) Pravda, the government's mouthpiece in Soviet times now acting rather critically towards state policies from a leftwinger point of view. Though polemic in style, this observation says it all where Central Asia's economic direction is concerned, and explains to a large extent the reasons for the region's outstanding economic performance, including the "Russian dimension" connected with it. Now in a multi-phase and multi-gear process, varying from country to country, to wrestle itself away from "capital-dictated" global mechanisms and consolidate within a global alternative economic constellation which comprises not just Russia but also China, India, Latin America and a wide variety of other non-western economies, Central Asia has not just grasped the chance to sustain its regional economy but even opened opportunities to increase the respective countries' economic independence. The report reads as follows. 83)

Do not be to taken in by all the apocalyptic news coming out of the western press about Russia's economic demise. If this journalist's memory still serves him the country produces some pretty good chess players, engineers and mathematicians. Yes, the Russian economy is on a bumpy toboggan ride downhill having to deal with a shrinking GDP, devalued rouble and high inflation. But so what - is the rest of the world picking golden apples off the tree of unending prosperity? In fact, of late the IMF has been warning that the world appears to be stuck in permanent stagnation. This would appear to be the case since virtually all of the recent economic indicators worldwide are pointing downward. Russia has no reason to don the dunce cap and sit in the corner to be flogged by dart-throwing propagandists, opponents that are pushing for the collapse of the country. Has the Euro not also been slashed in value along with every other currency versus the dollar? Yes and beyond that, the Euro-Union has a very high GDP to National Debt ratio, about 90% in 2014. By contrast, Russia's GDP to Debt ratio was 13.74%

percent of the G D P in 2014. Government Debt to GDP in Russia averaged 26.60% from 1999 until 2013, reaching an all time high of 99% in 1999, and a record low of 7.90% in 2008 (keep that in mind and recall the western financial collapse). According to the mass media Russia is going over a cliff, but how so when America has an $18 trillion national debt to Russia's $600 billion. The US debt is now 106% of GDP, whereas Russia's is closer to 15% so who comes out of the next crash in better shape? The globalist movers and shakers -- the western bankers at the apex of world's financial system -- have chosen to make their minions portray the half-empty side of Russia's glass. However, nobody in the international financial world, in their right mind, believes that America will ever be able to repay its national debt, so why is the dollar on a tear? For the very same reason the rouble's value has been slashed, geopolitics. There are a number of key variables that go into determining the relative value of a currency. Those include debt levels, inflation, unemployment, monetary policy and balance-of-trade among them. The latter is another key factor which shows that Russia's cup is half-full, not all empty. Russia runs regular trade surpluses primarily due to high exports of commodities like crude oil and natural gas. Now contrast that to America and even Japan. The US is not only noted as the world's largest debtor nation but also the biggest trade deadbeat. America has been running consistent trade deficits since 1976. Normally, a country would not be able to pull this off as its currency would get devalued to the point that import prices would soar. However, the formation of the petrodollar in the 1970's made it the worlds, de facto, reserve currency which has kept demand for it artificially high. That is the geopolitical factor at work offsetting the real underlying weakness of the dollar. Japan had, like Russia, run trade surpluses for decades until 2013 when it racked up its first trade deficit, which it did again last year. With a 240% debt to GDP ratio and a growing negative trade imbalance, the yen is also a very weak currency with no fundamentals to prop it up. The rouble was choked over the last 12 months but it is rebounding. It has some strong fundamentals supporting it. Unlike the central banks of the US, Japan and the Euro-Union, their Russian counterpart is not printing money like a half-comatose methamphetamine addict in desperate need of a constant fix. Even Russians seem to be caught in the negative perception trap that the global elite have set for the nation's collective identity. Yes, there is high inflation, yes the rouble crashed and yes the economy is shrinking, all true. Okay, we should add that the price of oil has also collapsed. But shift the perspective for a moment. Perhaps the Moscow strategist's saw the writing on the wall years ago. Russia is pursuing a pathway opposite to that of the rest of the world. Instead of zero interest rates it has high interest rates. What does that do? It attracts capital, supports the rouble and it squeezes financial bubbles out of the system. In addition, it deleverages debt and imposes a level of national austerity. As noted above, instead of drowning in red ink Russia has a low national debt, a positive trade balance and ample foreign reserves. Most other nations are just the opposite. They continue to go deeper into debt and spend money they don't really have. Soon that party will end. The rest of the world is one big financial bubble waiting for a pin -- some kind of 2008 type of trigger-- to pop it. Could the brain trust in Moscow have seen this all coming? (Do bears poop in the woods?) The world was told that Russia was threatening to sell its US treasury holdings only after the events in Ukraine occurred. In fact, they started selling them off in 2011, and slowly but steadily have unwound their share of US debt obligations over the past 4 years. This insulates Russia from any kind of US financial shock. Russia cut its holdings of U.S. debt by 20 percent in December, 2014 the Treasury data show. Its stake amounted to $86 billion, the lowest level since 2008 and down from the 2010 high of $176 billion. Note that in 2011 commodities prices peaked and have been declining ever since. In spite of what western economists (cheerleaders) have been saying about their being a recovery, that is only due to smoke and mirrors manipulations of statistics. There has not been any global recovery, ask any ordinary, working person in America or Europe or Brazil or Canada or the UK and so on. Oil was simply the last commodity to fall. Even more interesting this also happened before the crash of '08. Now in this context we see Russia's behavior has a lot of common sense to it. If there were a global recovery there would be rising, not falling demand, for commodities. In addition, central banks would not be shoveling money out the door at near zero interest rates; and banks would not be charging customers to hold their deposits. negative interest rates. What has really been going on? And why does it feel like our world governments are asking us to suspend the laws of physics, economics and common sense? The short answer: a soft- war of the almost imperceptible, financial kind. The brain-trusts in Russia and China saw what happened in 2001 and 2008 and decided that they were not going to idly watch a 2015 rerun. The western propaganda machine always casts every financial collapse as being caused by random events. These accidents they claim just came out of nowhere; however that is false imagery, propaganda in short. The global, financial elite engineered both of those collapses. The FED, central bankers in general, eased the credit reins and pumped up bubbles first in the dot.coms and then in real estate derivatives. At least that is the generally accepted narrative. Be that as it may, the end result was financial collapses and recessions. Why should it be any different this time around? The stock and bond markets are the current bubbles. There is no reason they won't follow the path of commodities and fall off a cliff, they will. It will happen when the rest of the world wakes up and realizes that Russia and China are serious about ditching the petrodollar. The US has essentially dug its own grave on this score by pressing forward in Syria and the Ukraine and also encircling China militarily. Add to this the madmen in the FED and other central banks futilely trying to pump up their economies now for 6 years by printing money. In reality, this is just a Ponzi scheme to transfer wealth to the privately held central banksters like the FED. Why should Russia and China finance the debt of a country that considers them the enemy? They would be dumb to do so and they are not stupid by any stretch. China has also been dumping treasuries, albeit, fairly slowly given its massive holdings. In addition, both countries have been net purchasers of gold for years now. Though the western propaganda machine casts these actions as aggressive attempts to destroy the dollar, the FED has shown it needs no help with that task. The Russian and Chinese leaders are simply doing what they have to do to protect their own countries; and being flooded in petrodollars and US debt obligations runs counter to that aim. Enter the final stages of the soft-war, i.e., skirting around the petrodollar when selling or buying oil, creating an alternative to the World Bank. What we are seeing is rather amazing, the oldest cultures on the planet finally exercising their adult authority and stepping in to supervise the reckless teens (leaders of the West) ever staggering from one drunken rampage and violent orgy to another. The petrodollar, fiat currency, western central bank conspiracy has been the biggest financial scam in history. But now the BRICS are putting their foot down, no more silly games, no more turning most of the planet's population into sweat- shop serfs. The currents running beneath the waves we see on the surface are changing. There is a fiat to non-fiat currency shift that is in motion. Accompanying that is the replacement of an un-backed reserve currency, the dollar, with one that will be backed by gold. At this point in time we are in maximum instability and chaos but there is an attempt to restore the historical equilibrium in the works. There is a reason that even US allies joined China's new bank. A gold backed reserve currency comes with automatic restraints built into it. Nobody really appreciated the monopoly the US has had on international trade due to the fiat petrodollar. The new system will at least give the global community some semblance of a level playing field. The US and Europe know they are losing their grip; another empire is fading into the sunset. But the future is by no means guaranteed. The chaos and carnage we see in various countries are all a part of the western financial elite's desperate attempt to keep the status quo intact at any cost. Unfortunately the soft, financial war could become a shooting war...“

CHAPTER 8

WEST GOES EAST – EAST GOES WEST

Pavel Filonov. Landscape. Wind. 1907. Oil on cardboard. 20.5 × 30.5 cm. The Russian Museum, St. Petersburg, Russia

While America had been pushing forth – first of all into Georgia turning it into an anti-Russian bastion, and now to Ukraine more or less considered "captured" and scheming to push further ahead taking Azerbaijan as a bridgehead into Central Asia, Russia had remained on the defensive except for accepting the Crimea's entry into the Russian Federation, wrongly described as "annexation". But in Ukraine, where in summer 2015 hundreds of American officers had arrived to "train" a colourful band of military and paramilitary forces, including some of the country's oligarchs' private armed forces and those belonging neonazi organisations preparing to rebel against the government, a further split-up of the country into domains under control of rival groups and individuals threatened – reminding one of the fragmentation of Lebanon, including that of its capital, curing the civil war. This threatened to throw Washington and its allies back westward. But there were other problems barring the master scheme to encircle Russia and destroy it from within, and it was time to face them – or at least try to do so.

During the winter of 2014/'15, two major "rehearsals" were held for what is clearly intended to become the next round of upheavals initiated by America's "family of troublemakers" meant to subdue, bit by bit, the former Soviet Union, to begin with its outskirts and eventually ending up in Russia itself. The first took place in the tiny former Yugoslavian republic of Macedonia, outside the former USSR but "resistant" to join America's club of anti-Russian hysterics. The second attempt came in the former Soviet republic of Armenia, located on the conglomerate's very outskirts but still significant because of its membership of the Eurasian Economic Union. As for Macedonia, the sequence consisted of a terrorist attack in the hinterland, allegedly carried out by Albanian nationalists who are striving for a "Greater Albania" (the parallel to Armenian radicals campaigning for a "Greater Armenia" looks striking – see below), led to Maidan-like scenes in the capital, besieging the ruling coalition dominated by ethnic Slavs with protesters claiming that rather than seeking cooperation with Russia and other former Soviet republics, Macedonia should seek EU and NATO membership instead. But behind the demonstrations and subsequent clashes with law and order forces a fresh wave of information on the ones really behind the string of events was soon to be unleashed.

1.   The next move east takes off: Macedonia and Armenia

Pavel Filonov: Composition. Ships, Tretyakov Gallery, Moscow

The former member states of Yugoslavia, emerged from the country's tragic disintegration at the cost of the lives of tens of thousands, may have found their national sovereignty but not their independence in the sense that local governments can make up their own minds where it comes to loyalties and strategic choices on the international political chessboard. Ethnic hard feelings and misplaced ambitions go deep. With a number of states having become NATO members all but at gunpoint, others, in particular Serbia and Macedonia, show reluctance despite repeated provocations to join the US anti-Russian hysteria chorus. And guess what: Washington decides that it is time for a coloured revolution – little hindered by detailed knowledge of the complex situation on the ground.

"Macedonia's ethnic divide between Albanians and Macedonians came to a head on May 9, when an attack by Albanian gunmen in the town of Kumanovo left at least 18 people dead. A Macedonian opposition member alleged that the attack was faked, and that the government had attacked itself. Violent opposition protests in the country's capital on May 6 injured 38 police officers and at least two protesters," Sputnik News was to report on May 15. "Although the Macedonian opposition talks of democracy and anti-corruption campaigns, its actual political discourse, such as in the prominent Societas Civilis group which has received US government funding, focuses primarily on issues of ethnicity and nationalism. Particular emphasis is given to the study of Bosnia and Herzegovina, where ethnic groups live in a separated country which is on track to EU and NATO membership. If there is any difference with the situation in Ukraine's Russian minority, it is that US-sponsored interests favor the recognition of the Albanian minority in Macedonia. Unlike Russia, Albania is a US ally and NATO member."

The strategy pursued by the CIA and other American agencies in Macedonia looks all too "Ukrainian". Some of the names and connections are news, while others look all too familiar. "There is increasing concern about potential outside influence involved in recent political demonstrations in Macedonia following reports that students were offered up to $1,500 by an activist group to come up with the best ideas on how to protest against the country's government," Sputnik News reported on May 21, 2015. "The concern about overseas hands being involved in sparking protests in the country has been heightened by recent reports in Macedonian media, which claimed that activist group, CANVAS (Centre for Applied Nonviolent Action and Strategies), had sent out a memo to Macedonian students encouraging them to come up with effective protest ideas. The leaked memo, sent three weeks before last Sunday's mass demonstrations against Nikola Gruevski's government, purportedly shows CANVAS offering students who could come up with the best protest ideas for a grant of $1,500. The issue of CANVAS being involved in Macedonia is another matter of discontent among some within the country. The Belgrade-based group was formed by Slobodan Djinovic and Srdja Popovic — activists who were considered to have played an instrumental role in deposing former Yugoslav leader Slobodan Milosevic in 2000. [...] The group, which is considered to be a terrorist organization in the UAE, has also been accused of collaborating and sharing information with intelligence agencies in the past, further raising questions about Canvas' motives of their work in Macedonia. Canvas' actions in Macedonia has also been coupled with reports the group is teaming up with non-government organisations (NGOs) in the country, who are allegedly determined to see the overthrow of Nikola Gruevski's government over what has been seen as a lack of cooperation by not imposing sanctions on Russia. Among these groups is the 'Open Society Foundations,' which is one of the many NGOs set up by controversial investor George Soros, while US government agency USAID also runs various programmes in Macedonia." 84)

The appearance of CANVAS amply illustrates that Macedonia is not an isolated case but part of a conspiracy XX Century novelists would have delighted in. "Serbia's Srdja Popovic is known by many as a leading architect of regime changes in Eastern Europe and elsewhere since the late-1990s, and as one of the co-founders of Otpor!, the U.S.-funded Serbian activist group which overthrew Slobodan Milošević in 2000," in the words of a report by Occupy.com, emerged from the Occupy Wall Street movement, published in 2011. "CANVAS (Centre for Applied Nonviolent Action and Strategies) [has] also maintained close ties with a Goldman Sachs executive and the private intelligence firm Stratfor (Strategic Forecasting, Inc.), as well as the U.S. government. Popovic's wife also worked at Stratfor for a year. These revelations come in the aftermath of thousands of new emails released by Wikileaks' Golbal Intelligence Files. The emails reveal Popovic worked closely with Stratfor, an Austin, Texas-based private firm that gathers intelligence on geopolitical events and activists for clients ranging from the American Petroleum Institute and Archer Daniels Midland to

Dow Chemical, Duke Energy, Northrop Grumman, Intel and Coca-Cola. Referred to in emails under the moniker "SR501," Popovic was first approached by Stratfor in 2007 to give a lecture in the firm›s office about events transpiring in Eastern Europe, according to a Stratfor source who asked to remain confidential for this story. In one of the emails, Popovic forwarded information about activists harmed or killed by the U.S.-armed Bahraini government, obtained from the Bahrain Center for Human Rights during the regime's crackdown on pro-democracy activists in fall 2011. Popovic also penned a blueprint for Stratfor on how to unseat the now-deceased Venezuelan president Hugo Chavez in September 2010. Using his celebrated activist status, Popovic opened many doors for Stratfor to meet with activists globally. In turn, the information Stratfor intended to gain from Popovic's contacts would serve as "actionable intelligence" — the firm billed itself as a "Shadow CIA" — for its corporate clients. Popovic passed information to Stratfor about on-the-ground activist events in countries around the world, ranging from the Philippines, Libya, Tunisia, Vietnam, Iran, Azerbaijan, Egypt, Tibet, Zimbabwe, Poland and Belarus, Georgia, Bahrain, Venezuela and Malaysia."

Once more, it appears here that not just America's political and bureaucratic elites are the engines of gangs such as CANVAS. Apart from taxpayers' money, there is big money from private sources in it as well – raising the spectre of Skull and Bones to those who may well guess all to near. "One of CANVAS's major allies is Muneer Satter, a former Goldman Sachs executive who stepped down from that position in June 2012 and now owns Satter Investment Management LLC. Stratfor CEO Shea Morenz worked for ten years at Goldman Sachs as well, where he served as Managing Director in the Investment Management Division and Region Head for Private Wealth Management for the Southwest Region. Satter is meanwhile a major funder of the Republican Party, giving over $300,000 to Karl Rove's Super PAC Crossroads GPS before the 2012 election, and another $100,000 to the Republican Governors Association in the first half of 2013 prior to the

2014 mid-term elections. Living in a massive, $9.5 million mansion in Chicago›s North Shore suburb of Lake Michigan, Muneer also gave $50,000 toward President Obama's inaugural fund in 2009. When it came time to connect Muneer with the global intelligence firm, Popovic served as the middle man introducing Satter to Stratfor Chairman George Friedman. […] A powerful individual who lobbied the U.S. government to give money to CANVAS early on was Michael McFaul, the current U.S. Ambassador to Russia for the State Department and someone who "worked closely with" Popovic while serving as a Senior Fellow at the right-wing Hoover Institution at Stanford University."

In an in-depth background report published under the headline "A New Gladio in Action: Ukrainian Postmodern Coup Completes Testing of New Template" as early as spring 2005, in the midst of the first "colour revolution" wave, author Jonathan Mowat not only demonstrates that the architecture of America's campaign to submit the former communist block once and for all and annihilate its economic clout goes back to late Soviet and early post-Soviet times, but he also already gives an impressive nomenclature of America's brainbosses behind the campaign. It includes Dr. Peter Ackerman, the author of "Strategic Nonviolent Conflict" (Praeger 1994). Writing in the "National Catholic Reporter" on April 26, 2002, he "…elaborated on the concept involved," in Mowat's words. "He proposed that youth movements, such as those used to bring down Serbia, could bring down Iran and North Korea, and could have been used to bring down Iraq—thereby accomplishing all of Bush's objectives without relying on military means. And he reported that he has been working with the top US weapons designer, Lawrence Livermore Laboratories, on developing new communications technologies that could be used in other youth movement insurgencies."

The name Ackerman evokes sinister scenarios including the notorious Hidden Persuaders, pop-ups lasting a tiny fraction of a second thereby subconsciously penetrating the minds of viewers and listeners. Such practices are outlawed in most countries including the United States. "Dr. Ackerman is the founding chairman of International Center on Nonviolent Conflicts of Washington, DC, of which former US Air Force officer Jack DuVall is president. Together with former CIA director James Woolsey, DuVall also directs the Arlington Institute of Washington, DC, which was created by former Chief of Naval Operations advisor John L. Peterson in 1989 'to help redefine the concept of national security in much larger, comprehensive terms' it reports, through introducing "social value shifts into the traditional national defense equation. As in the case of the new communication technologies, the potential effectiveness of angry youth in postmodern coups has long been under study. As far back as 1967, Dr. Fred Emery, then director of the Tavistock Institute, and an expert on the 'hypnotic effects' of television, specified that the then new phenomenon of 'swarming adolescents' found at rock concerts could be effectively used to bring down the nation-state by the end of the 1990s."

So how to get from thee laboratory to the ground – other than through the Internet? Once more, the case of Macedonia with its far-reaching connections proves to be an incredible eyeopener. "The creation and deployment of coups of any kind requires agents on the ground. The main handler of these coups on the 'street side' has been the Albert Einstein Institution, which was formed in 1983 as an offshoot of Harvard University under the impetus of Dr. Gene Sharp, and which specialises in 'nonviolence as a form of warfare'. Dr. Sharp had been the executive secretary of A.J. Muste, the famous U.S. Trotskyite labor organizer and peacenik. The group is funded by Soros and the NED. Albert Einstein's president is Col. Robert Helvey, a former US Army officer with 30 years of experience in Southeast Asia. He has served as the case officer for youth groups active in the Balkans and Eastern Europe since at least 1999. [...] According to B. Raman, the former director of India's foreign intelligence agency, RAW, in a December 2001 paper published by his institute entitled 'The USA's National Endowment For Democracy (NED): An Update', Helvey 'was an officer of the Defence Intelligence Agency of the Pentagon, who had served in Vietnam and, subsequently, as the US Defence Attache in Yangon, Myanmar (1983 to 85), during which he clandestinely organised the Myanmar students to work behind Aung San Suu Kyi and in collaboration with Bo Mya's Karen insurgent group.... He also trained in Hong Kong the student leaders from Beijing in mass demonstration techniques which they were to subsequently use in the Tiananmen Square incident of June 1989' and 'is now believed to be acting as an adviser to the Falun Gong, the religious sect of China, in similar civil disobedience techniques.' Col. Helvey nominally retired from the army in 1991, but had been working with Albert Einstein and Soros long before then."

From Macedonia, the second wave of "colour revolutions" spearheaded straight to Armenia. In striking comparison with the uprising in Kyrgyzstan back in 2005 which brought the usurping regime under Kurmanbek Bakiyev to power, the spark that made Armenia plunge into its current turmoil was a rise in electricity tariffs of a (relatively modest) 16.7 per cent – announced by the government and meant to cope with the heavy losses made by the national power grid. But history varying from Honduras to Kyrgyzstan amply demonstrates that there is always more behind what meets the eye. Since Armenia is part of the Eurasian Economic Union, which the USA seeks to break up, it was obviously on top of Washington's list – together with fellow-member states Kyrgyzstan, Kazakhstan and Belarus, with the final aim to cripple the economic, political and ultimately territorial integrity of the Russian Federation, the EEU's largest member.

The prelude to Armenia's accession to the EEU looks indeed like a spitting image of the developments that led to Ukraine's upheaval – even though so far the results have been its opposite. Speaking at a NATO seminar in troubled Yerevan last week, Armenian Foreign Minister Edward Nalbandian reportedly reminded an Association Agreement which was all but finalised by Brussels and Yerevan in the summer of 2013. "Nalbandian said that when the Armenian government began association talks with Brussels in

2010 it made clear that it wants to combine European integration with Armenia's involvement in Eurasian integration processes championed by Russia," the independent local news agency Azatutyun reported. "He said the EU initially accepted this complementary policy but suddenly changed its stance during the final stage of the negotiating process.

"EU leaders told Armenia and five other ex-Soviet states involved in the EU's Eastern Partnership program: You must make a choice - either the EU or Russia," the agency quoted Nalbandian as saying. "At meetings of the foreign ministers of EU member and partner states ... I said I don't think it's a good approach to demand that we make an 'either-or' choice and that that approach could lead to new escalations." Only months later, Ukraine imploded exactly like that...

Not unlike the events in Macedonia, the latest trouble in Armenia has opened yet one more Pandora's box of agencies operating in the country with the aim to pave the way for a fresh "revolution" to pull the country out of the Eurasian Economic Union and replace the government by a "pro-western" regime. Among them is an organisation known as "The Choice is Yours", which is fully funded by Washington, actually performs in the election processes outside the territory of Armenia since 2010, Russia Today reported in late June on Armenia and its "electric revolution". Officially, "The Choice is Yours" has sent hundreds of volunteers as observers to presidential and parliamentary elections in a number of former Soviet states ever since, under supervision of the Organisation for Security and Cooperation in Europe (OSCE). The main aim of this, however, is to get a foothold in such countries in order to spread agitation among the poorer parts of the population with the end goal to have governments toppled in so-called coloured revolutions. "A number of pro-Western NGOs in Armenia perform various functions, including the support of political processes and even overseeing foreign elections," in the news report's words. "Now, as protests against an electricity rate hike drag on, these groups are getting a second look."

According to Dr Paul Craig Roberts, the former US assistant secretary of the Treasury for economic policy and interviewed in the RT report, the suggestion that money stolen by "dissidents" could have been used to co-fund agitators throughout the former USSR and beyond should not come as any sort of surprise at all. "It is part of the destabilisation of Russia," Roberts told Russia Today, while commenting on the role of non-governmental lobbies in so-called coloured revolutions in the region and beyond. "It is part of the regime change that neoconservatives in Washington desire to accomplish. So it was obvious that Armenia would be subject to this type of thing. Now this particular protest, it might be innocent, it may be a legitimate protest. But even if it is, Washington will make an effort to turn it into more. And the same thing is going to happen in Kyrgyzstan, Azerbaijan. If possible, Washington will destabilise Kazakhstan, they would love to do that because then they can also put pressure on China." 85)

From a purely strategic point of view, the choice of Armenia as a link in the coloured-revolutionary chain looks somewhat less than clever. While the large Armenian diasporas concentrated in France and California but spread all over the world give a much higher level of western-cosmopolitical sense among the Armenians as a whole, their clout in Russia is hardly less significant. At home, Armenia's relations with its neighbours to the north and the south – meaning Georgia and Iran – are lukewarm while those with Turkey to the west and Azerbaijan to the east are bluntly hostile. Embracing the USA and the EU will do little to change that situation. Armenia also happens to occupy one-sixth of the territory of neighbouring Azerbaijan, having chased over a million ethnic Azeris from their homes while killing tens of thousands in the process. On more than one occasion, the government of Azerbaijan has sent a clear message to Moscow concerning the eventuality of Azerbaijan's membership of the Eurasian Economic Union: give us our lands back and we join the club. This means that when Armenia quits the EEU today, Azerbaijan is likely to jump in the next morning, and the USA must give up all hopes of ever gaining a foothold on the Caspian Sea, from which it can dispatch fresh "revolutionary" waves through Central Asia. The response could well be a "coloured revolution" in Baku, and subsequently a wave of similar movements throughout Central Asia. Repression of such movements by the countries' respective authorities can subsequently give western media serving Washington's purposes the perfect excuse to cry wolf once more over "despotic", "authoritarian" and "anti-democratic" regimes in the region hit by such "revolutions".

2. Countermoves: across the Mediterranean to the Caribbean

*Pavel Filonov: Flowers of the Universal Flowering,
Russian Museum, St. Petersburg.*

The First Cold War, apart from the war of words by proxy, was by and large fought out by proxy on the ground. It started with Khrushchev taking one of Levon Trotsky's strategic tools out of the mothballs: the "exportation of revolution" – to begin with to newly independent states as a result of a global decolonisation trend. It started not with one of those, though, but with Korea, in then still friendly cooperation with the People's Republic of China. The "victory" of communism in Korea came halfway, and resulted pretty much in the situation it remains in today. In Cuba, right on America's very doorstep, success was striking. In Vietnam, the revolution which took place after the departure of the French colonial regime was more successful – but it came at a high price. An attempt to trigger a revolution in newly

227

independent Indonesia, a well over a decade after the country's independence from The Netherlands, was doomed to fail. Later attempts in Latin America and Africa remained unsuccessful with the exception of Angola. Counter-coups staged by the CIA, using local jungle commanders and other military and paramilitary butchers, remained equally unimpressive. Only in the Middle East leftist revolutions left tangible results in the form of Soviet-friendly states such as Syria, Egypt, Libya and South Yemen.

What the policy pursued by Khrushchev did achieve, though, was a worldwide network of Soviet military strongholds, and fleets carrying the flag of the USSR were now freely sailing on every ocean – something which filled each and every Soviet citizen with enormous pride. That pride was all the more boosted for the fact that the response from the western powers, more or less united in NATO, remained halfhearted. One attempt to trigger what today would be dubbed a coloured revolution in Hungary in 1956 utterly failed – as did the one in Czechosolvakia twelve years later. In Europe, NATO was on the defensive. Today, the situation has been reversed, and Russia and those former Soviet republics resisting western provocations are on the defensive. As described in earlier chapters, revolutions these days are no longer made in the USSR but made in USA – and they represent a much more serious threat to peace and stability in the world than the former ever did.

But the overall "eastward" trend counterplaying that game is not without response. Though their motivations are far more commercial than political, Turkey, Egypt, Cyprus and Greece have already abandoned their unconditional support for US policies and are cooperating with Russia concerning gas supplies to southern Europe and other economic domains. And the growing resistance against Washington's roll-back moves does not stop there. Politicians from Italy, Spain and Portugal increasingly voiced their concerns over Europe's docility towards America into the year 2015. Malta has had its reservations versus NATO-driven policies ever since it declared itself independent from the UK under the left-wing government of Dom Mintoff back in the 1960s. Syria, Egypt and Algeria have been staunch allies of the Soviet Union ever since the rise of Hafez el-Assad and Zhemal abdel Nasser little earlier, followed by Algeria's independence from France.

The "first to fall" and closest to home in Russia's alleged "counter-domino", however, was not an old friend but an old enemy – namely Turkey. Following the Ukrainian "revolution" and resistance against the regime it produced in the east of the country and on the Crimea, gas supplies from Russia to Europe got into jeopardy. Whereas the Crimea swiftly adhered to the Russian Federation allowing it to get pacified, the other two "rebel" (in US propaganda terminology) provinces, namely Lugansk and Donetsk, slipped into a stalemate which was consolidated with the cease-fire agreed upon in Minsk in February 2015. The ruling government in Kiev led by President Peter Poroshenko had inherited an unpaid gas bill from the regime it had ousted topping 200 billion Russian rouble for domestic gas supplies which it would have to pay before gas supplies could be resumed. But more than a third of the gas destined to the European Union also flew through pipelines crossing Ukrainian territory, both under government control and held by resistance forces. This prompted Gazprom to look for alternatives circumventing the troublesome area altogether. The easiest (though also the most expensive) solution was to pick up an old plan, mothballed half a decade earlier, that consisted of an offshore pipeline leading from the Russian Black Sea coast to Bulgaria, from where it could be connected with the European grid through Macedonia and Albania, from where a newly built trans-Adriatic pipeline could carry gas straight into Italy. Known as South Stream, the track in Russia's territorial waters was already under construction when the trouble in Kiev, followed by that in eastern Ukraine, broke out. Beyond doubt under American pressure, the government of Bulgaria broke off its agreement to cooperate in the project. It was then decided to redirect the last offshore track towards Turkey, cooperation of which was ensured in subsequent formal agreements. There already was a supply pipeline across the Black Sea from Russia to the northern Turkish port of Supsa, known as Blue Stream, but its capacity is limited and there is no high-capacity transportation facility to the west of the country where both the population and the industry are concentrated.

"Turkish Stream, a new gas pipeline from Russia to Turkey will run across the Black Sea from the Russkaya CS near Anapa to Kiyikoy village in the European part of Turkey and further via Luleburgaz to Ipsala on the border between Turkey and Greece," Gazprom information reads.

"660 kilometre of the offshore pipeline route will be laid within the old corridor of South Stream and 250 kilometre – within a new corridor towards the European part of Turkey. The onshore gas pipeline section will stretch for 180 kilometers from the Black Sea coast of Turkey to the border between Turkey and Greece. The annual gas pipeline capacity will total 63 billion cubic metre of gas. The offshore gas pipeline will consist of four strings with the capacity of 15.75 billion cubic metre each. Gas from the first string is intended exclusively for the Turkish market. On December 1, 2014 Gazprom and Turkish company Botaş Petroleum Pipeline Corporation signed the Memorandum of Understanding on constructing the Turkish Stream gas pipeline. In February 2015 the key reference points of the route and technical solutions for the gas pipeline in Turkey were approved. In particular, the landfall location was defined near Kiyikoy village, the gas delivery point for Turkish consumers in Luleburgaz and a border crossing between Turkey and Greece in Ipsala. On May 8, 2015 Gazprom moved on to the construction stage of the Turkish Stream offshore gas pipeline. Gazprom will be solely responsible for the construction of the offshore section. Turkish gas transportation facilities will be built jointly. The first string is forecast to be constructed by December 2016. The first string's throughput of 15.75 billion cubic metre will be exclusively intended for Turkish consumers. The growing demand for natural gas in the Istanbul district will be taken into account in the gas pipeline design."

There can be little doubt that the "revolution" attempt in Macedonia, was intended to undermine the Turkish Stream device. Macedonia into 2015 still hoped for a chance to get a northern branch, meant to serve the former Yugoslavian republics through its territory. But the Macedonians are at odds not just with Albania but with Greece as well. Reaching out to Moscow means also reaching out to Athens in the new geopolitical mapping of a region where hard feelings of old tend to be staunch. 86)

After Turkey, it was Cyprus' turn to open up. The island-state, a one-time British colony which shortly after its independence got split up, following military coups in Greece and Turkey respectively, resulting in the forced creation of the so-called Republic of Northern Cyprus – a phantom state only recognised by Ankara. In both tutor states, democracy has returned ever since, but on the island itself wounds have prove hard to heal. It is all too likely, though, that Turkey's decision to accept the Russian gas transit deal made it easier for the government of Cyprus (proper, that is) to seek a way out of the strangling grip the European Commission holds on it because of a debt burden far beyond the country's repayment capacity.

"Russia has signed an agreement with Cyprus to give Russian navy ships access to Cypriot ports, the BBC reported on February 26, 2015. "Russian President Vladimir Putin agreed the deal after talks with Cypriot President Nicos Anastasiades. The deal comes as tensions between Russia and Western countries over the Ukrainian conflict continue. President Putin said that other countries should not be concerned and that the port's main use would be for counter-terrorism and anti-piracy. The island already hosts British military bases. Britain announced on Tuesday that it would be deploying troops to Ukraine as trainers. Tensions remain high between Russia and other European countries but the Russian leader was not concerned that the deal could be misconstrued. 'Our friendly ties are not aimed against anyone,' President Putin said. 'I do not think it should cause worries anywhere.' Russia has sought to strengthen ties with a number of individual

EU members - including Cyprus, Hungary and Greece, after the bloc, along with the US, imposed sanctions on Moscow over its role in Ukraine. President Anastasiades also revealed that the two countries were discussing the possibility of Russia using an air base on Cyprus for humanitarian relief missions."

"At a time when the European Union has imposed harsh economic sanctions on Russia and is trying to isolate the Russian government, the Kremlin is clearly relishing every opportunity to draw attention to cracks in Europe's unity. Russian President Vladimir Putin's recent visit to Hungary — complete with a natural gas supply deal — is one example of this; the Cyprus talks are another," a Middle East newsreel called Al-Monitor commented on the deal. "What makes Moscow's pursuit of this political symbolism most obvious is how Russia's official media are handling the story. The headline at Sputnik — a relatively new government-sponsored media organisation targeted at foreign audiences — conveys this quite directly: Russia Signs Military Deal with EU Member State. In other words, Sputnik is telling Europeans you may think you can isolate us, but you cannot even keep your own members from hosting Russian military forces. Of course, Russian officials likely want to reach audiences beyond the EU or the West in general. Another audience is domestic — to whom the deal says, "We are not quite as isolated as Western leaders claim." Beyond this, given the island nation's strategic location, regularized Russian naval access to Cypriot ports sends a message across the eastern Mediterranean region of the Middle East: We are here to stay."

"The deal, which cuts interest rates on a 2.5 billion euro Russian bailout loan to Cyprus and extends payments from 2016 to as late as 2021, also makes two other important statements in the eastern Mediterranean," the report reads further down. "The first is that the Kremlin takes care of its friends; Cyprus is a particularly special friend as an offshore banking haven and the second-ranking source of foreign investment in Russia, though as even Putin acknowledges, a large part of this is repatriated capital. The second message is that Russia is able to help friends like Cyprus even at a time of great economic distress. Russian officials may see this as the most consequential idea to communicate at a time when most news from Moscow is assessing the impacts of low energy prices and a much-reduced rouble. Cyprus President Nicos Anastasiades has perhaps unintentionally reinforced the case that the deal is more symbolic than substantive by insisting that it was a renewed agreement rather than a new one. Still, the agreement is not exclusively about symbolism — access to ports in Cyprus does have value for Russia's navy, even if only for what Anastasiades described as port "calls with humanitarian aims, which are supplies of provision and refueling of vessels, as well as for rescue of lives of Russian nationals and their evacuation from neighboring countries."

"After all, Russia's naval replenishment facility at Syria's port of Tartus is only about 241 kilometre from Limassol, a major port on the southern coast of Cyprus," the article continues. "With Syria's civil war continuing with no end in sight, having an alternative to Tartous makes good sense (particularly since no one knows what the outcome of the war will be). Moreover, despite much excitement early in the conflict about the strategic role of the Tartous facility, in reality it offers little more than what Cyprus is willing to provide. The port access is especially important in view of Defense Minister Sergei Shoigu's declaration, it has been decided to set up a navy department task force in the Mediterranean zone where naval forces will stay on a permanent basis. The Moscow Times suggested that this permanent presence would allow Russia to secure shipping access to the Suez Canal and extend its influence in the Middle East. The paper added that the force would operate from either Sevastopol or Novorossiysk in the Black Sea, because Tartus could not support it. A press officer from Russia's Black Sea Fleet describes Russia's current Mediterranean presence as a task force of 10 ships led by the destroyer Severomorsk, which has been detached from the Northern Fleet. It also includes vessels from the Black Sea Fleet and the Pacific Fleet. As Al-Monitor has previously reported, some of them participated in live-fire exercises with Cypriot and Israeli ships last fall. Anastasiades said that Putin approached the agreement delicately and without putting Cyprus in a complicated position with its EU partners. He likewise made clear that Russia will not have a military base; some press reports had suggested this possibility. (Indeed, some Greek patriots hope for a permanent Russian naval base on this island. Before the trip, Anastasiades even suggested that Cyprus might provide Moscow with access to an air base for humanitarian missions, though subsequent reports do not suggest this was in the final agreement.) What remains unclear is how Turkey — a major Russian economic partner and a NATO member — will react if Greek Cyprus becomes a key logistical node for the Russian navy in the Mediterranean. Ultimately, however, Moscow doesn't need much from Turkey beyond its treaty-based access to the Mediterranean; Ankara, by contrast, genuinely needs Russian natural gas. And Turkey's role in NATO imposes sharp limits on its ties to Russia anyway, as does Cyprus' EU membership. With both of these realities in mind, Putin may expect that he can manage the issue. After all, as Czar Alexander III famously said, Russia has only two allies, its army and its navy. Having signed the latest agreement with Cyprus, Putin has assured that one of those two long-standing allies will be in a somewhat better position to operate in the Mediterranean Sea." 87)

From Cyprus, the step to Greece was predictable and not very hard to take. Having been hit hard by the financial crunch of 2008, Greece had seen itself lured to accept astronomic loans offered by the European Commission, the European Central Bank and the International Monetary Fund (IMF). Greece's total debt is currently estimated at $350 billion, with some $270 billion owed to the international lenders. There is little chance that Greece's economy will enable it to pay such sums back within a short period of time. In fact, such loans are junk – not unlike the ones currently offered to Ukraine with a similar outlook for the future.

This was not just causing financial losses, but it would also turn out to be a blow to such global lending institutions' authority in the world. Lending huge lump sums without holding sufficient collateral that can be collected in case of a major long-term default is something no banker with his mind in the right place would even remotely think of doing. This is where Greece's lenders differ from alternatives: both the Eurasian Economic Union and China are building up funds for the survival of damsels in distress on the geopolitical scene but they are all allocated against tangible collateral with sustainable asset value – varying from railway tracks and seaports to oil fields and gold mines. This, in turn, allows long-term engagement which allows borrowers to depend on longer-term economic growth to cover debt instead of cutting into national reserves.

It is therefore that Greece's determination to go shopping elsewhere should its current fund suppliers back off has been in the air for some time now. "There have been proposals, offers I would say, from Russia, recently after the election, for economic support as well as from China, regarding help, investment possibilities," The Daily Telegraph in a report published on February 10 quoted Panos Kammenos, the defence minister and head of the Independent Greeks party in the ruling coalition as saying on the national television. "We have not asked for it. It is on the table. We are discussing it, [...] We want a deal. But if there is no deal, and if we see that Germany remains rigid and wants to blow Europe apart, then we will have to go to Plan B."

Though a long shot, such a plan is not entirely without perspective. Greece's reliance on Russian energy makes Moscow is its largest trading partner, with bilateral trade amounting to nearly $10bn a year. In 2009, China's state-backed firm Cosco took control of a third of the country's largest port, Piraeus – thereby putting a wedge into the series of kick-back privatisations of state assets reminding one of the scams clinched with Russia's oligarchs at the time of Boris Yeltsin. Among the remedies to stop that flow was the taming of federal states' governors, decided by Vladimir Putin, by depriving them from the right to sell of public assets to private parties and leave that to the central government. It helped weaker Russian regions to save their collateral, enabling them to apply for federal state support. It is this kind of state impact that makes policies carried out by the likes of the World Bank, the IMF and the ECB look obsolete and the Eurozone as a solidarity pact like a failure should current policies be maintained.

It may look ironic (which it is) but this could make Russia, unwittingly, into the undeclared Master of the Mediterranean, Algeria and Morocco, the last remaining northern-African states having remained aloof from the so-called Arab Spring which further east brought "Islamic" terror to power, show no sympathy for America's moves to isolate the Russian Federation. France's support against Russia was halfhearted from the very beginning. Thus, with an increasing number of reservations in Central Europe, Washington could find itself with only Germany and the United Kingdom as "reliable allies" while running the Second Cold War. And even they might in the end decide that sacrificing the European Union for the sake of Ukraine, let alone Armenia, is asking a bit too much.

But even the Atlantic Ocean appears to be no barrier where it comes to the east-west wave of counter-movements against America's multiple "revolution" push from west to east, and by summer 2015 had come to end up right on the USA's doorstep. In the course of last winter, popular movements have risen in Guatemala and Honduras featuring scenes that remind one all too well of those in Kiev, Skopje and now Yerevan – with the only crucial difference that America found itself on the wrong side of the barricade. It toppled the (democratic) Hondurese government as late as 2009 (rehearsal for Ukraine?), suspecting it of "defection".

Further south, Russia can depend on a longstanding ally which is Nicaragua. Since late 2014 works on a new canal linking the Atlantic to the Pacific, with capacity to allow vessels three to four times larger, including warships and even submarines, to cross the continent have started last autumn in Nicaragua, threatening the US-controlled (though no longer US-owned) Panama Canal out of business. The canal is being built using modern methodology: waste resulting from digging is being stored, cleaned and used for landfill on a number of strategic islands on which farmers and fishermen will be resettled. "The Nicaragua Canal project now under construction is expected not only to link the Atlantic and Pacific oceans but be a green project as well, [according to] an adviser with China's HKND Group that holds the concession for the canal, a Chinese newsreel reported on June 26 2015. "The 279-km-long mega project, which began at the end of 2014, will take five years to build with a total cost of US$50 billion. It will provide a more convenient interoceanic passage for large vessels that can not go through the Panama Canal, such as 25,000-TEU container ships, said Bill Wild, HKND Group's chief project adviser. Moreover, over the past two years, HKND has also made great efforts on the environmental and social impact assessment, which has been submitted to the local government and is waiting for approval. Wild said the company will launch a reforestation program for watersheds along the canal. The canal will also serve as a protective barrier once the program is completed. There will be a 10-km-wide "no-go area" in the Mesoamerican Biological Corridor so that no human activities will affect wildlife in this area. Material excavated during construction will be used to create some 30,000 to 40,000 hectares of land for agriculture, Wild said. He said two islands with rock walls will be built in Cocibolca or Nicaragua Lake, the country's largest lake and part of the canal route, where the extracted material can be deposited. The material will be extracted through a system that uses giant suction tubes, with a mechanism similar to a vacuum cleaner, ensuring the sediment is not simply disrupted and floating around, he said. The lake is one of the people's biggest concerns. We will make sure to protect it, Wild said." 88)

Investments in various other sectors of Nicaragua's economy have come from China, and Nicaragua has signed long-term strategic pacts with both

China and Russia. As well as infrastructure, trade also features high on the agenda where both the Russian Federation and the People's Republic of China are concerned. Following the 21-26 January visit to Moscow by a Nicaraguan delegation led by deputy foreign minister, Valdrack Jaentschke, and Ortega's son, Laureano, in representation of ProNicaragua, the official investment and export promotion agency; the head of Nicaragua's trade & industry ministry (Mific), Orlando Solórzano, announced various accords. These include the continuation of Russian shipments of wheat to Nicaragua, which first arrived in November 2011, aimed at improving nutrition and boosting the bread industry. Solórzano said that a further four Russian shipments of wheat, each of 25,000 tonnes (t), would arrive this year. He also said that the Russians had pledged 1,000 tractors and 1,000 mowers. Meanwhile, on 21 March Ortega announced that Russia had donated 130 public buses, bringing the total number to 485 since 2009.

The most recent report on foreign cooperation by Nicaragua's central bank, published in March 2013, revealed that Russia remained the biggest single foreign donor for Nicaragua's public sector in 2012, accounting for US$37.4m (28.8%) of the US$130.1m in bilateral donations for the public sector. Yet there is room for improvement. Last October the two countries announced they were negotiating a trade agreement. Bilateral trade reached US$94.5m in the first ten months of 2012 on the latest figures from the Central American economic integration system (Sieca) – just over 1% of Nicaragua's total US$8.7bn. This follows US$87.8m in 2011, up on the US$46.4m registered in 2010. Russia has also yet to feature as a significant source of foreign direct investment (FDI). The top five sources of FDI in the first half of 2012, on the latest figures from ProNicaragua were the US, Panama, Mexico, Switzerland and Venezuela, accounting for 73% of the total US$584m over the period. 89)

EPILOGUE: COLD WAR II IN A
MULTI-DIMENSIONAL PERSPECTIVE

*El Greco. The Annunciation. 1590s. Oil on canvas. Thyssen-Bornemisza
Collection, Lugano-Castagnola, Switzerland*

The main question staying in place after this modest survey of pros and
contras remains why the overall bulk within the western media establishment
staunchly keeps advocating anti-Russian hysteria among western audiences,
echoing blunt lies and covering up for "inconvenient" facts and events. "The
frantic spell of Western media behaviour could be a case-study in how it is
centrally manipulated with a political agenda and thought-control. Editors
at major Western media corporations are evidently following a political line

cast by Washington and its European allies," an article posted on April 20 2015 by Sputnik and written by Finian Cunningham who has a Master's graduate in Agricultural Chemistry and worked as a scientific editor for the Royal Society of Chemistry, Cambridge, England, before pursuing a career in newspaper journalism an who for nearly 20 years worked as an editor and writer in major news media organisations, including The Mirror, Irish Times and Independent, was to read. "The multi-billion-dollar Western news media networks are replete with an unquestioning, unwavering anti-Russian agenda. This agenda is recklessly inflaming international tensions to the point of inciting further conflict and even an all-out global war. The roll of dishonour includes stellar corporate names, from CNN, New York Times, Washington Post, BBC, Financial Times, Guardian, France 24, Deutsche Welle, and many more. It is a veritable troll army marching in lockstep with their governments' agenda of disinformation. In unison, they are functioning as a global ministry of propaganda." 90) "Paradoxically, the charge of propaganda and media trolls is actually substantiated if applied to the gamut of Western corporate news media. We are not talking about clandestine media impostors, bloggers and cyber-trolls on the payroll of the CIA or MI6 who infest the media. We are referring to the entire professional media industry — a multi-billion-dollar global industry. [...] This frantic spell of Western media behaviour, based on that incident alone, could be a case-study in how it is centrally manipulated with a political agenda and thought-control. Editors at major Western media corporations are evidently following a political line cast by Washington and its European allies. That line is: demonise Putin and destabilise Russia. It may be a subtle form of control, and partly also down to lazy follow-the-herd editorial instinct, but nevertheless the behaviour amounts to spectacular control. And this in a supposedly 'free thinking, independent' industry. Rather than investigating the real political climate under the Western-backed regime in Kiev — neonazi, anti-Russia, illegal, fascistic, war criminality, proven gangsterism — the Western media swing into denial mode, whitewash mode and disinformation mode to cast aspersions on Moscow. Western media may pride itself with vain self-congratulating descriptions of 'independent news, freedom of thought and expression, fearless defenders of truth' and so on. But the truth is that Western corporate so-called news media are simply this: one giant troll army marching in lockstep with the political agenda of Washington and its coterie of Western allies. Ukraine and Russia are merely one manifestation among many of the Western media's total propaganda function. That function has been around for decades, but it is only now becoming abundantly transparent. Western politicians may fret about the Western public being invaded by an alleged Russian troll army and Kremlin propaganda. When the reality is that the Western public is already under oppressive occupation of a troll army — otherwise known as Western corporate 'news media'."

Even though the outspoken dilemma noted here is relatively new, the phenomenon is rather old. "What is new? What is happening?" It is a question which drives a herd of does into hiding on signals that the lion is in a hunting mood. On the other side, the presence of the does provokes the lion's appetite since without hunting he and his family will be doomed to starve. Knowledge how things work, experience how to take advantage of it in order to survive are in animals' instincts and that peculiar animal called human is no exception to it. However, the human is the only animal on earth (as far as known, that is, since it is widely believed that other mammals such as whales and dolphins possess brain capacities similar to that of men) who questions his instincts and direct information, thereby making him able to design strategies based on logic rather than mere observation.

Curiosity beyond the direct needs of the body, therefore, have marked humans throughout history, and what we call journalism today is a consistent result of that capacity. Another element not to overlook is the interest of gathering and divulging information the bearer of that information carries. This interest is only abstract in theory - a theory that betrays the real motives behind the spreading of information, the information's explanation and the vast grey zone that lies between them. In this respect, journalism is like music, poetry or visual arts: art for art's sake has been widely professed since well over a century. Before that, nobody took the idea seriously. As things appear to stand, it never existed except in academic professors' imagination. Whether a chorus sings Halleluyah for half an hour or *Alle Menschen werden Brùder* for a couple of minutes, it is clear that the sweet tune that would melt a heart of stone is there to pass on a message - not just to serve the pleasure of the human ear.

The same terrible truth is valid for news: the one who thrusts it into the public dominion seldom, if ever, does it without a reason. True: in order to look genuine, arguments pro and contra must be reflected - but then again, this is only with the purpose of making a stronger point rather than to spread doubt. Where does that leave the journalist? Exactly: in the orchestra - whether he plays the first violin or hammers on the kettle drum matters little. A journalist can dream of holding the conductor's stick, and in some cases such dreams can come true. But even then, the tune is set by what is written in the score under his musical nose, and what is written there is NOT written by journalists.

It may seem funny looking back from where we are today, but at the cradle of "news", "reporting' and other journalic jargon stood not newsgatherers, copy-writers, editors or publishers. It may well be a bit disappointing for those romantics who still view the journalist as the brave knight-in-arms riding against armies of evil spokespeople, interviewees and public relations demons, the light in the dark consisting of intrigue and secrecy mongers and the defender of sacred truth and immortal integrity amidst a world full of deceit and cover-ups. Fact is that in reality the origin of news divulging has been plain and straight with potentates in ancient times who felt the need to warn the public to obey their orders - or else.

Both the Roman Emperors and their Chinese peers were systematically divulging their *acta* (in Rome) *ti-pao* (in China) reporting on official decrees, appointments and dismissals, stocks of commodities and other news from above worth knowing for the obedient subjects. The main reason for those in power was to combat gossip and its subsequent doubt in such a way that no one could any longer be uncertain regarding where the truth lay, and society could live in order and stability. Across the Atlantic, long before the Spanish and Portugese "discovered" it, the Inca and Aztek empires are reputed to have had, though they had no script as such, official messengers who reported trouble in the vast empires to warn travellers and other people who needed to know about the situation. The usefulness of such information has never been put in doubt - nor have the advantages of knowing trouble and its outcome up till our very days. Many centuries after the Empires of Rome and the Chinese Han Dynasty had come to an end, a London-based banker called Nathan Rothschild had his own information links to the continent whereby he knew hours before both newspapers and official proclamation broke the news that the allied forces had won the battle of Waterloo. By using that information to speculate on the London Stock Exchange, he reputedly used those hours to make a handsome fortune.

Independent reporting, along with its self-imposed standards of "fair" reporting including passing on more than one side of a story, appears to have existed at times when potentates still ruled the known world and peace used to be little more than a run-up of the next war. On page 54 of his classic "A History of News", New York based mass media scholar Mitchell Stephens refers to the text on tablets found in Mesopotamia and dating from the late XVth or early XIVth Century BC. "The tablets display a series of charges against the mayor, named Kushiharbe, of the town of Nuzu in Mesopotamia," the text reads. "He is accused primarily of theft and extortion: 'So declares Ninuari: Kushiharbe robbed me from my own storehouse. Two shekels of gold, one ox, and two rams I paid to Kushiharbe, then he restored to me [what he had stolen].' But an additional charge was also leveled against the mayor: that he had had illicit intercourse with a married woman named Humerelli. Apparently mindful of the need of impartiality, the writer of the tablets includes not only the damaging testimony of Palteya, who says he procured the woman for the mayor, but Kushiharbe's response to the charges: "I swear that Palteya did not bring Humerelli to the trysting house of Tilunnaya, nor did I have intercourse with her!" 91)

The rise in Europe, starting in the middle of the XVIth Century AD, of private-held post services, mainly paid for by merchant and banking families in order to check what was going on with their merchandise and investments at greater distances, triggered a wave of news exchange, independent from state propaganda. Such services, though, were expensive and the price paid by clients for information correspondingly high. For the broader public, still by and large suffering from illiteracy, the public heralds, usually under strict control of the cleric and secular authorities, remained the main tool for divulging news among commoners. In England, this lead to the development of the so-called news ballad: popular poetry in which events were related and often accompanied by a patriotic undertone. One example, quoted by Stephens, is a news ballad in circulation in England during the campaign against it by the Spanish Armada in 1588, and telling the capture of one of the latter's flagships:

The chiefest Captaine, of this Gallion so hie:
Don Hugo de Moncaldo he, within this fight did die.
Who was the Generall, of all the Gallions great:
But through his brains w' pouders force, a bullet strong did beat.
And manie more, by sword did loose their breath:
And manie more within the sea, did swimme and took their death.
There you might see the salt and foming flood:
Died and staind like scarlet red, with store of Spanish blood.

Periodicals under their publishers' and editors' personal signature and free from censorship by either the Church or the authorities first appeared in Europe in the late XVIth and early XVIIth Century, almost simultaneously in Venice and Amsterdam. The Netherlands, engaged in a war of exhaustion against Spain of which, according to Spanish law, their territory still formed part but in effect by and large enjoying independence from both the Spanish Crown and the Vatican's oppression, had become a federal republic (the first of its kind in the world) where freedom of religious conscience and (to some extent) freedom of opinion and its expression on worldly affairs was protected by the law. This brought a constant flow of dissidents from all parts of Europe into the country, and thereby turned its cities into centres bursting with information and exchange of thought. Soon, the first periodical was started up, dubbed *coranto* ("current") in Italian. They found their way all over Europe, since they were the only printed source on the state of affairs on the continent that came from independent sources.

The establishment of the Amsterdam Stock Exchange in 1608, the Dutch national currency exchange bank in 1609, its first credit bank in 1610 and 1616, all fully private though working on the basis of state guarantees, made the city a boomtown for trade and investments, all the more for it with the establishment of the East India Company in 1602, an outsourced state monopoly with the colonial empire Holland was building up in Southeast Asia. Similar developments took place in Venice, which controlled trade with the Middle East and Central Asia. The Venetian *gazetas* mainly served the city-state's powerful merchant class, which also controlled much of its political hierarchy, with military and maritime information in order to secure trade and hedge stocks against the risks of war and instability. Cologne, finally became a temporary centre for the newborn press, thanks to the fact that it managed to stay aloof from the looming civil war in Germany (which was to break out in 1618) for quite some time and thereby served as a neutral ground and a bridgehead to The Netherlands.

The rise of "independent" journalism in The Netherlands and Italy and gradually conquering Europe's autocratic monarchies in the process, in the end was poised to create a press industry, meaning people who made money on presenting events and developments in the community to the community's broader audiences. The journalist by profession as we know him or her these days, has effectively been a latecomer in the news industry. Until well into the XVIIIth Century, publishers were their own editor or hired people gifted with the art of wording for the job. Some of them, especially in the second half of the XVIIth Century as demand for information expanded with a strong growth in literacy in Europe, hired informers, who used to hang out in docks, at post stations or any other place where messages from abroad arrived, to come up with information. Such information, though, remained by and large dependent on the source which, in turn, often failed to come up with first-hand information to begin with. In modern-day journalism, those "news collectors" are known as stringers. Poorly paid, such people could hardly be expected to do independent research or analysis.

Yet, editorial skills at the desk made the formula work for a long time. "Correspondents" abroad, on whom the corantos were dependent for their news updates, were not professionals either, but often traders of diplomats who could, thanks to their position, could provide information gathered outside the public domain. Finally, quite a number of postmen and courriers who were not all too scrupulous to take their plight of confidence seriously, made their small fortune by selling information to publishers of periodicals taken from letters entrusted to them which they had discretely opened and read in the process. Journalism at large consisted of scrambling information, trying to make sense of it to a major or a minor extent, and present it to readers accompanied with comments - often mixed with the information since, free press or not, Europe in all remained a heavily moralist society. The reason was clear: there was no point to have professional correspondents on the spot as long as it took weeks if not months for the information they came up with to the place where it could be made ready to print. It was only the appearance of electronic ways to transfer information, telegraph first, telephone later followed by even more advanced means of transfer, that the journalist/reporter made his/her appearence. This was not before halfway the XIXth Century - even though before, especially in the Napoleonic wars, reporters were sent down to Europe's battlefields to write eyewitness reports on them. Logistics remained a bottleneck: hardly had a report made the headlines, or the next war had already started or even ended.

In most European countries, therefore, with the best example being the French literary salons' periodicals, there was hardly a way to tell where bellettrie ended and journalism began. A trend which, couriously, has started returning in the world of late with the opening-up of news sources to the general public through the Internet, thereby crushing news media's exclusivity in terms of access to news and pushing them back into the position of think-tanks rather than information channels. But in the century-and-a-half laying between those two instants, the media in general, and journalists in particular, have been lifted on pedestals to the extent that they used to be, and in many places still are, dubbed the "sixth power" after Montesquieu's trias politica - the legislative, executive and judicial powers - state bureacracy and corporate enterprise. In some cases, the role attributed to the media actually made democratically elected people's representatives wonder who was supposed to be the real decision-maker: they or self-proclaimed judges of what went on in society from behind their news desks.

The rise of the "sixth power" brought about morality, formerly imposed by society, into the inner veins of the journalistic community. Sensationalism, which had never been absent in reporting stretching from the Tudor era's news ballads to the early XXth Century penny papers, today known as tabloids, with their screaming headers, was by and large responsible for the need felt by the media to polish their tarned image. In the process, confrontations between the "facts-and-nothing-but-the-facts" movement on the rise and the opposition to it also raised the question in how far the information should be "genuine", "unbiased", "truthful", "impartial" - just to name a few qualifications and characteristics journalists were, and to staunchly large extents still are, supposed to adhere to.

Stephens on page 265 of his book traces the polemics regarding journalists' position in these respects back to the XVIIIth Century from where on they never ceased to be omnipresent both in public debates and in media circles: "Reporters may initially be in the position of the messenger, returned from the battle, in Euripides' *The Suppliant Women* who exclaims: 'I know the many horrors there, but nowhere to begin.' But, like that messenger, reporters do begin, and where they begin and where they and, and how they travel from beginning to end, helps condition their audiences' response to the news. [...] As they tell their stories, journalists are encumbered with belief systems, social positions, workaday routines and professional obligations - all of which affect their selection and presentation of facts. [...] The [American] Federalist editor William Cobbett called claims of impartiality "perfect nonsense" in 1797. Since then the biases journalists impose on the news have grown subtler and, given the forest of facts in which modern reporters operate, more difficult to discern; but despite reporters' great show of reverence for those facts, these biases have not been eliminated. 'To hear people talk about the facts you would think that they lay about like pieces of gold ore in the Yukon days waiting to be picked up,' the British journalist Claud Cockburn wrote in 1967; '...all stories are written backwards - they are supposed to begin with the facts and develop from there, but in reality they begin with a journalist's point of view, a conception'." In all: if there is one domain in the world in which it always was and always will be a hopeless task to determine where integrity ends and hypocricy begins, it is bound to be journalism.

A classical view on journalism, but yet way ahead of its time, was formulated under the looming threat of the Second World War when the world had hardly recovered from the mental and economic shocks that the first one had triggered in its wake. This was the thesis, later popularised into a booklet, by Wickham Steed, under the straightforward title "The Press". He actually virtually predicted the crisis in information flows and their accessibility to the public which today makes - or rather should make and in too many cases fails to do so - journalists realise that the world is changing and that without meeting that changing the spectre of massive unemployment is looming above their pretty little heads. 92)

"No newspaper can long be produced without the help of of its editorial staff, or journalist," Steed states. "Who and what are 'journalists'?, he proceeds. "Though efforts have been and are made to train journalists for their work and 'schools of journalism' exist, it is broadly true that journalists pass no professional examination, take no special degrees and hold no charter. The news they gather and the comment they write has to be sold to the public, usually under stress of competition. As news-getters and news-sellers, journalists may hardly seem entitled to claim a higher status than that of any cheapjack whose vociferations draw pence from passers-by. Yet the function they actually discharge give them a public standing above that of men whose only aim is to catch the eye or the star of their fellow men. Whence comes this standing? In the last resort I think it comes from instinctive public recognition that journalism proper is in the nature of a vocation, that it is something more than a craft, something other than an industry, something between an art and a ministry. Journalist proper are unofficial public servants whose purpose it is to serve the community. Such journalists are born, not made. They may need training and experience; yet no degree of training and no amount of experience can make make journalists of the unless they have in them the vital spark that distinguishes the journalist proper from the newspaper hand. [...] Of newspapermen without the vital spark there is no lack. Journalists by vocation are rare. They are men and women with minds and standards of judgement of their own, with an (often unconfessed) zeal for the spread of educational knowledge, and with a determination to go through the newspaper mill in the hope of finding one day a chance to tell the public what they believe it ought to know. These journalists are 'the press' in the true sense of the term; and if ever the 'newspaper industry' seeks to dispense with them and to look upon itself solely or chiefly as a business for the enrichment of its owners or shareholders, it will be doomed as a public institution. Yet journalists by vocation are often reminded of the gap that divides their ideal from the practical approach to it. Experience teaches them that their craft may be an industry, a business, as well as a liberal profession, an art or a vocation; that it may be all these things by turns and, at moments, all of them together. They know that, as its name implies, journalism consists in gathering, printing and publishing news of events, day by day, with or without comment or opinion. They know that this is responsible work, that news is expected to be true and the comment upon it to be honest." In all: the true journalist is the one that does his homework in order to enter the bright realm of revelation, which entitles him or her to bring the facts as they are and if he or she feels like it add his or her observations and interpretations to them - with a clear distinction between the facts as they are and the way the author feels about them.

Scientists have argued for a long time that it is impossible to predict the unpredictable. But as even mathematics have now entered the zone of the invisible, the unperceivable (as far as it goes beyond the limits of our present perception, that is) becomes perceivable, and the unimaginable imaginable. Some would call the process science fiction not without (perfectly plausible) disdain for Hollywood circuses, and even though men of great learning and science up to this day try to figure out scenarios according to which there could be something truthful in the myriad of stories about space monsters, their input is widely being considered entertainment of varying level and quality.

So if the physical dimension of the unknown has been by and large commercialised, what is left to explore in order to remain within the realm of thought and in order to expand that realm? The answer could well have to be sought in the psychological areas beyond our horizon. Because if there is anything unpredictable left in society, it is whim – wit's bad twin brother, the "dark" (read: unperceived, not necessarily evil) side of the human animal's ego. It represents the constant challenge to any perception, theory, explanation and all other things belonging to the realm of thought. This complementary antagonism could be compared with a psychodrama verses an ordinary drama. Whereas the latter gradually leads from intrigue to outcome in which the entire intrigue is being unraveled, in a psychodrama, if there is an outcome at all, it leaves all questions how it came to be open to many interpretations, if any interpretation at all. The spectator is left with riddles which can only be accepted and motivations which are left to mere guesswork.

The same distinction exists in the world of thought, and the world of economic thought is no exception to it. Opposite to the side of the explainable, the explicable and the understandable (even though here imagination does play a role not to be neglected) is a world that gives no answers, offers no systematic perception – only chaos too strong, too stubborn to submit itself to any human logical observation. Those who want to get to know it have to accept *a priori* that they will have to acknowledge things they cannot understand, to take dimensions for granted the existence of which can only be imagined (and then only with a lot of effort) and never be proven. Any axiom at least bears the comfort of human consensus. This luxury is not at the disposition of those who are entering a wild world which therefore, meaning for the sake of relating, could be dubbed psychoeconomics: a non-cosmos of flying thoughts, disorderly outcries to which philosophy has no answers. Even the most cautious tread over its threshold will generate confusion, indignation, even anger. Yet, if the human mind pretends to exist in order to control, it cannot be ignored.

So is spirit an original phenomenon that simply adapted itself to physical restrictions and used it to take physical shape? Or is spirit a product – or even byproduct – of physical processes which by whatever force generated themselves in the cosmos? Whatever the case, among the most remarkable results has been that uncommon creature dubbed (by itself) human, the one both blessed and cursed with a mind of its own. The credulous dimension in human intellect (the word was always ill-defined for all it matters) has been the very intruder of the universal perception from the very beginning. As soon as imagination was born, the animal side in this strange character's nature started to stir. Like the little bird that cleans the crocodile's teeth at the risk of being taken for lunch in the aftermath of a sheer yawn without much notice, the human character poked around in the world it knew and observed and in the world it imagined.

In this way, while being left in the dark about its own origin – either mere physical and chemical coincidence or something else – the human mind gets carried away by speculation to the extent that it forgets that his observations on the imaginary side of the cosmos are the products of its own imagination and that of the minds of fellow-humans to begin with. Ignorance regarding the fact that this peculiar phenomenon called imagination is the human mind's strength and weakness at the same time reinforces its latter quality more than its former one. The tendency to create structures so powerful that they threaten to absorb mankind's control is in fact as old as Mankind itself. There has always been an inclination, stretching from prehistoric cave-dwellers to modern-day state or corporate structures to confine forces that really pull the strings to obscurity and instead put puppets in the limelight – thereby creating mindless zombies directed by faceless minds. Whether those hidden forces are real humans, divine beings that do not physically exist but the power of which imposes itself on communities' minds nonetheless, or machines - it matters little and the result has always been the same. One could say that these days, brands have taken the place of the idols of old. Is this an original observation? Probably not – but then, so what? If a cow needs four stomachs to re-digest her food three times, how many minds it should take to re-digest that ever-stirring brew called thought is hard to imagine indeed. Human brain has always been slow to react to observations – with the exceptions of those very occasional and almost exclusively individual leaps forward that opened the eyes of the world's population a bit wider. These were brought about by the creative minds – in the very ancient times of the Sumerian, Egyptian, Toltek, early Chinese and contemporaries of people whose names have gone into oblivion, and later on of those like Aristotle, Descartes, Da Vinci, Montesquieu, Kant, Nietzsche, Einstein.

Since the middle of the XXth Century, the phenomenon master-mind seems to have started to retreat and such quantum leaps have not occurred in spite of unseen technological advances. This growing absence of sublimated imagination could well have fatal consequences for human subsistence on earth as the world has known it so far – since this kind of imagination is exactly what helped the human race survive for millions of years. Without it, Man could possibly lose its only resource to survive the forces of nature, and follow the example of the giant prehistoric reptiles who became extinct not for lack of physical force but for lack of advance thought through the tool of an independent mind. This possible outlook is frightening enough indeed. Vision has always been the very power that pushed mankind into the next gear and helped it survive in spite of the most dramatic setbacks throughout its existence. Vision means guidance. Guidance means subsistence. The individual thought that generates ideas has been the only way so far communities could look ahead of their immediate observations and think of the imaginable – thereby enabling themselves to take the necessary precautions in the fact of dangers and challenges imposed by their environment. Such thought often goes against all the logic imposed by known realities.

It all illustrates too much that raising the question of western media prostrating themselves in subordination to the instructions of NATO commanders – either dressed up in operetta uniforms or in those of Hollywood jungle captains – or white-collar "intelligence" officials raises more other questions than it provides straight answers, especially if one looks at the universal psychology behind it which we tried to do in this open-end epilogue of our journey through the realms of words. Ever since the downfall of the Iron Curtain, there have been attempts to change the political landscape of the world. As noticed earlier, there were initially two trends that could be discerned: that towards a multipolar world and its adversary trend towards a unipolar world, ruled by the USA without any defiance from any rival force. Now, the clock is being turned back and the bipolar world notion is back on the scene. Russia, China and India are combining their economic, political and military clout to counter the USA's while the latter struggles to make friends with unlikely bedmates such as Iran and Cuba on the shortlist, while the European Union is slowly moving away from Washington in the direction of the position of a neutral force which is Washington's very nightmare since rather than "isolating Russia" as official stragety explanations maintain, it is America which is getting more and more isolated by the day – and all that because of a place called Ukraine which reportedly hardly any American citizen has been able to find on the map and further spearheading through the southern Caucasus into Central Asia, names of states of which sound even more exotic to American ears. Within this psychological whirlwind, it can hardly come as a surprise that news managers are at a loss and take the easy way: the old pattern of heroes and villains. That may well be a snapshot of the current situation, but it leaves all in the dark regarding what could be in store next...

NOTES

1. http://www.theses.fr/2011EHES0468
2. http://www.newrepublic.com/authors/maria-snegovaya
3. http://thediplomat.com/2015/03/silk-road-reporters-an-independent-news-site-for-central-asia/
4. ibid.
5. https://www.americanambassadors.org/publications/ambassadors-review/fall-2014/democracy-in-central-asia-supporting-kyrgyzstan-s-island-of-democracy
6. http://en.tass.ru/russia/761146
7. http://www.globalresearch.ca/ukraine-through-the-us-looking-glass-anti-russian-propaganda-in-the-mainstream-media/5378303
8. http://www.opednews.com/articles/A-Family-Business-of-Perpe-by-Robert-Parry-Neocons_Perpetual-War_Political_Putin-150320-170.html
9. http://www.bilderberg.org/skulbone.htm
10. ibid.
11. see numerous articles on the Ablyazov affair by the author on www.kazworld.info
12. http://www.themoscowtimes.com/news/article/russian-investigators-target-ukraine-minister-in-organized-murder-probe/502135.html
13. http://theanondog.i2p.us/cgi-bin/src.py?140627000
14. http://sputniknews.com/europe/20150411/1020768456.html
15. http://sputniknews.com/europe/20150411/1020763134.html
16. http://www.bbc.com/news/world-europe-28357880
17. http://www.theguardian.com/world/2014/dec/25/mh17-russia-claims-to-have-airfield-witness-who-blames-ukrainian-pilot
18. http://sputniknews.com/europe/20150506/1021764384.html
19. http://sputniknews.com/europe/20150410/1020730266.html

20. http://sputniknews.com/europe/20150320/1019748871.html
21. http://www.eurasiareview.com/30012011-washington-intensifies-push-into-central-asia/
22. http://www.washingtonpost.com/wp-dyn/content/article/2010/08/06/AR2010080606148.html
23. http://nikpress.com/article_read.php?a=8384
24. www.eng.24.kg/parliament/172308-news24.html
25. www.eng.24.kg/community/172334-news24.html
26. http://www.4thmedia.org/2014/05/biggest-german-newspapers-say-blackwater-behind-massacres/
27. http://www.huffingtonpost.com/jeremy-scahill/blackwater-still-working_b_213835.html
28. http://www.4thmedia.org/2014/05/biggest-german-newspapers-say-blackwater-behind-massacres/
29. http://www.newtimes.co.rw/section/article/2015-01-13/184899/
30. http://thediplomat.com/2014/10/russias-chokehold-on-kyrgyzstan/
31. http://www.youroilandgasnews.com/gazprom+kyrgyzstan+to+provide+reliable+gas+supply+to+kyrgyz+republic_104887.html
32. http://www.gazprom.com/about/production/projects/deposits/kyrgyzstan/
33. http://foreignpolicy.com/2015/03/03/central-asias-cheap-oil-double-whammy-russia-china-silk-road/
34. http://www.eurasiareview.com/19112014-kyrgyzstan-no-alternative-closer-russia-ties-prime-minister/
35. www.eng.kremlin.ru/transcripts/22404
36. http://www.eurasiareview.com/19112014-kyrgyzstan-no-alternative-closer-russia-ties-prime-minister/
37. http://en.wikipedia.org/wiki/George_Soros
38. http://www.nytimes.com/2014/10/06/opinion/masha-gessen-putinspeak-in-kyrgyzstan.html?_r=0
39. www.eng.kremlin.ru/transcripts/22404

40. http://www.faz.net/aktuell/politik/ausland/eurasische-wirtschaftsunion-gegruendet-zum-unterschreiben-verdammt-12961389.html

41. http://internacional.elpais.com/internacional/2014/05/29/actualidad/1401390938_978952.htm

42. http://www.nytimes.com/2014/05/30/world/europe/putin-signs-economic-alliance-with-presidents-of-kazakhstan-and-belarus.html?_r=0

43. http://www.businessweek.com/articles/2014-05-29/putins-eurasian-union-looks-like-a-bad-deal-even-for-russia

44. http://www.lemonde.fr/idees/article/2014/04/15/les-republiques-d-asie-centrale-vont-elles-etre-une-nouvelle-crimee_4401396_3232.html

45. http://www.rferl.org/content/dozens-of-anti-ees-activists-detained-in-astana/25402607.html

46. https://www.foreignaffairs.com/articles/armenia/2014-12-26/eurasian-disunion

47. ibid.

48. http://www.eng.24.kg/economics/174363-news24.html

49. sputniknews.com/business/20150205/1017798717.html

50. http://thediplomat.com/2015/02/central-asias-ruble-awakening/

51. en.alalam.ir/news/1651560

52. https://www.khaama.com/clash-between-radicals-isil-vs-taliban-in-afghanistan-9341

53. http://www.theguardian.com/world/2015/feb/18/kyrgyzstan-imam-encouraging-followers-fight-for-isis
http://www.ft.com/cms/s/0/35a081fa-bea9-11e4-8d9e-00144feab7de.html

54. http://www.csmonitor.com/World/Europe/2015/0220/Islamic-State-not-just-a-Western-problem-says-top-Russian-spy

55. http://minchenko.ru/netcat_files/File/Political_risks_CA_2014.pdf

56. http://articles.economictimes.indiatimes.com/2015-02-02/news/58711799_1_shanghai-cooperation-organisation-trilateral-cooperation-early-conclusion]

57. http://www.globalresearch.ca/fifty-years-of-imperial-wars-global-neoliberalism-and-americas-drive-for-world-domination/5434305

58. http://www.dailymail.co.uk/news/article-2572449/The-United-States-Hatred-From-KKK-black-separatists-939-hate-groups-America-mapped.html

59. http://www.dailymail.co.uk/news/article-2572449/The-United-States-Hatred-From-KKK-black-separatists-939-hate-groups-America-mapped.html

60. http://www.theguardian.com/world/2014/oct/28/eurasian-economic-union-russia-belarus-kazakhstan

61. http://mandrillapp.com/track/click/7958185/www.stratfor.com?p=eyJz
IjoiaXBUa1RDSlVMOW9TSzgtdjVBSWhwVUZmY0xnIiwidiI6MS
wicCI6IntcInVcIjo3OTU4MTg1LFwidlwiOjEsXCJ1cmxcIjpcImh0dH
BzOlxcXC9cXFwvd3d3LnN0cmF0Zm9yLmNvbVxcXC9mb3JlY2Fzd
FxcXC9kZWNhGUtZm9yZWNhc3QtMjAxNS0yMDI1XCIsXCJp
ZFwiOlwiZWFlY2VmYTVlZmJhNGU2ZGJiN2ZlMWVhNGQ3NT
c4MTFcIixcInVybF9pZHNcIjpbXCJkNWE2ZTYzODUwN2RmZT
RkZDlkODY1ZDg5YjA3NjdmNmJmNTU5OTgxXCJdfSJ9

62. http://www.rferl.org/content/kyrgyzstan-signs-eurasian-union-deal/26759237.html

63. http://en.tengrinews.kz/politics_sub/Nazarbayev-speaks-about-launching-Eurasian-Economic-Union-258082/

64. http://thediplomat.com/2014/11/kyrgyzstan-to-reluctantly-join-the-eeu/

65. http://eng.kremlin.ru/transcripts/22404

66. http://www.economist.com/news/asia/21586304-vast-region-chinas-economic-clout-more-match-russias-rising-china-sinking

67. http://www.ciis.org.cn/english/2014-01/26/content_6640226.htm

68. http://blogs.ft.com/brusselsblog/files/2015/01/Russia.pdf

69. http://www.dailysabah.com/opinion/2015/01/29/russias-increasing-ties-with-china-vitalize-the-eurasian-union

70. http://www.silkroadreporters.com/2015/01/24/central-asian-republics-perceive-emerging-eurasian-union/

71. http://www.eng.24.kg/glance/174407-news24.html

72. http://journal-neo.org/2014/06/24/what-us-ambassadors-to-georgia-really-say-about-american-values/

73. http://www.rense.com/general45/bet.htm

74. http://www.mintpressnews.com/erik-prince-americas-harbinger-death-democracy/200325/

75. http://larouchepub.com/pr/2015/150125_blackwater_ukraine.html

76. http://sputniknews.com/analysis/20150119/1013509345.html #ixzz3Rk4QNLPP

77. http://www.rferl.org/content/central-asia-us-reassess-strategy/26911854.html

78. http://russia-insider.com/en/2015/03/18/4656

79. http://www.opednews.com/articles/Russia-Under-Attack-by-Paul-Craig-Roberts-NATO_Propaganda_Putin_Russia-And-China-150320-747.html

80. http://akipress.com/news:546355/

81. http://theunobservednews.blogspot.com/2015/03/china-and-russia-vs-united-states.html

82. http://csis.org/publication/vision-shared-prosperity-central-asia

83. http://sputniknews.com/columnists/20150420/1021135202.html

84. http://english.pravda.ru/world/americas/14-05-2015/130599-usa_lose_soft_war-0/#sthash.FrJIde3F.dpuf

85. http://sputniknews.com/europe/20150521/1022421659.html
http://sputniknews.com/politics/20150515/1022197471.html
http://www.occupy.com/article/exposed-globally-renowned-activist-collaborated-intelligence-firm-stratfor
http://colorrevolutionsandgeopolitics.blogspot.com/2011/04/from-archives-jonathan-mowat-new-gladio.html

86. http://www.azatutyun.am/content/article/27079876.html
http://rt.com/op-edge/269566-armenia-protests-energy-ngos/

87. http://www.gazprom.com/about/production/projects/pipelines/turkish-stream/

88. http://www.bbc.com/news/world-europe-31632259
http://www.al-monitor.com/pulse/originals/2015/03/russia-sanctions-europe-nato-economy-cyprus-mediterranean.html

89. http://www.wantchinatimes.com/news-subclass-cnt.
aspx?id=20150625000003&cid=1202

90. http://www.latinnews.com/services/item/55794-nicaragua-boosting-ties-with-russia.html

91. Mitchell Stephens: A history of news, Harcourt Brace, 1996. FIRST EDITION, Viking, 1988; paperback, Penguin, 1989

92. Wickham Steed: The Press, Penguin, London 1938

HERTFORDSHIRE PRESS

Titles List

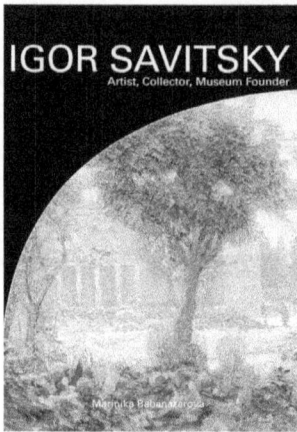

Igor Savitsky: Artist, Collector, Museum Founder
by MarinikaBabanazarova (2011)

Since the early 2000s, Igor Savitsky's life and accomplishments have earned increasing international recognition. He and the museum he founded in Nukus, the capital of Karakalpakstan in the far northwest of Uzbekistan. Marinika Babanazarova's memoir is based on her 1990 graduate dissertation at the Tashkent Theatre and Art Institute. It draws upon correspondence, official records, and other documents about the Savitsky family that have become available during the last few years, as well as the recollections of a wide range of people who knew Igor Savitsky personally.

Игорь Савитский: Художник, Собиратель, Основатель музея

С начала 2000-х годов, жизнь и достижения Игоря Савицкого получили широкое признание во всем мире. Он и его музей, основанный в Нукусе, столице Каракалпакстана, стали предметом многочисленных статей в мировых газетах и журналах, таких как TheGuardian и NewYorkTimes, телевизионных программ в Австралии, Германии и Японии. Книга издана на русском, английском и французском языках.

Igor Savitski: Peintre, collectionneur, fondateur du Muse

Le mémoire de Mme Babanazarova, basé sur sa thèse de 1990 à l'Institut de Théâtre et D'art de Tachkent, s'appuie sur la correspondance, les dossiers officiels et d'autres documents d'Igor Savitsky et de sa famille, qui sont devenus disponibles dernièrement, ainsi que sur les souvenirs de nombreuses personnes ayant connu Savistky personellement, ainsi que sur sa propre expérience de travail a ses cotés, en tant que successeur designé. son nom a titre posthume.

ISBN: 978-0955754999
RRP: £10.00

Savitsky Collection Selected Masterpieces.
Poster set of 8 posters (2014)

Limited edition of prints from the world-renowned Museum of Igor Savitsky in Nukus, Uzbekistan. The set includs nine of the most famous works from the Savitsky collection wrapped in a colourful envelope. Selected Masterpieces of the Savitsky Collection.
 [Cover] BullVasily Lysenko
1. Oriental Café Aleksei Isupov
 2. Rendezvous Sergei Luppov
3. By the Sea. Marie-LouiseKliment Red'ko
4. Apocalypse Aleksei Rybnikov
5. Rain Irina Shtange
6. Purple Autumn Ural Tansykbayaev
7. To the Train Viktor Ufimtsev
8. Brigade to the fields Alexander Volkov This museum, also known as the Nukus Museum or the Savitsky.

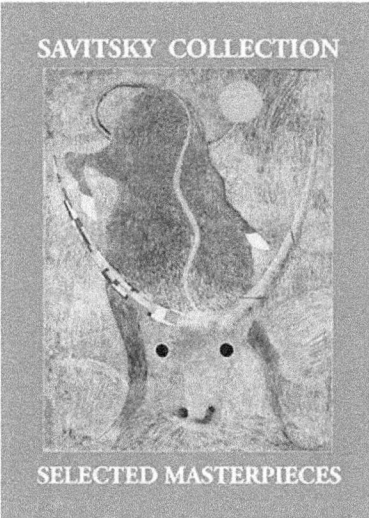

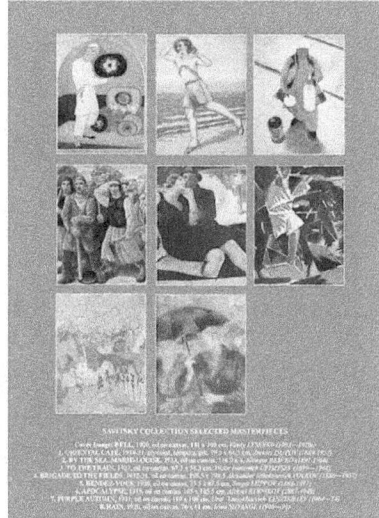

ISBN: 9780992787387
RRP: £25.00

Friendly Steppes. A Silk Road Journey
by Nick Rowan

This is the chronicle of an extraordinary adventure that led Nick Rowan to some of the world's most incredible and hidden places. Intertwined with the magic of 2,000 years of Silk Road history, he recounts his experiences coupled with a remarkable realisation of just what an impact this trade route has had on our society as we know it today. Containing colourful stories, beautiful photography and vivid characters, and wrapped in the local myths and legends told by the people Nick met and who live along the route, this is both a travelogue and an education of a part of the world that has remained hidden for hundreds of years.

ISBN: 978-0-955754944
RRP: £14.95

Птицы Узбекистана

ФОТОАЛЬБОМ

THE PHOTOALBUM **BIRDS OF UZBEKISTAN**

Birds of Uzbeksitan
by Nedosekov (2012)

FIRST AND ONLY PHOTOALBUM
OF UZBEKISTAN BIRDS!

This book, which provides an introduction to the birdlife of Uzbekistan, is a welcome addition to the tools available to those working to conserve the natural heritage of the country. In addition to being the first photographic guide to the birds of Uzbekistan, the book is unique in only using photographs taken within the country. The compilers are to be congratulated on preparing an attractive and accessible work which hopefully will encourage more people to discover the rich birdlife of the country and want to protect it for future generations

ISBN: 978-0-955754913
RRP: 25.00

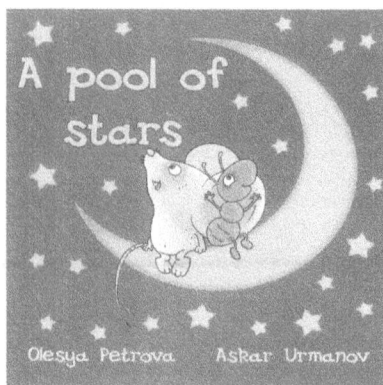

Pool of Stars

by Olesya Petrova, Askar Urmanov,
English Edition (2007)

It is the first publication of a young writer Olesya Petrova, a talented and creative person. Fairy-tale characters dwell on this book's pages. Lovely illustrations make this book even more interesting to kids, thanks to a remarkable artist Askar Urmanov. We hope that our young readers will be very happy with such a gift. It's a book that everyone will appreciate. For the young, innocent ones - it's a good source of lessons they'll need in life. For the not-so-young but young at heart, it's a great book to remind us that life is so much more than work.

ISBN: 978-0955754906

«Звёздная лужица»

Первая книга для детей, изданная британским издательством Hertfordshire Press. Это также первая публикация молодой талантливой писательницы Олеси Петровой. Сказочные персонажи живут на страницах этой книги. Прекрасные иллюстрации делают книгу еще более интересной и красочной для детей, благодаря замечательному художнику Аскару Урманову. Вместе Аскар и Олеся составляют удивительный творческий тандем, который привнес жизнь в эту маленькую книгу

ISBN: 978-0955754906
RRP: £4.95

Buyuk Temurhon (Tamerlane)

by C. Marlowe, Uzbek Edition (2010)

Hertfordshire based publisher Silk Road Media, run by Marat Akhmedjanov, and the BBC Uzbek Service have published one of Christopher Marlowe's famous plays, Tamburlaine the Great, translated into the Uzbek language. It is the first of Christopher Marlowe's plays to be translated into Uzbek, which is Tamburlaine's native language. Translated by Hamid Ismailov, the current BBC World Service Writer-in-Residence, this new publication seeks to introduce English classics to Uzbek readers worldwide.

ISBN: 9780955754982
RRP: £10.00

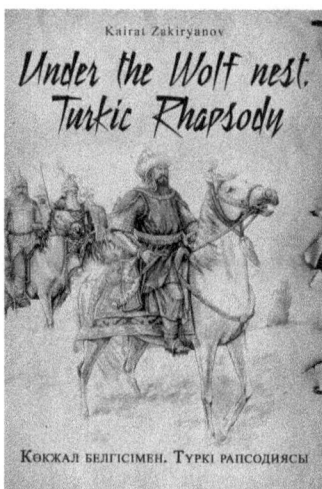

Under Wolf's Nest
by KairatZakiryanov
English –Kazakh edition

Were the origins of Islam, Christianity and the legend of King Arthur all influenced by steppe nomads from Kazakhstan? Ranging through thousands of years of history, and drawing on sources from Herodotus through to contemporary Kazakh and Russian research, the crucial role in the creation of modern civilisation played by the Turkic people is revealed in this detailed yet highly accessible work. Professor Kairat Zakiryanov, President of the Kazakh Academy of Sport and Tourism, explains how generations of steppe nomads, including Genghis Khan, have helped shape the language, culture and populations of Asia, Europe, the Middle East and America through migrations taking place over millennia.

ISBN: 9780957480728
RRP: £17.50

268

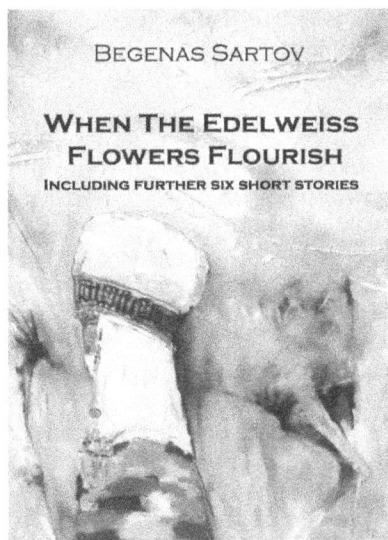

When Edelweiss flowers flourish

by Begenas Saratov

English edition (2012)

A spectacular insight into life in the Soviet Union in the late 1960's made all the more intriguing by its setting within the Sovet Republic of Kyrgyzstan. The story explores Soviet life, traditional Kyrgyz life and life on planet Earth through a Science Fiction story based around an alien nations plundering of the planet for life giving herbs. The author reveals far sighted thoughts and concerns for conservation, management of natural resources and dialogue to achieve peace yet at the same time shows extraordinary foresight with ideas for future technologies and the progress of science. The whole style of the writing gives a fascinating insight into the many facets of life in a highly civilised yet rarely known part of the world.

ISBN: 978-0955754951

Mamyry gyldogon maalda

Это фантастический рассказ, повествующий о советской жизни, жизни кыргызского народа и о жизни на планете в целом. Автор рассказывает об инопланетных народах, которые пришли на нашу планету, чтобы разграбить ее. Автор раскрывает дальновидность мысли о сохранение и рациональном использовании природных ресурсов, а также диалога для достижения мира и в то же время показывает необычайную дальновидность с идеями для будущих технологий и прогресса науки. Книга также издана на **кыргызском языке**.

ISBN: 97809555754951
RRP: £12.95

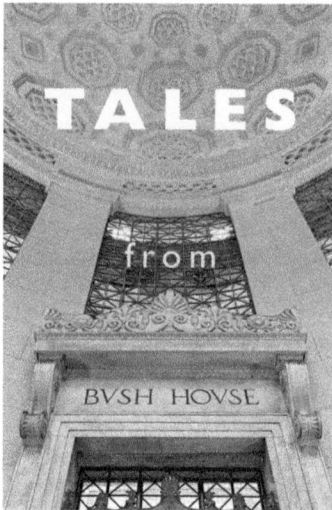

Tales from Bush House

(BBC Wolrd Service)
by Hamid Ismailov
(2012)

Tales From Bush House is a collection of short narratives about working lives, mostly real and comic, sometimes poignant or apocryphal, gifted to the editors by former and current BBC World Service employees. They are tales from inside Bush House - the home of the World Service since 1941 - escaping through its marble-clad walls at a time when its staff begin their departure to new premises in Portland Place. In July 2012, the grand doors of this imposing building will close on a vibrant chapter in the history of Britain's most cosmopolitan organisation. So this is a timely book.

ISBN: 9780955754975
RRP: £12.95

Chants of Dark Fire
(Песни темного огня)

by Zhulduz Baizakova
Russian edition (2012)

This contemporary work of poetry contains the deep and inspirational rhythms of the ancient Steppe. It combines the nomad, modern, postmodern influences in Kazakhstani culture in the early 21st century, and reveals the hidden depths of contrasts, darkness, and longing for light that breathes both ice and fire to inspire a rich form of poetry worthy of reading and contemplating. It is also distinguished by the uniqueness of its style and substance. Simply sublime, it has to be read and felt for real.

ISBN: 978-0957480711
RRP: £10.00

Kamila

by R. Karimov
Kyrgyz – Uzbek Edition (2013)

«Камила» - это история о сироте, растущей на юге Кыргызстана. Наряду с личной трагедией Камилы и ее родителей, Рахим Каримов описывает очень реалистично и подробно местный образ жизни. Роман выиграл конкурс "Искусство книги-2005" в Бишкеке и был признан национальным бестселлером Книжной палаты Кыргызской Республики.

ISBN: 978-0957480773
RRP: £10.00

Gods of the Middle World
by Galina Dolgaya (2013)

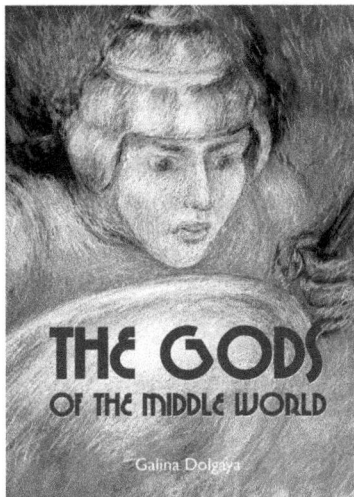

The Gods of the Middle World tells the story of Sima, a student of archaeology for whom the old lore and ways of the Central Asian steppe peoples are as vivid as the present. When she joints a group of archaeologists in southern Kazakhstan, asking all the time whether it is really possible to 'commune with the spirits', she soon discovers the answer first hand, setting in motion events in the spirit world that have been frozen for centuries. Meanwhile three millennia earlier, on the same spot, a young woman and her companion struggle to survive and amend wrongs that have caused the neighbouring tribe to take revenge. The two narratives mirror one another, and Sima's destiny is to resolve the ancient wrongs in her own lifetime and so restore the proper balance of the forces of good and evil

ISBN: 978-0957480797
RRP: £14.95

Jazz Book, poetry
by Alma Sharipova , Russian Edition

Сборник стихов Алмы Шариповой JazzCafe, в котором предлагаются стихотворения, написанные в разное время и посвященые различным событиям из жизни автора. Стихотворения Алмы содержательные и эмоциональные одновременно, отражают философию ее отношения к происходящему. Почти каждое стихотворение представляет собой законченный рассказ в миниатюре. Сюжет разворачивается последовательно и завершается небольшим резюме в последних строках. Стихотворения раскрываются, как готовые «формулы» жизни. Читатель невольно задумывается над ними и может найти как что-то знакомое, так и новое для себя.

ISBN: 978-0-957480797
RRP: £10.00

13 steps of Erika Klaus
by Kazat Akmatov (2013)

KAZAT AKMATOV

THIRTEEN STEPS
TOWARDS THE FATE
OF ERIKA KLAUS

The story involves the harrowing experiences of a young and very na ve Norwegian woman who has come to Kyrgyzstan to teach English to schoolchildren in a remote mountain outpost. Governed by the megalomaniac Colonel Bronza, the community barely survives under a cruel and unjust neo-fascist regime. Immersed in the local culture, Erika is initially both enchanted and apprehensive but soon becomes disillusioned as day after day, she is forbidden to teach. Alongside Erika's story, are the personal tragedies experienced by former soldier Sovietbek , Stalbek, the local policeman, the Principal of the school and a young man who has married a Kyrgyz refugee from Afghanistan . Each tries in vain, to challenge and change the corrupt political situation in which they are forced to live.

ISBN: 978-0957480766
RRP: £12.95

100 experiences of Kazakhstan

by Vitaly Shuptar, Nick Rowan and Dagmar Schreiber (2014)

The original land of the nomads, landlocked Kazakhstan and its expansive steppes present an intriguing border between Europe and Asia. Dispel the notion of oil barons and Borat and be prepared for a warm welcome into a land full of contrasts. A visit to this newly independent country will transport you to a bygone era to discover a country full of legends and wonders. Whether searching for the descendants of Genghis Khan - who left his mark on this land seven hundred years ago - or looking to discover the futuristic architecture of its capital Astana, visitors cannot fail but be impressed by what they experience. For those seeking adventure, the formidable Altai and Tien Shan mountains provide challenges for novices and experts alike

ISBN: 978-0-992787356
RRP: £19.95

Shahidka/ Munabia
by KazatAkmatov (2013)

Munabiya and Shahidka by Kazat Akmatov National Writer of Kyrgyzstan Recently translated into English Akmatov's two love stories are set in rural Kyrgyzstan, where the natural environment, local culture, traditions and political climate all play an integral part in the dramas which unfold. Munabiya is a tale of a family's frustration, fury, sadness and eventual acceptance of a long term love affair between the widowed father and his mistress. In contrast, Shahidka is a multi-stranded story which focuses on the ties which bind a series of individuals to the tragic and ill-fated union between a local Russian girl and her Chechen lover, within a multi-cultural community where violence, corruption and propaganda are part of everyday life.

ISBN: 978-0957480759
RRP: £12.95

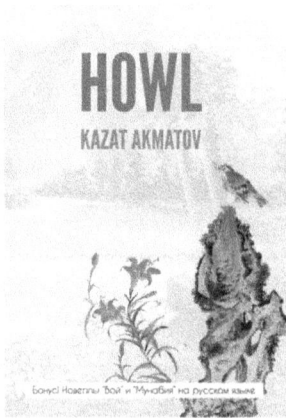

Howl *novel*
by Kazat Akmatov (2014)
English –Russian

The "Howl" by Kazat Akmatov is a beautifully crafted novel centred on life in rural Kyrgyzstan. Characteristic of the country's national writer, the simple plot is imbued with descriptions of the spectacular landscape, wildlife and local customs. The theme however, is universal and the contradictory emotions experienced by Kalen the shepherd must surely ring true to young men, and their parents, the world over. Here is a haunting and sensitively written story of a bitter -sweet rite of passage from boyhood to manhood.

ISBN: 978-0993044410
RRP: £12.50

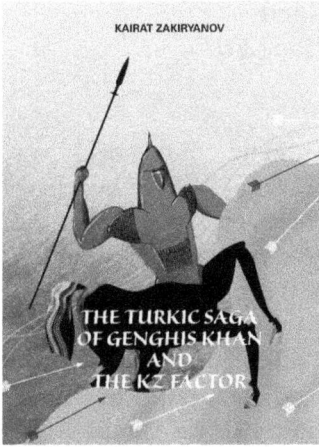

The Turkic Saga of Genghis Khan and the KZ Factor
by Dr.Kairat Zakiryanov (2014)

An in-depth study of Genghis Khan from a Kazakh perspective, The Turkic Saga of Genghis Khan presupposes that the great Mongol leader and his tribal setting had more in common with the ancestors of the Kazakhs than with the people who today identify as Mongols. This idea is growing in currency in both western and eastern scholarship and is challenging both old Western assumptions and the long-obsolete Soviet perspective. This is an academic work that draws on many Central Asian and Russian sources and often has a Eurasianist bias - while also paying attention to new accounts by Western authors such as Jack Weatherford and John Man. It bears the mark of an independent, unorthodox and passionate scholar.

ISBN: 978-0992787370
RRP: £17.50

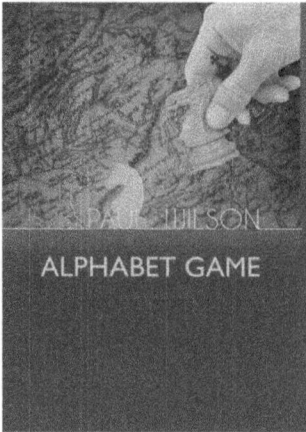

Alphabet Game
by Paul Wilson (2014)

Travelling around the world may appear as easy as ABC, but looks can be deceptive: there is no 'X' for a start. Not since Xidakistan was struck from the map. Yet post 9/11, with the War on Terror going global, could 'The Valley' be about to regain its place on the political stage? Xidakistan's fate is inextricably linked with that of Graham Ruff, founder of Ruff Guides. Setting sail where Around the World in Eighty Days and Lost Horizon weighed anchor, our not-quite-a-hero suffers all in pursuit of his golden triangle: The Game, The Guidebook, The Girl. With the future of printed Guidebooks increasingly in question, As Evelyn Waugh's Scoop did for Foreign Correspondents the world over, so this novel lifts the lid on Travel Writers for good.

ISBN: 978-0-992787325
RRP: £14.95

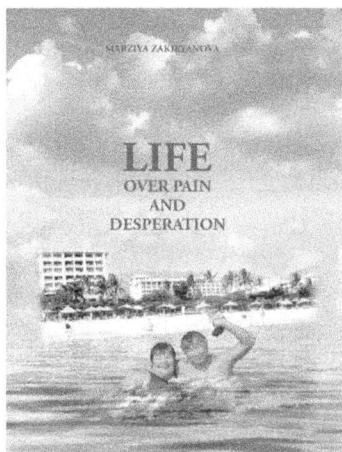

Life over pain and desperation
by Marziya Zakiryanova (2014)

This book was written by someone on the fringe of death. Her life had been split in two: before and after the first day of August 1991 when she, a mother of two small children and full of hopes and plans for the future, became disabled in a single twist of fate. Narrating her tale of self-conquest, the author speaks about how she managed to hold her family together, win the respect and recognition of people around her and above all, protect the fragile concept of 'love' from fortune's cruel turns. By the time the book was submitted to print, Marziya Zakiryanova had passed away. She died after making the last correction to her script. We bid farewell to this remarkable and powerfully creative woman.

ISBN: 978-0-99278733-2
RRP: £14.95

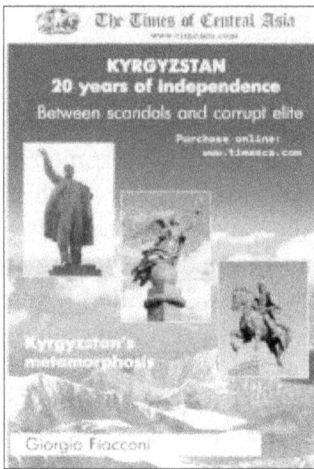

Kyrgyzstan - 20 Years of Independence: Between scandals and corrupt elite by Giorgio Fiacconi, 2012

The book chronicles not only the birth of an independent sovereign nation, The Kyrgyz Republic, and its struggle to come to terms with a forced separation from its communist parent, the former Soviet Union, a foundling seeking to establishment a new governmental constitution based on democratic principles and a quest for a national identity, but also the trials (at times literally!) of a businessman with a vision to see opportunities, with a bravery of his own conviction to invest considerable sums of money in a country at a time of great uncertainty economically. It's a story of love and hate, success and despair.

ISBN: 9789967265578
RRP: £29.95

282

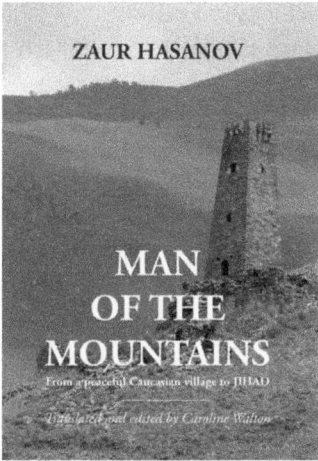

Man of the Mountains
by Abudlla Isa (2014)
(OCABF 2013 Winner)

Man of the Mountains" is a book about a young Muslim Chechen boy, Zaur who becomes a central figure representing the fight of local indigenous people against both the Russians invading the country and Islamic radicals trying to take a leverage of the situation, using it to push their narrow political agenda on the eve of collapse of the USSR. After 9/11 and the invasion of Iraq and Afghanistan by coalition forces, the subject of the Islamic jihadi movement has become an important subject for the Western readers. But few know about the resistance movement from the local intellectuals and moderates against radical Islamists taking strong hold in the area.

ISBN: 978-0-9930444-5-8
RRP: £14.95

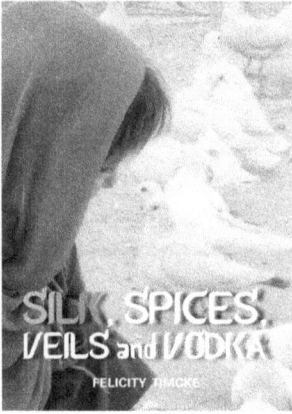

Silk, Spice, Veils and Vodka
by Felicity Timcke (2014)

Felicity Timcke's missive publication, "Silk, Spices, Veils and Vodka" brings both a refreshing and new approach to life on the expat trail. South African by origin, Timcke has lived in some very exotic places, mostly along the more challenging countries of the Silk Road. Although the book's content, which is entirely composed of letters to the author's friends and family, is directed primarily at this group, it provides "20 years of musings" that will enthral and delight those who have either experienced a similar expatriate existence or who are nervously about to depart for one.

ISBN: 978-0992787318
RRP: £12.50

Finding the Holy Path
by Shahsanem Murray (2014)

"Murray's first book provides an enticing and novel link between her adopted home town of Edinburgh and her origins form Central Asia. Beginning with an investigation into a mysterious lamp that turns up in an antiques shop in Edinburgh, and is bought on impulse, we are quickly brought to the fertile Ferghana valley in Uzbekistan to witness the birth of Kara-Choro, and the start of an enthralling story that links past and present. Told through a vivid and passionate dialogue, this is a tale of parallel discovery and intrigue. The beautifully translated text, interspersed by regional poetry, cannot fail to impress any reader, especially those new to the region who will be affectionately drawn into its heart in this page-turning cultural thriller."

В поисках святого перевала – удивительный приключенческий роман, основанный на исторических источниках. Произведение Мюррей – это временной мостик между эпохами, который помогает нам переместиться в прошлое и уносит нас далеко в 16 век. Закрученный сюжет предоставляет нам уникальную возможность, познакомиться с историейи культурой Центральной Азии. «Первая книга Мюррей предлагает заманчивый роман, связывающий между её приемным городом Эдинбургом и Центральной Азией, откуда настоящее происхождение автора.

RUS ISBN: 978-0-9930444-8-9
ENGL ISBN: 978-0992787394

RRP: £12.50

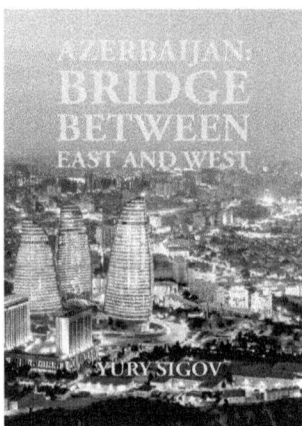

Azerbaijan:
Bridge between East and West
by Yury Sigov, 2015

Azerbaijan: Bridge between East and West, Yury Sigov narrates a comprehensive and compelling story about Azerbaijan. He balances the country's rich cultural heritage, wonderful people and vibrant environment with its modern political and economic strategies. Readers will get the chance to thoroughly explore Azerbaijan from many different perspectives and discover a plethora of innovations and idea, including the recipe for Azerbaijan's success as a nation and its strategies for the future. The book also explores the history of relationships between United Kingdom and Azerbaijan.

ISBN: 978-0-9930444-9-6
RRP: £24.50

Kashmir Song
by Sharaf Rashidov
(translation by Alexey Ulko, OCABF 2014 Winner). 2015

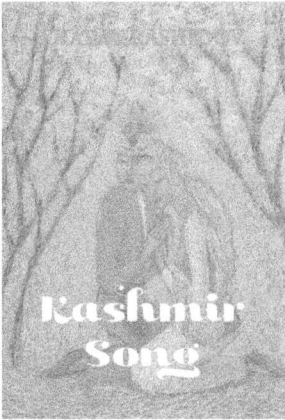

This beautiful illustrated novella offers a sensitive reworking of an ancient and enchanting folk story which although rooted in Kashmir is, by nature of its theme, universal in its appeal.

Alternative interpretations of this tale are explored by Alexey Ulko in his introduction, with references to both politics and contemporary literature, and the author's epilogue further reiterates its philosophical dimension.

The Kashmir Song is a timeless tale, which true to the tradition of classical folklore, can be enjoyed on a number of levels by readers of all ages.

ISBN: 978-0-9930444-2-7
RRP: £29.50

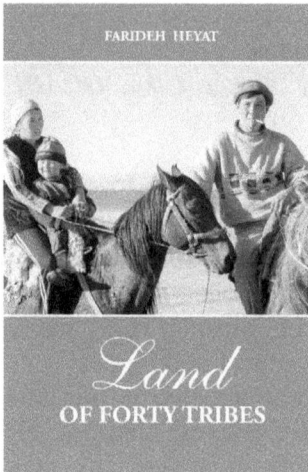

Land of forty tribes
by Farideh Heyat, 2015

Sima Omid, a British-Iranian anthropologist in search of her Turkic roots, takes on a university teaching post in Kyrgyzstan. It is the year following 9/11, when the US is asserting its influence in the region. Disillusioned with her long-standing relationship, Sima is looking for a new man in her life. But the foreign men she meets are mostly involved in relationships with local women half their age, and the Central Asian men she finds highly male chauvinist and aggressive towards women.

ISBN: 978-0-9930444-4-1
RRP: £14.95

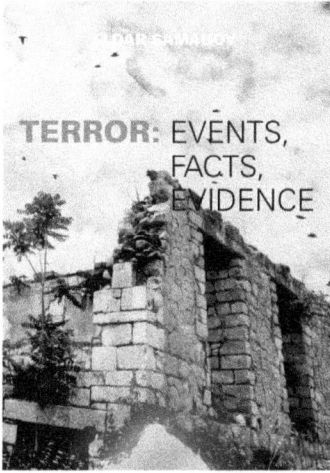

Terror: events, facts, evidence.
by Eldar Samadov

This book is based on research carried out since 1988 on territorial claims of Armenia against Azerbaijan, which led to the escalation of the conflict over Nagorno-Karabakh. This escalation included acts of terror by Armenian terrorist and other armed gangs not only in areas where intensive armed confrontations took place but also away from the fighting zones. This book, not for the first time, reflects upon the results of numerous acts of premeditated murder, robbery, armed attack and other crimes through collected material related to criminal cases which have been opened at various stages following such crimes. The book is meant for political scientists, historians, lawyers, diplomats and a broader audience.

ISBN: 978-1-910886-00-7
RRP: £9.99